Palgrave Studies in Performa[illegible]

Series Editors

Susan Broadhurst
School of Arts
Brunel University
Uxbridge, United Kingdom

Josephine Machon
Middlesex University
London, United Kingdom

Aim of the Series

This exciting and timely series features cutting-edge books which centre on global and embodied approaches to performance and technology. As well as focussing on digital performance and art, the series includes the theoretical and historical context relevant to these practices. Not only does the series offer fresh artistic and theoretical perspectives on this exciting and growing area of contemporary performance practice, but it also aims to include contributors from a wide range of international locations working within this varied discipline. The series includes edited collections and monographs on issues including (but not limited to): identity and live art; intimacy and engagement with technology; biotechnology and artistic practices; technology, architecture and performance; performance, gender and technology; and space and performance. The Editorial Advisory Board is: Philip Auslander, Carol Brown, Sita Popat, and Tracey Warr. We welcome all ideas for new books and have provided guidelines for submitting proposals in the Authors section of our website. To discuss project ideas and proposals for this series please contact the series editors: Susan Broadhurst: susan.broadhurst@brunel.ac.uk and Josephine Machon: j.machon@mdx.ac.uk.

More information about this series at
http://www.springer.com/series/14604

Julie Holledge • Jonathan Bollen • Frode Helland • Joanne Tompkins

A Global Doll's House

Ibsen and Distant Visions

palgrave
macmillan

Julie Holledge
Centre for Ibsen Studies
University of Oslo
Norway

Jonathan Bollen
School of the Arts and Media
University of New South Wales
Sydney, Australia

Frode Helland
Centre for Ibsen Studies
University of Oslo
Norway

Joanne Tompkins
Humanities and Social Sciences
University of Queensland
St Lucia, Australia

Palgrave Studies in Performance and Technology
ISBN 978-1-349-68378-9 ISBN 978-1-137-43899-7 (eBook)
DOI 10.1057/978-1-137-43899-7

Library of Congress Control Number: 2016953093

Softcover reprint of the hardcover 1st edition 2016 978-1-137-43898-0

Cover illustration: Nora, Train Station II, Oslo. From *Nora's Story* directed by Jules Wright, photographer Thomas Zanon-Larcher. The Wapping Project London, October 2006 – February 2007 (Source: © Thomas Zanon-Larcher, 2016).

Printed on acid-free paper

This Palgrave Macmillan imprint is published by Springer Nature
The registered company is Macmillan Publishers Ltd. London

Acknowledgements

Researching the global production history of a canonical play requires a collaborative methodology. The idea for this book came out of part of a chapter in *Women's Intercultural Performance* (2000), which was co-authored by Julie Holledge and Joanne Tompkins. Ten years ago it was conceived as a conventional monograph on *Et dukkehjem* authored by Holledge, but the existence of a database of productions of the play lodged in Ibsen.net at the National Library in Oslo shifted the methodology of the project into the digital humanities. At that time Holledge, Bollen, and Tompkins were all involved in the development of AusStage, the Australian database for researching performance. Bollen was transforming the capabilities of AusStage to include mapping and network analyses, and the *Et dukkehjem* production records were used as an experimental data set. By this time, Holledge had begun collaborating with Helland at the Centre for Ibsen Studies at the University of Oslo. The roles of all the authors of this study were defined by this history: Holledge led the project and travelled the world watching productions of *Et dukkehjem*, and drafted the text; Bollen interrogated the production data and authored the visualisations; Helland co-wrote Chapter 3 and contributed his broad knowledge of Ibsen scholarship and Norwegian culture throughout the remaining text; and Tompkins provided the strong editorial guidance that unified these elements into the book. Although this study is published under four names, the success of the project has been dependent on contributions from myriad international scholars and artists. The first acknowledgement must be to Jens-Morten Hanssen, who was responsible for gathering the production records on global performances of *Et dukkehjem* in Ibsen.net, the database held at the National Library in Oslo. The second must go to Asgeir Nesøen, Øystein Bjarne Ekevik, Damir Nedic, and Heidi Løken, who created IbsenStage at the University of Oslo with the help of Jenny Fewster at AusStage, and to Sean Weatherly, who transferred the *Et dukkehjem* data into IbsenStage. Data visualisations were created using software from Visone (http://visone.info) for networks and QGIS (http://www.qgis.org) for maps.

The research in this project would not have been possible without the help of scholars, artists, and research assistants from around the world. Scholars from the *Ibsen Between Cultures* project (supported by the Norwegian Research Council) generously shared their knowledge about *Et dukkehjem* histories in their countries: Tapati Gupta and Krishna Sen (India); Sun Jian, He Chengzhou, Liu Minghou, and Xia Liyang (China); Kwok-kan Tam (Hong Kong); and Kamaluddin Nilu, Sabiha Huq, and Ahmed Ahsanuzzaman (Bangladesh). In Africa, we owe thanks to the adaptors of *Et dukkehjem* who agreed to attend a symposium we co-convened in Lusaka: Robert McLaren, Stephen Chifunyise, and Sithokozile Mhlanga (Zimbabwe); Ian Mbugua (Kenya); Cheela Chilala (Zambia); Msgun Zerai (Eritrea); Melissa Eveleigh, Karl Hoff, and Thoko Kapiri (Malawi); Manuela Soeiro (Mozambique); and Claire Stopford (South Africa). We would also like to thank Hilde Guri Bohlin and the Ibsen Award Scholarship committee for funding this symposium and Helge Rønning for using his extensive networks to make the event happen. An international team of research assistants, funded through a grant from the Australian Research Council, have proved invaluable to the project; they have gathered material, translated, and organised interviews: Dr Mona Khedr (Arabic); Gabriela Espinosa and Alirio Zavarce (Spanish); Alethea Silvestre (Portuguese); Saranya Mukhopadhyay (Bangla); Chong Zhou (Chinese); May-Brit Akerholt (Norwegian, Danish, Swedish); Catherine Fitzgerald, Chris Hurrell, Lily Carrodus, Alex Vickery-Howe, and Brad Williams. We would also like to thank all the artists who generously gave up their time to be interviewed: Maude Mitchell and Richard Newton (USA); Alexandra von Hummel and Bastián Bodenhöfer (Chile); Sunil Pokharel and Nisha Sharma Pokharel (Nepal); Mumbi Kaigwa (Kenya); Sheema Kermani and Anwer Jafri (Pakistan); Gerrit Timmers (Netherlands); Tonje Gotschalksen, Hanne Tømta, Marit Synnøve Berg, Vivi Sunde, Marit Østbye, Monna Tandberg, Gisken Armand, Gro Ann Uthaug, Edith Roger, Joachim Calmeyer, and Espen Skjønberg (Norway); Karl Eric Schollhammer, José Fernando Peixoto de Azevedo, and Teth

Maiello (Brazil); and Gamal Yakout (Egypt). Throughout the project, the staff and postgraduate students in the Centre for Ibsen Studies at the University of Oslo have been fantastically supportive. We would like to thank staff members Astrid Sæther and Ellen Rees, administrator Laila Y. Henriksen, librarians Randi Meyer and Maria Faskerti, and research assistants Janicke S. Kaasa, Ingeborg Dalby, and Hedda Solberg Rui, as well as all the masters and doctoral students who have engaged in discussions at various stages in this research. Our next thanks go to all the people who have worked to produce this book: Sarah Thomasson for all the copy-editing, William Dunstone for work on earlier stages of the draft, and Linda Brainwood for picture research and permissions; and to everyone at Palgrave Macmillan: Paula Kennedy for all her support in the early commissioning stages of the project, Peter Cary and April James for their work as editorial assistants, and to the Performance and Technology series editors, Susan Broadhurst and Josephine Machon.

Finally, we would like to thank a group of friends, artists, and scholars who have given wonderful advice and used their networks to help us track down information: Mark Sandberg, Michiko Aoki, Mitsuya Mori, Eugene Van Erven, Richard Back, Rita Braga, Juan Cameron, Jeebesh Rayamajhi, and Elisabeth Sødal; and last but not least, for emotional and culinary support, Chen Yen Hui, Thyra Knudsen, Alan Lawson, and Mary Moore.

Contents

List of Figures

CHAPTER 1

Introduction

A Global Doll's House aims to answer a very simple question: what accounts for the global success of Henrik Ibsen's most popular play? We consider the question from two angles: cultural transmission and adaptation. By tracing the cultural transmission of the play through its global performances, we uncover the social, economic, and political forces that have secured it a place in the canon of world drama; by looking at multiple adaptations we reveal how artists have been able to re-create the play successfully in so many cultural contexts.

When Ibsen wrote the play that he named *Et dukkehjem*, he was hardly known outside Scandinavia and Germany, and it became his passport to international fame. Its protagonist, Nora Helmer, rivals Antigone, Carmen, Medea, and Juliet as the most performed, discussed, and debated female character on the international stage. The play premiered in Copenhagen in 1879.[1] It has since been performed in thirty-five languages in eighty-seven countries, thirty-nine of which are outside Europe; with 3787 records of productions it has become one of the world's most produced dramas (see Figs. 1.1 and 1.2). It has been adapted into eight silent films and seven feature films; been televised at least twenty-five times and had numerous radio broadcasts; and more recently, a plethora of extracts have appeared on YouTube. The play is known by multiple titles, the most familiar in English being the mistranslation *A Doll's House* (Sandberg 2015, 72). In 1880, Ibsen wrote to his Swedish translator, Erik af Edholm, '[i]t is quite rightly

J. Holledge et al., *A Global Doll's House*, Palgrave Studies in Performance and Technology, DOI 10.1057/978-1-137-43899-7_1

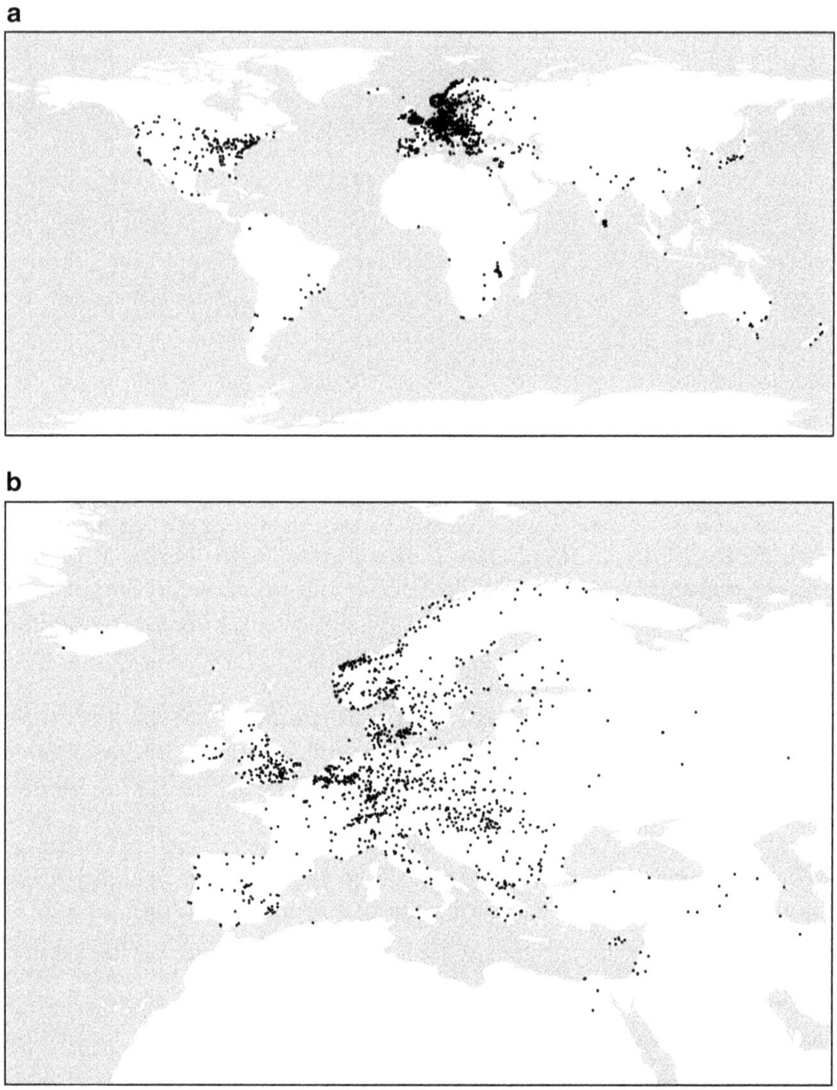

Fig. 1.1 (**a–b**) The distribution of *Et dukkehjem* by venue, 1879–2015 (Source: IbsenStage)

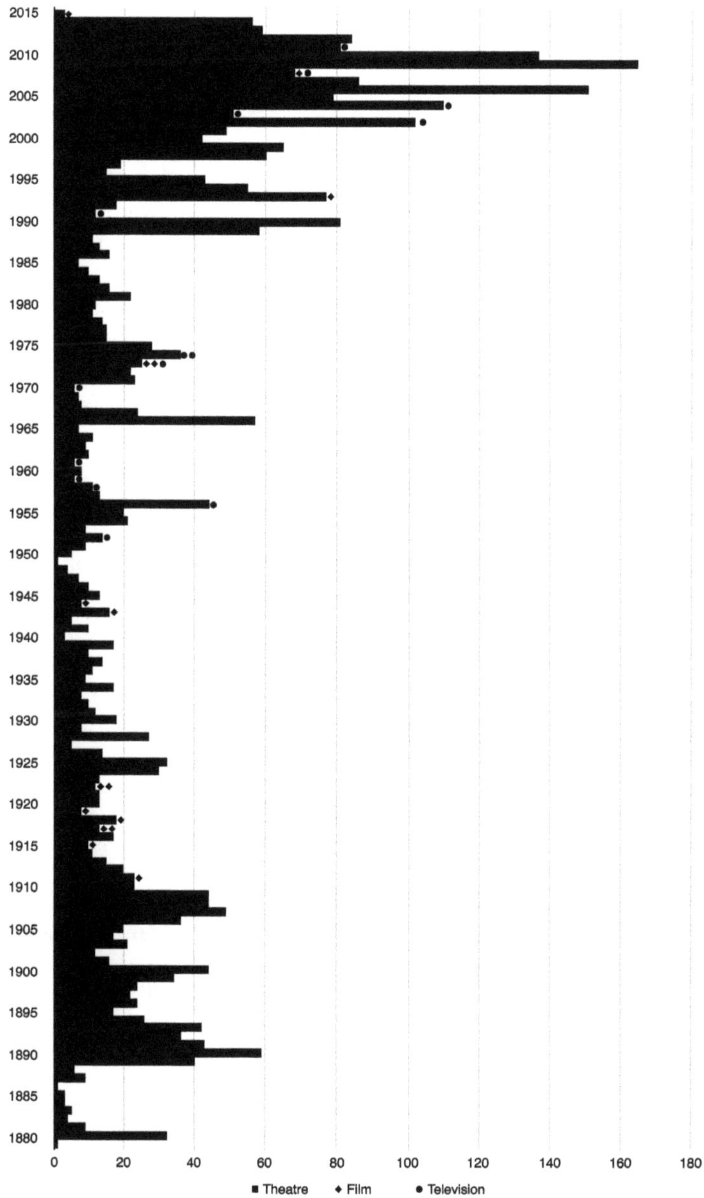

Fig. 1.2 The number of *Et dukkehjem* events by year, 1879–2015 (Source: IbsenStage)

the case, as you assume, that my play's title, *Et dukkehjem* [dukkehjem = dollhome] is a new phrase, which I myself have made up, and I am very pleased that they will repeat the phrase in Swedish in a direct translation' (Ibsen 1880b, 11–12).[2] Rather than *A Doll Home*, the title given to the play by William Archer was *A Doll's House*, which has become the standard title used in English bibliographies and digital archives, and we follow this convention in the title of this book.[3] But within this study we use the original Dano-Norwegian title, *Et dukkehjem*, to refer both to the play-script and the entire 'work': this is the play in all its versions, translations, and adaptations, and all the productions presented live on stage or recorded for transmission by film, radio, television, Internet, and so on. This all-encompassing 'work' is our focus, as we aim to avoid what Pierre Bourdieu has called the 'ideology of the inexhaustible work of art', and instead take as our point of departure 'the fact that the work of art is in fact made not twice, but hundreds of times, thousands of times, by all those who have an interest in it' (1993, 111). When we refer to individual productions we use their advertised titles if they conform to the Roman alphabet and translate them into English as *A Doll Home* when the original is in a different script.

As *Et dukkehjem* appears on school and university curricula worldwide, we assume that most of our readers will have encountered it on stage, on film, or in the classroom. To renew this acquaintance, we begin with Ibsen's 'Notes for a Modern Tragedy', written a month after he moved to Rome and began working on the play in September 1878[4]:

> There are two kinds of spiritual law, two kinds of conscience, one in man and another, altogether different, in woman. They do not understand each other; but in practical life the woman is judged by man's law, as though she were not a woman but a man.
>
> The wife in the play ends by having no idea of what is right or wrong; natural feeling on the one hand and belief in authority on the other have altogether bewildered her.
>
> A woman cannot be herself in the society of the present day, which is an exclusively masculine society, with laws framed by men and with a judicial system that judges feminine conduct from a masculine point of view.
>
> She has committed forgery, [and it is her pride]; for she did it out of love for her husband, to save his life. But this husband with his commonplace principles of honour is on the side of the law and regards the question with masculine eyes.
>
> Spiritual conflicts. Oppressed and bewildered by the belief in authority, she loses faith in her moral right and ability to bring up her children. Bitterness. A mother in modern society, like certain insects who go away and

> die when she has done her duty in the propagation of the race. Love of life, of home, of husband and children and family. Here and there a womanly shaking-off of her thoughts. Sudden return of anxiety and terror. She must bear it all alone. The catastrophe approaches, inexorably, inevitably. Despair, conflict and destruction. (Krogstad has acted dishonourably and thereby become well-to-do; now his prosperity does not help him, he cannot recover his honour.) (Ibsen ([1878b] 1917, 91)[5]

A year later when he delivered the manuscript of *Et dukkehjem* to his publisher, Frederik Hegel, he wrote, 'I cannot remember that any of my books have given me greater satisfaction in the development of the details than this particular one' (Ibsen 1879b, 505–06). These meticulously crafted details were cemented into a plot line that manipulated familiar nineteenth-century tropes of illness, financial corruption, blackmail, and sexual desire. It was not until the second half of the play that Ibsen confounded the narrative expectations of his audience. The shift from the predictable to the unpredictable is evident in the final two sentences of our summary of the *Et dukkehjem* plot:

> Nora, a happily married woman with three small children, has a closely guarded secret. Early in her marriage, her husband developed a serious illness; his recovery was dependent on leaving the cold climate of the North. Nora forged her dying father's signature to secure a loan to finance this journey. Eight years have passed and she is still secretly paying off the loan. Torvald, her husband, has just been appointed as the manager of a bank and the family's finances are changing; it is Christmas and there is plenty to celebrate. Nora has never told Torvald about the loan. It is only when Krogstad, the loan shark, tries to blackmail her, that she realises her forgery was a criminal act. She suddenly understands the enormity of her crime and begins to believe that she is morally corrupt and unfit to raise her children. Krogstad now works at the bank, but with his history of financial indiscretions, he fears that he will lose his position. He tells Nora to persuade Torvald to secure his future employment, but she fails and Krogstad is sacked. Nora decides to seek help from Dr Rank, a close family friend, but she changes her mind when he confides his love for her and reveals that he is suffering from a terminal disease. The blackmail plot escalates when Krogstad writes a threatening letter to Torvald. While this letter sits in a letterbox, waiting to be opened, Nora asks Mrs Linde, her old school friend, for help. Mrs Linde agrees to use her influence over Krogstad to thwart the blackmail plot, but she insists that Torvald is told the truth. Nora is terrified that Torvald will sacrifice himself rather than see her prosecuted for a criminal act, but when he reads Krogstad's letter, he capitulates to its demands, and blames Nora for ruining his life. Nora is deeply

> shocked to discover Torvald's true nature. Through Mrs Linde's intervention, the blackmail threat is removed, but Nora realises that her childlike dependency and ignorance of the world have made her incapable of raising her children. She decides to leave her husband and her children, educate herself, and strive to live as a self-determining human being.

The *International Ibsen Bibliography* lists 3540 items with material on *Et dukkehjem* that are attributed to 2085 authors; they include 1076 books, and 2392 journal and newspaper articles (Nasjonalbiblioteket 2012). Readers could be forgiven for assuming that there is nothing more worth saying about this theatrical phenomenon, but the underlying premise of our book is that *new ways of looking produce new ways of thinking*. IbsenStage, the database that holds over 15,000 production records of Ibsen's plays, has made these new ways of looking possible.

The 'distant reading' developed by literary historian Franco Moretti is central to our approach: he notes that 'distance is however not an obstacle, but a specific form of knowledge: fewer elements, hence a sharper sense of their overall interconnection. Shapes, relations, structures. Forms. Models' (2005, 1). Looking from a distance at the 3787 records of *Et dukkehjem* productions in the IbsenStage database, we see patterns in the data that guide us towards new sites of enquiry. When we reach these sites, we zoom in to look at the work and lives of particular artists, commercial and government funding, specific performances, genres of adaptation, and multiple versions of a single scene to find the evidence that can help explain the global success of the play. No single performance is examined at great length, but full details of all the productions mentioned are held in IbsenStage. Before describing the database and the methodology we use to analyse patterns in its records, we first locate our study within the wider frameworks of digital humanities and contemporary Ibsen scholarship.

Digital Humanities

Digital humanities opens up new avenues for theatre scholarship. Sarah Bay-Cheng proposes that theatre historiography must take account of the digital; she advocates that theatre historians embrace 'the digital records of past performances and the digital circulation of images in the present' (2010, 133). This book takes up her challenge in applying a digital approach to interrogating the production history of one of the most popular plays in the global repertoire. We use techniques of data analysis, quantification, and visualisation in an attempt to understand the dynamic forces that have shaped, and continue to shape, the production of world drama.

Audiences for performance are now accustomed to the use of computer technologies in the theatre. Computers are used to control light, sound, and the projection of text and images in performance, and companies use digital media to transmit images and video of live productions to audiences around the world. The use of computers in theatre research has also become widespread. Databases assist in analysing information about performance events and artefacts; sound, image, and video are incorporated into digital multimedia to represent the production history of a play or new genres of performance; and three-dimensional theatre models provide virtual venues for re-creating performance from the past or simulating future prospects for production (Herbert 1986; Donohue 1989; Saltz 2004). Theatre scholars have become optimistic about the new kinds of teaching, research, and performance that digital technologies enable as the convergence of digital archives, broadband media, and Internet services provide distributed access to performance, and previously dispersed materials become increasingly accessible (Carson 2005; Causey 2006; Dixon 2007).

Across the arts and humanities, researchers have taken up the potential that computers provide, borrowing methodologies from the sciences, where data have been analysed using digital methods since the advent of computers. Investigating cultural data produces significant discoveries and using computers in the humanities complements 'traditional' reading and research, but it is important to recognise the distinct findings that digital methods uncover (McGann 2001; McCarty 2005). There is nothing fundamentally new about digital methods of data analysis in the humanities, even if current proponents take advantage of tools that were unavailable until quite recently: researchers who developed concordances of the Bible or Shakespeare's plays used precursor technology to search for specific words or patterns across large corpora of texts (Hockey 2000). Since then, ways of using computers to interrogate documents have proliferated with tools for quantifying written texts, analysing content, recognising topics, detecting sentiment, and characterising style (Schreibman et al. 2004). These quantitative techniques were developed over decades through journals like *Computers and the Humanities* (from 1966) and *Literary and Linguistic Computing* (from 1986; now *Digital Scholarship in the Humanities*). In recent years, a broadening of interest has seen the uptake of digital methods and ensuing critical debate across many fields of research in the humanities (Gold 2012; Berry 2012; Burdick et al. 2012; Arthur and Bode 2014).

In looking for ways to analyse the transmission and adaptation of *Et dukkehjem* around the world, we were impressed by Franco Moretti's visualisations of literary genres in *Graphs, Maps, Trees: Abstract Models for a Literary History* (2005), which depicts quantitative and spatial analyses of texts and titles that demonstrate their distribution in space and evolution over time. More recently, in *Distant Reading* (2013), Moretti consolidates the value of pursuing a quantitative approach to literary history, as distinct from the 'close reading' that has characterised the study of literature for decades. In the 'form' of diagrams that quantify the history of literary texts, Moretti finds evidence of the operations of social force on literary production; his graphs, maps, and diagrams are constructs of empirical analysis, hitherto 'invisible objects' having 'no equivalent within lived experience' (2013, 157). As distant visions, Moretti's diagrams 'zoom out' from the detail to reveal unexpected patterns that we do not see 'up-close'. For Moretti, their value as departures within a critical tradition may be measured by the 'new, irreverent hypotheses' that they permit him to advance (2013, 158). In terms that will be familiar to theatre scholars, the empirical abstraction of Moretti's diagrams serves a function that is akin to Brecht's *Verfremdungseffekt*: visualisations invoke an inquisitive stance by presenting what we know in a way that makes it strange.

It is one thing to amass information in a database and visualise its content. It is another actually to interrogate what these data tell us: what new research possibilities emerge from the accumulation of information? No diagram can show us why an artist chose to produce this play, or how an audience received it; nor can it reveal the complexities and extraordinary richness of the adaptations and translations of the play. Yet visualisations of production data can indicate the transmission of Ibsen's play through time, across space, and between artists working in the theatre. They can reveal patterns that provoke further investigation. The methods used in the digital humanities provide the opportunity to ask questions that were not previously imaginable. Digitising cultural data can be costly, but if data sets are gathered effectively, they can be interrogated by many projects, each asking different questions.

Building on the Past

Digital humanities offers possibilities for extending the bounds of Ibsen scholarship. Data analysis and visualisation add new interpretative perspectives to the strengths of conventional scholarship. Before we introduce the *Et dukkehjem* data set, we provide a brief overview of the rich scholarly history (produced by means of conventional research) relevant to our enquiry into the global success of the play. Numerous close readings of Ibsen's play-script have sought to explain its global appeal. Barbara Herrnstein Smith's model for analysing the spread of canonical works has informed explorations into its global success for the last thirty years: '[a]t a given time and under the contemporary conditions of available materials, technology, and techniques, a particular object—let us say a verbal artefact or text—may perform certain desired/able functions quite well for some set of subjects. It will do so by virtue of certain of its "properties"' (1984, 30). In the critical literature on *Et dukkehjem*, there are three major 'properties' frequently cited as responsible for the global impact on multiple 'sets of subjects': the theatrical representation of a human being striving for individual freedom and self-realisation (Northam 1953); the iconic status of the character of Nora as a representation of an emergent female subjectivity tied to modernity (Templeton 1997; Holledge and Tompkins 2000); and the development of theatrical modernism and aesthetics (Moi 2006). All of these approaches have provided valuable, though partial, explanations for the success of the play-script; but, as we demonstrate, difficulties arise when any of them acquires universal applicability.

A Human Striving for Individual Freedom

The claim for a universal significance of the play rests on its representation of a non-gender-specific human being striving for individual freedom and authentic existence. According to the eminent scholar John Northam, 'the play is a deep study of the tormented yet consistent development of an individual mind under the pressure of forces at once inevitable and adequately symbolic of the forces we experience in ordinary life' (1953, 38). This view is still held by some critics and is prominent in the recent critical edition of Ibsen's writings: the introduction states that it is fundamental to the meaning of the play that 'the decisive point is that the individual human being lives authentically, in accordance with the core of its inner personality' (Ystad and Aarseth 2008, 204). This 'Kierkegaardian' conception allows for the possibility that the social ethical norms framing the individual's struggle for self-authentication may vary between cultures, but asserts that the aim of incorporating the true self within the social realm remains constant across all human culture; it suggests that social conditions can change only through individuals striving for self-expression.

While an analysis of Ibsen's representation of self-authentication may reveal the philosophical subtext beneath his fictional creations, it is problematic when this interpretative strategy is taken out of a literary context and used to explain the success of the play with global audiences. It is difficult to argue that the successful reception of *Et dukkehjem* is reliant on the depiction of a character's struggle to actualise an authentic existence as defined by a nineteenth-century philosophical discourse.

Nora as Emergent Modern Female Subject

The second 'property' also concerns Nora, but instead of interpreting her as a symbol of humanity striving for self-realisation, this approach sees the character as an iconic representation of an emergent female subjectivity tied to modernity. Nora's personal struggle becomes a metaphor for demands by nineteenth-century women for subjective freedoms enjoyed by men. Jürgen Habermas defines this subjectivity as 'the space secured by civil law for the rational pursuit of one's own interests: in the state, as the in principle equal rights to participation in the formation of political will; in the private sphere, as ethical autonomy and self-realisation' (1985, 83). This argument suggests that the play's cultural setting within nineteenth-century Europe—where women were agitating for financial independence, the vote, equality before the law, access to education, and a place in the work force—can be substituted by any cultural context of modernity in which women struggle for equality. Yet 'ethical autonomy and self-realisation' are slippery concepts, even in the polemical writings of the famous female activists who cited Nora as an icon for the nineteenth-century 'new woman': Olive Schreiner (the South African liberal feminist and pacifist), Alexandra Kollontai (the Russian Bolshevik), Emma Goldman (the American anarcho-communist), and Eleanor Marx (the British socialist) would have been hard pressed to agree on a common vision of women's self-realisation.[6] When we move away from Europe and North America, this quality becomes even more difficult to define, as is demonstrated by the constantly changing embodiments of Nora in China. The first of the many subjectivities represented by Chinese Noras was tied to an emergent modernity linked to the May Fourth movement, but then she morphed into a quintessential icon of revolutionary consciousness for the Communist Party, and still later represented a retrograde Western feudalism (Holledge and Tompkins 2000, 31). With so many variations in the reception of Nora in China, let alone the rest of the world, it is impossible to pin fixed properties associated with the struggle for gender equality to the character and claim that they are responsible for the play's global reach. There may be causal relationships between local gender politics and the choice of the play for production; but the interpretative leaps made by diverse actors, directors, adaptors, and producers of the play demonstrate that gender relations are lived realities tied to specific times and places. It is not just gender relations that are culturally specific; the emotional responses of audiences to interpretative strategies, as embodied in characters, are equally tied to cultural particularities. The variable nature of audiences makes it difficult to argue that the reception of a character is a defining property in the global success of a dramatic text. The character of Nora has been a major attraction for female artists, particularly at the end of the nineteenth century; our reservation concerns the supposedly universal lure of the character removed from the specificities of time and place.

Theatrical Modernism and Aesthetics

The third property is that *Et dukkehjem* represents a major innovation in theatre aesthetics. The publication of Toril Moi's portrait of Ibsen as a founder of European modernism has added considerable weight to this claim (2006). Her argument relies on a re-evaluation of theatrical realism that places it as central, rather than oppositional, to modernist aesthetics. Certainly, the shift that Moi describes—from a popular theatre of romantic spectacle to a theatre reflecting the everyday domestic life of the bourgeoisie—represents a seismic aesthetic shift in late nineteenth-century European theatre. Her argument fits perfectly within British theatre history, where Ibsen's plays were central to the transition of female characters from melodrama to psychological realism.[7] Yet any argument that attributes the global success of the play to the aesthetics of realism falters even within Europe. Kirsten Shepherd-Barr's meticulous study of the early reception of Ibsen in Europe contrasts the realist productions in Britain with the approaches used by the French avant-garde (1997). The same plays were produced as naturalist drama at André Antoine's Théâtre Libre and symbolist drama at Aurélien-Marie Lugné-Poë's Théâtre de l'Oeuvre, while the first mainstream theatrical success was Gabrielle Réjane's performance as Nora in *Maison de Poupée*, which 'steered away from either of these two dominant modes of presenting Ibsen' (Shepherd-Barr 2012, 62). In Russia the aesthetic history of the play was equally diverse: one of the most critically acclaimed of the early

Noras, Vera Komissarzhevskaya, was influenced by symbolist approaches to theatre. Her contemporaries observed that '[s]he opened wide the window to another world by intonation alone [...] that immersed the spectator in mysticism and transformed her, inadvertently and unconsciously, into a symbol' (qtd in Senelick 1980, 478).[8]

All of these studies have created new knowledge about Ibsen's dramaturgy and the meanings embedded in *Et dukkehjem*, but their attempts to identify unique properties to explain the global popularity of the play are doomed to fail, not only because of the diversity of cultural, geographical, and temporal locations of production, but also because of the transformative processes inherent in theatrical adaptation. Genres mutate into new aesthetic forms, gendered relations are culturally specific, and theatrical characters change when they adapt to new theatre cultures. It is for these reasons that recent investigations into the global transmission of *Et dukkehjem* have shifted from close readings of the written text to close readings of performances. This approach stresses the cultural specificity of performances rather than looking for universal properties in the written text, and relies on empirical studies either of isolated productions or of the impact of the play within particular theatre cultures of cities, nations, or geographical regions. Performance analyses of productions of *Et dukkehjem* now abound in papers delivered at Ibsen conferences, within collections of Ibsen-related scholarship, and in the international journal *Ibsen Studies*. Authors have a tendency to frame these studies by using geographical, temporal, or aesthetic criteria to limit the parameters of their analyses. When viewed together, all the case studies have added significant knowledge to our understanding of the adaptation of *Et dukkehjem* in multiple cultural contexts. They all provide deep contextual knowledge of specific performances, but, like all case studies, they are framed by their own geographical and temporal specificity.

Four major collections of performance analyses have appeared in recent years. *The Relevance of* A Doll's House*—Translation and Adaptation* (Nilu 2003), the proceedings from a conference held at the Centre for Asian Theatre in Dhaka, Bangladesh in 2002, focuses on productions of the play from the Indian subcontinent. 'Ibsen Intercultural: Nora's Door Slamming around the Globe' (Budde 2011), a special issue of *Canadian Review of Comparative Literature*, includes performance analyses of stage and screen productions from Egypt, Iran, the Netherlands, Germany, and China, together with studies of comparative literature considering the influence of the play on Nigerian and Canadian dramatists, and parallel narratives from Inuit legends. *Global Ibsen: Performing Multiple Modernities*, the proceedings from a conference marking the centenary of Ibsen's death held at the Academy of the Arts in Berlin in 2006, is framed by the theoretical premise that Ibsen's major plays are global successes because they address 'problems modern or modernizing societies all over the world were and still are facing' (Fischer-Lichte et al. 2011, 1). Most of the contributors in this volume take one play and describe its transformation over time into multiple performance texts in a single country. The articles on *Et dukkehjem* come from South Africa, the USA, Australia, Canada, Japan, and Scandinavia. All these publications open up fresh areas for Ibsen scholarship; not only do they offer new knowledge about the previously hidden influence of Ibsen on the world's theatre cultures, they also include new voices of scholar/artists. Particularly prominent are directors of recent productions of *Et dukkehjem*, including Mitsuya Mori (Japan), Kamaluddin Nilu (Bangladesh), and Sunil Pokharel (Nepal).

If there is a common structure to these three collections, it is the organising principle of the nation state. In an attempt to cross national boundaries, the Centre for Ibsen Studies in Oslo invited a team of international Ibsen scholars and scholar/artists to conduct comparative research into Ibsen productions in the Indian subcontinent and East Asia. A fourth collection of essays, *Ibsen Between Cultures* (Helland and Holledge 2016), includes valuable material on the transnational history of *Et dukkehjem*, particularly with regard to a shared Bengali theatre culture in India and Bangladesh, and the influence of Tokyo theatre on the introduction of spoken word drama in Shanghai and Beijing. Like the earlier publications, the strength of the articles in this collection comes from the authors' in-depth knowledge of their local theatre cultures. Another publication tied to this research project, *Ibsen in Practice* (Helland 2015), is the first monograph with a global view of contemporary Ibsen productions; it has substantial chapters on performances of *Et dukkehjem* in China and Chile.

We owe a debt to the combined efforts of these authors, and to all the scholars who have given papers on productions of *Et dukkehjem* at the triennial International Ibsen Conference since its inception in 1965. They have addressed the history of Ibsen productions in many different theatre cultures, and references to their research will be found throughout this book, but they only cover a tiny fraction of the *Et dukkehjem* productions recorded in the IbsenStage database. It has only become possible to attempt a study of all of these productions because of the methods of data analysis and visualisation developed in the digital humanities.

The *Et dukkehjem* Data Set

How do we read *Et dukkehjem*, the entire work, at a distance? How do we 'zoom out' to see the connections between all productions of the play, instead of limiting our scope to the work of significant artists and critically acclaimed performances? What methods of analysis will quantify the history of the play in production, track its transmission around the world, and reveal the diversity of its adaptations?

The innovation of our Ibsen study is that no previous research team has had access to such a rich and extensive data set on the production of an Ibsen play within the global canon. The global data set on *Et dukkehjem* has been digitised over the last ten years, largely due to the efforts of Jens-Morten Hanssen at the National Library of Norway in Oslo, who initiated an Ibsen database. He began gathering Ibsen performance data from the programmes and posters held at the Centre for Ibsen Studies; subsequently he added data from theatre archives in the Nordic countries, Germany, the UK, Italy, France, the USA, Russia, the Netherlands, Belgium, and the Czech Republic. By mid-2008, he had entered 6000 records, which he estimated to be approximately 60% of the past productions of Ibsen's plays. Data on productions outside Europe and North America have been gathered with the assistance of international scholars from the Indian subcontinent, China, South America, and Africa; this is an ongoing process. In 2013, the data held at the National Library was entered into IbsenStage, a research database with complex searching, mapping, and network functions that is located in the Centre for Ibsen Studies at the University of Oslo. The global performance history of *Et dukkehjem* exists as a subset of 3787 records within IbsenStage. When looking at the visualisations included in this book, readers need to remember that this data set, though extensive, is still not complete. It will continue to grow, not just with records of future productions, but with records of past performances still to be collected.[9]

The IbsenStage database uses a conceptual schema for managing information about theatre productions.[10] We adopt this schema in quantifying the production history of *Et dukkehjem*. At a basic level, it determines the things we can count and the quantities we can show in graphs and diagrams. We have already introduced the concept of a **work** in referring to *Et dukkehjem*. For our purposes, the concept of the work provides a mechanism for selection: it determines the set of events to be analysed in this book. An **event** in the IbsenStage database is a distinct happening, defined by title, date, and venue: typically, a performance or a consecutive series of performances at a venue. A **venue** is defined as a place where an event happens: typically, a theatre building located at a street address or identified by geographical coordinates. IbsenStage defines **contributors** as individuals who contribute in some capacity—actors, directors, designers, producers, writers, and so on—to the conception, production, or presentation of an event. Likewise, **organisations** are defined as a group or company involved in the conception, production, or presentation of an event (see Figs. 1.3 and 1.4).

This schema also forms a basis for mapping the history of *Et dukkehjem* in production. In representing the spatial aspects of theatre, scholars have drawn on a range of visual techniques: architectural designs of theatre buildings, photographs and sketches of set designs, three-dimensional models, graphical representations of action on stage, textual mark-up of spatial indications in play-scripts, and a descriptive vocabulary rich in spatial metaphors (McAuley 2000; Wiles 2003; Tompkins 2006). To these we add cartography to represent the geographical transmission of the play by plotting the spatial distribution of theatre productions and the intersecting trajectories of artists (Bollen and Holledge 2011). Historical maps are synoptic by convention: events from different times are arrayed on a continuous terrain. Yet our approach to the cartography of theatre production brings the temporality of events to the fore. Events are characterised by their relatively brief duration at a venue: events appear briefly, flashing on and off, here and there. Venues persist between events as locations on a geographical terrain; a venue's duration is defined by its first and last events, and patterned by the rhythm of events occurring during its timespan. Contributors are mobile agents, attracted to a venue for the duration of an event and then released; their patterns of convergence, dispersal, and reconvergence in different combinations distribute a dynamic network of artistic collaboration across space and time. These patterns are fundamental to the art form: theatre production brings people together in time and space. Yet without the use of computer-assisted data management and cartographic software, the scale and significance of these patterns were difficult to determine and an empirical analysis of their structure was practically impossible.

In analysing patterns of distribution in theatre production, we also adopt techniques of visualisation from social network analysis (Scott 2000). As artists move from production to production, their trajectories may be analysed as forming networks of collaboration. By visualising how

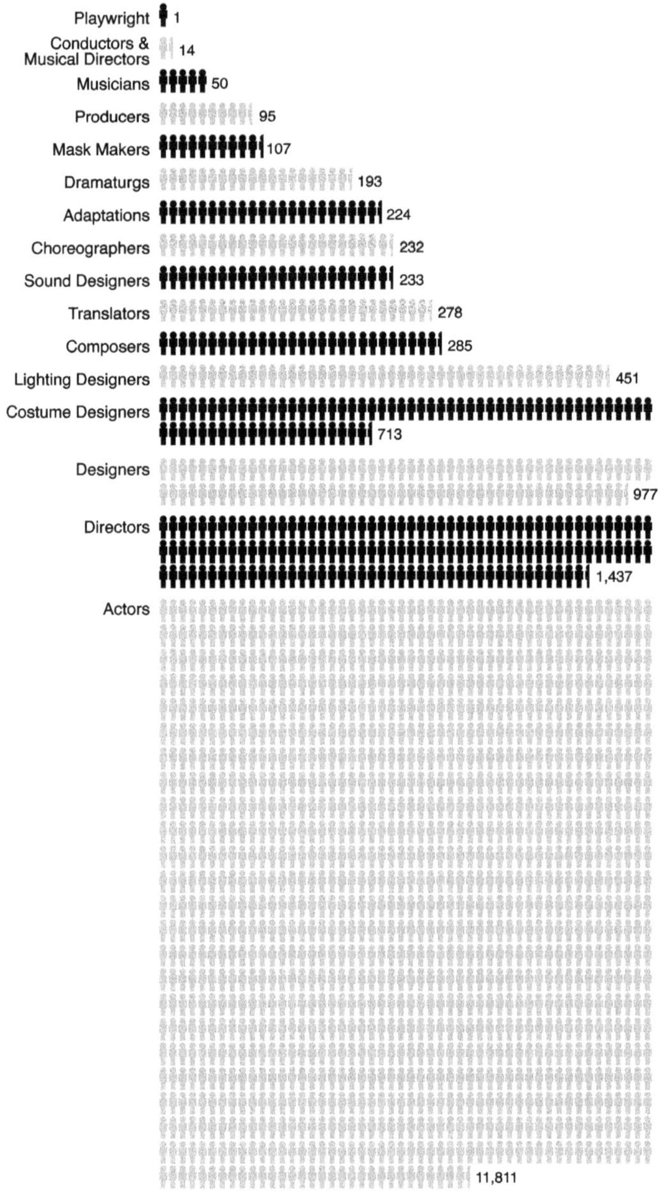

Fig. 1.3 Contributors to *Et dukkehjem* by artistic function, 1879–2015, as recorded in performance credits (Source: IbsenStage)

Country	First Year	**Organisations by chronology** [truncated, with count]
Denmark	1879	August Rasmussens Teaterselskab, Vilhelm Petersens Selskab, August Lindbergs turnéer, Betty Hennings Turne, Teater Mungo, Johanne Dybwad-Turneen, Fahlstrøms Theater, Den norske Ibsen Tourné... [21]
Germany	1880	Vilhelm Petersens Selskab, Kieler Stadttheater, Süddeutsches Hoftheater-Ensemble, Stadttheater Mainz, Stadttheater Magdeburg, Großherzogliches Hoftheater Weimar, Stadttheater Glogau, Stadttheater Lübeck... [99]
Norway	1880	Christian Wilhelm Foght Teaterselskab, Christiania Folketheater, Den Skandinaviska Gästspelsturneen, Nordlandstourneen, Teater Mungo, Nationalturneen, Johanne Dybwad-Turneen, Nationaltheatret... [40]
Poland	1880	Trupa operetkowa Juliana Grabińskiego, Tournée Gabrieli Zapolskiej, Stadttheater Stettin, Stadttheater Bromberg, Stadttheater Posen, Stadttheater Glogau, Elysium-Theater, Stadttheater Kolberg, Stadttheater Leignitz... [19]
Sweden	1880	August Rasmussens Teaterselskab, Emil Hillbergs teatersällskap, August Lindbergs Sällskap, Den Skandinaviska Gästspelsturneen, Betty Hennings Turne, Albert Ranfts Sällskap, Knut Lindroths sällskap... [18]
Austria	1881	Ensemble-Gastspiel der königlich württembergischen Hoffschauspieler, Compagnia di Roma città Drammatica, Vereinigte städtische Theater Graz, Dr. Carl Heines Ibsen-Theater, Agnes Sorma Ensemble... [13]
United States	1882	Richard Mansfields Company, Novelty Theatre, Deutsches Theater, Agnes Sorma und die Irving Place Theatergesellschaft, N.Y., Nazimova Company, Mme Vera F Komisarzhevskaya Repertory, Thanhouser, Allan Holubar... [104]
United Kingdom	1884	The Scriblers Dramatic Society, Novelty Theatre, Lydia Yavorskas (princess Bariatinsky) Matinees, Birmingham Repertory Theatre Company, Clarion Dramatic Club, J. T. Grein's Cosmopolitan Theatre, Arts Theatre Club... [54]
Hungary	1889	Egry Kálmán társulata, Somogyi Károly társulata, Valentin Lajos társulata, Csóka Sándor társulata, Makó Lajos társulata, Aradi Gerő társulata, Miklósy Gyula társulata, Halmai Imre Társulata, Bokodyné Máté Róza társulata... [48]
Australia	1889	Novelty Theatre, Stage Society, Adelaide Repertory Theatre Incorporated, Brisbane Repertory Theatre, Five Arts Club, Tin Alley Players, Independent Theatre, Canberra Repertory Theatre, Melbourne Theatre Company... [31]
Italy	1889	Compagnia Emilia Aliprandi Pieri, Compagnia di Roma città Drammatica, Compagnia Buccellati, Compagnia Drammatica Giovan Battista Marini, Compagnia Paladini-Zampieri, Compagnia Reinach / Gramatica... [30]
Netherlands	1889	De Tooneelvereeniging, Kreukniet, Bigot, Poolman en Blaaser, Jan C. De Vos en Willem van Korlaar, Tournée Direktion Wilhelm Kupfer, Agnes Sorma Ensemble, Vereenigde Rotterdamsche Tooneelisten, Haagse Comedie... [15]
Slovak Republic	1889	Tiszay Dezső Társulata, Halmai Imre Társulata, Bokodyné Máté Róza társulata, Krecsányi Ignác társulata, Károlyi Lajos társulata, Szendrey Mihály társulata, Relle Iván társulata, Komjáthy János társulata, Mezey Béla társulata... [15]
Romania	1889	Aradi Gerő társulata, Miklósy Gyula társulata, Krecsányi Ignác társulata, Valentin Lajos társulata, Egry Kálmán társulata, Bokodyné Máté Róza társulata, Makó Lajos társulata, Zilahy Gyula társulata, Szendrey Mihály társulata... [14]
France	1891	Stadttheater Straßburg, Stadttheater Metz, Compagnie Pitoëff, Les Films la Boétie, World Film Services, Ensemble Théâtral Mobile, Comédie de Lyon, Compagnie Robert Cordier, Centre Dramatique National d'Aubervilliers... [14]
Brazil	1899	Companhia Lucinda Simões, Teatro Anchieta, Teatro 5 de Setembro, Teatro Paulista, Grêmio theatrical Casimiro de Amadores Cunha, Arósio, Garcia & Rangel Produtores e Associados, Banco do Brasil, Teatro de Narradores... [12]
Japan	1911	Bungei Kyokai (The Literary Society), Kindaigeki Kyokai (The Modern Theatre Society), Tokyo Geijutsuza/Gekijo (Tokyo Art Theatre), Yoshiko Okada Troupe, New Tsukiji Troupe/Chuo Theatre, Japan Actors' School Troupe... [22]
China	1914	Peking Normal College for Women, Ershiliu jushe 26 (26 Drama Society), Peking People's Art Drama College, Shanghai Amateur Actors Association, Bright China Drama Society, Chongqing Drama Society... [11]

Fig. 1.4 Organisations producing *Et dukkehjem* events arranged by country and chronology (Source: IbsenStage)

events link artists into networks, we can trace the pathways of transmission that artists embody in performing Ibsen's play. These visualisations indicate lines of descent from the earliest productions and clusters of closely related productions that consolidate traditions; they also indicate points of disconnection, including isolated clusters of production and breaks in transmission (see Fig. 1.5). In Moretti's terms, these patterns in the play's production history suggest the play of forces in theatrical production; for our purposes, they have prompted further investigations. We also apply methods of quantification, data visualisation, and pattern recognition to our study of diversity and adaptation in productions of Ibsen's plays, although here our methods have been more exploratory, inspired by the possibilities of image processing in 'cultural analytics' (Manovich 2011) and the prospects of visual recognition systems that are in development (Shih 2010).

Transmission and Adaptation

Cultural transmission and *adaptation* are the twin themes of our study. Distant visions provide the method that unites them: we use maps and networks to identify the external flows of *cultural transmission* connecting productions through time and across space, and we use graphs and networks to explore the internal workings of *adaptations* of *Et dukkehjem*. These visualisations reveal patterns, and it is these patterns that drive the direction of our research, our assumption being that they are symptoms of underlying political, social, economic, aesthetic, or technological forces that are connected in some way to the global success of *Et dukkehjem*. Interpreting these patterns in the data as symptomatic of forces operating on the play's productions is such a crucial premise for our work that it needs to be explained before we can proceed. This interpretation draws on a cross-disciplinary model proposed by philosopher Robert Brandon and paleobiologist Daniel McShea. They collaborate across cultural studies and the natural sciences to hypothesise new ways of thinking about diversity in biology and culture. Beginning with biology, they propose a new Zero-Force Evolutionary Law that challenges the conventional view that natural selection creates diversity (McShea and Brandon 2010, 4). They reverse this view to argue that natural selection is a force that gives shape to different species by constraining the diversity of ever-changing living matter. In other words, life is difference and requires no additional force to create new forms; life will continually proliferate unless an external force like

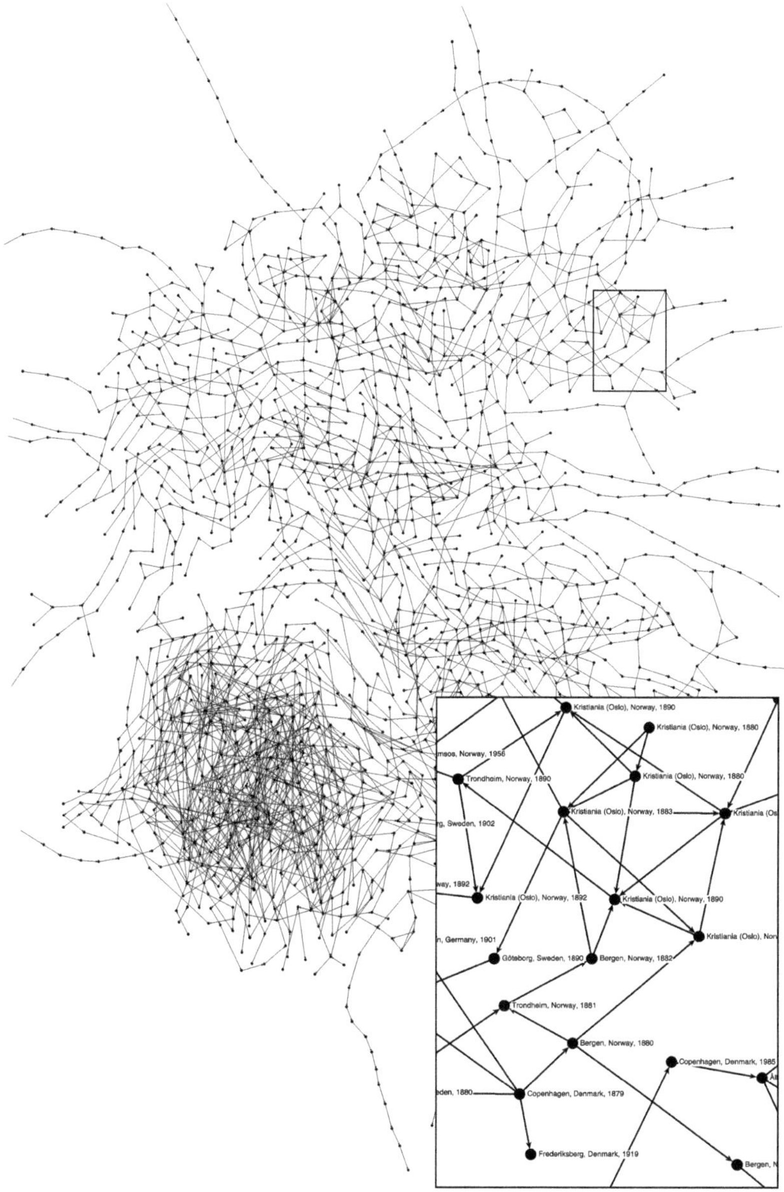

Fig. 1.5 Network of *Et dukkehjem* events linked by contributors, 1879–2015, excerpt with detail (Source: IbsenStage)

natural selection constrains or impedes such forms. The attraction of this model for our study is that we treat diversity in productions of *Et dukkehjem* as a given and concentrate on the forces of *constraint*: we look for the forces that have *constrained* the diversity of world theatre through the successful promotion of the play; we look for similarities between adaptations because they point to *constraining* forces that in some way influence the creative process.

We argue that *Et dukkehjem* conforms to the general formulation of McShea and Brandon's Law for non-biological systems where 'reproduction' and 'heredity' can be substituted with 'persistence, variation, and memory'. The general formation states that '[i]n any system in which there is persistence, variation, and memory, there is a tendency for diversity and complexity to increase, one that is always present but may be opposed or augmented by forces or constraints' (McShea and Brandon 2010, 111). *Et dukkehjem* has 'persistence, variation, and memory'. *Persistence* is difficult to define in this context, but its presence is obvious in a production history of a play that lasts for more than 135 years. As for *memory*, *Et dukkehjem* only exists through memory traces: cast lists, production scripts, prompt copies, programmes, reviews, photographs, electronic recordings, audiences' recollections, and so on. More importantly, it is through the collective memories of artists and audiences that aesthetic knowledge moves from production to production. Marvin Carlson suggests that all theatre 'is the repository of cultural memory, but, like the memory of each individual, it is also subject to continual adjustment and modification as the memory is recalled in new circumstances and contexts' (2003, 2). These adjustments and modifications can produce intentional *variation*, but there are also variations caused by 'unintentional drift', a term used by cultural anthropologists to explain random changes within cultural transmission (Stark et al. 2008, 6). This form of drift or change can be defined as 'any outcome that deviates from the expected outcome' (Stark et al. 2008, 91). As there are so many variables in any theatre production—from the artists, to the performance space and its audiences, to material elements used to create its fictional world—random variation will occur within the creative process even if the participating artists are trying to faithfully reproduce an earlier production. As persistence, variation, and memory are intrinsic to *Et dukkehjem*, we apply the logic of the McShea and Brandon schema and proceed on the basis that the condition of *Et dukkehjem* is one of increasing diversity and complexity. Diversity applies to every aspect of the production data: geographical, temporal, and aesthetic. Complexity is present in the pure sense of an increase in the 'number of part types or degree of differentiation among parts' (McShea and Brandon 2010, 7). In other words, an adaptation may be structurally more complex than Ibsen's text, but this does not necessarily result in any improved efficacy of performance.

By adopting the McShea and Brandon Law, we treat all the diversity and complexity that we find in the 3787 records of *Et dukkehjem* productions as unforced; it is the result of a collaborative art practice that interacts with live and unpredictable audiences. This makes sense in a study of the production history of a single play, as no two performances are ever the same, let alone two productions. We attend to the repetitions, echoes, and imitations between productions because they indicate a force at work influencing cultural dissemination, creative processes, and performance practices. If these repetitions are frequent enough to produce patterns in our visualisations, we surmise that the force behind them may be influencing the production of *Et dukkehjem*.

The thematic division of this book reflects the twin themes of our study: in Part I we look at the external forces responsible for the successful cultural transmission of *Et dukkehjem*, and in Part II we investigate the internal forces at work within the adaptation process. When considering external forces, we draw on theoretical models from the sociology of the arts to examine how constraints over the diversity of world theatre have secured a dominant position for *Et dukkehjem* in the global canon. Chapter 2 investigates the external social force generated by the European women's rights movements of the late nineteenth century: it increased the influence of women artists in the world markets of commercial theatre, changed their expectations in their public and private life, and created the market for *Et dukkehjem* as a play that addressed cultural changes in the social organisation of gender. This social force was crucial to the global success of *Et dukkehjem* before 1914. Norway is the source of the second force that we examine in Chapter 3. The Norwegian institutions that have constrained the diversity of world theatre by promoting *Et dukkehjem* include major theatres repeatedly selecting the play for production; established Norwegian theatre families using the play as a form of cultural inheritance; and government departments stimulating new domestic and foreign productions. This symbiotic relationship between a play and a nation is central to the success of *Et dukkehjem* from the early twentieth century to the present day.

Adaptation is the focus of Part II. In a short introduction we highlight the differences between our use of the McShea and Brandon model and the metaphors of natural selection as the wellspring of diversity that are currently used within adaptation studies to explain cultural production. In Chapter 4, we analyse visualisations of the inner workings of comparative adaptations to find patterns that indicate social or aesthetic forces at work in the creative process. We begin by looking for patterns that might indicate that there are core elements in multiple adaptations of *Et dukkehjem*. Our findings indicate that there are only a few common plot elements, some similarities in the practices of narrative relocation and changes in plot structures, and some parallels in the manipulation of characters. The forces that appear to be strong enough to constrain diversity in the creative process coalesce around four main areas: performance and narrative time; the links between the bricks and mortar of performance venues and the aesthetic choices made by artists; trans-cultural rigidities over ideological constructions of motherhood; and constraints over the representation of the female body in performance. Chapter 5 pursues this latter constraint by focusing solely on the physical score written into the play by Ibsen, and the social and aesthetic forces that have shaped its re-creations and re-imaginings. Our visualisations of the inner workings of comparative adaptations reveal a number of disparate forces. Where synergies do emerge between these constraining forces, they revolve around conventions governing theatrical representations of sexuality and gender. In themselves these forces do not contribute to the successful adaptation of *Et dukkehjem*, but they do stimulate the creative innovation of artists who decide to use the play to challenge or reinforce these representational conventions, particularly in eras marked by sexual vectors of social change.

What accounts for the global success of *Et dukkehjem*? The question is simple, but the answer is not. Multiple forces have shaped the *Et dukkehjem* cultural field; they are multi-faceted and contradictory. If there is a secret to the play's success it lies in their complex interactions; it is these dynamics that we aim to explore.

Notes

1. '*Et dukkehjem*'. 1879. Directed by H.P. Holst. Performed by Betty Hennings as Nora. Det Kongelige Teater, Copenhagen, Denmark. December 21. *IbsenStage*, Event 75660. https://ibsenstage.hf.uio.no/pages/event/75660.
2. All Ibsen's letters have been translated for this publication by May-Brit Akerholt direct from *Henrik Ibsen Skrifter* (*HIS*): http://www.ibsen.uio.no/.

3. In the earlier English translation by Henrietta Frances Lord, the German tradition of using *Nora* as the title was applied. In his review of her translation, William Archer wrote, '[i]t is difficult to understand why Ibsen's title, *A Doll's House*, which fits the play so perfectly, should have been discarded, in England as well as in Germany, for the meaningless and commonplace *Nora*' (Archer 1883, 5–6).
4. Henrik Ibsen to Edmund Gosse, 4 July 1879: 'I have lived here in Rome with my family since September and have during this time devoted myself to a new dramatic work, which will soon be finished, and which will come out in October. It is a serious play, a family drama, really, dealing with current conditions and problems in a marriage; the play will be divided into three rather long acts' (Ibsen 1879a, 498–99).
5. This is William Archer's translation of Ibsen's 'Notes for a Modern Tragedy'. All of Archer's translations within this book have been amended by Frode Helland and any changes are indicated with square brackets.
6. Eleanor Marx was so inspired by Ibsen that she learnt Norwegian and translated the first versions of *Enemy of the People* and *The Lady from the Sea* into English (Kapp 1972–76, 249); Emma Goldman published Ibsen's plays through her Earth Mother Publishing Association (Shulman 1998, 29); Olive Schreiner wrote about Nora in her journal (Kapp 1972, 101); and Alexandra Kollontai, in a public speech commemorating the anniversary of Ibsen's death in March 1928 in Oslo, spoke of the inspiration of Nora to her generation (Porter 1980, 447).
7. See Cima (1983) for a further discussion on the importance of Ibsen in the emergence of a new realist acting style in late nineteenth-century Britain.
8. Her brother, Fyodor Komissarzhevsky, designed an abstract set out of folded brown curtains, hanging at acute angles, for her performance as Nora (Komisarjevsky 1929, 90). We have used the more usual spelling of Komissarzhevsky, but that publication uses the older version of the surname.
9. This book analyses the data on productions of *Et dukkehjem* (1879–2015) that had been recorded in IbsenStage, https://ibsenstage.hf.uio.no, at 30 October 2015.
10. IbsenStage adopted the schema from AusStage (2003–15), http://www.ausstage.edu.au; see Bollen et al. (2009).

PART 1

Cultural Transmission

In Part I, we consider the *external forces* shaping the distribution of *Et dukkehjem*. We look at the geographical reach and the duration of the play over time to investigate the forces that have maintained it as a world drama. Recent scholarship has examined the distribution of Ibsen's plays for the reading public via the book market, and there is a growing interest in conducting comparative studies of translations (D'Amico 2014; Fulsås 2005–10). This is a particularly rich field: there are 155 translators listed as contributors in IbsenStage records prior to Ibsen's death in 1906. But our interest lies in performances and cultural transmission by artists across space and time: groups of artists travelling together in global touring productions, and individual artists moving between productions over the length of their careers. We use maps to visualise the major distribution routes used by artists to tour productions of *Et dukkehjem*. To create these maps we looked at the movements of 16,074 artists in productions of *Et dukkehjem* to find those connected with performances in three or more countries. This process identified 568 key individuals; the tours of the fifty-six Noras are represented in Fig. 1.6.

The first global expansion of *Et dukkehjem* happens at the end of the nineteenth century and beginning of the early twentieth century over a twenty-five-year span. During this period the play is performed in eighteen different languages. Fourteen major international touring productions in eleven European languages travel to thirty-five countries over five continents. Between the First and Second World Wars there is comparatively little touring: IbsenStage holds 431 records on productions with only five European tours from 1914 to 1945. Even if the records for these years are underrepresented in

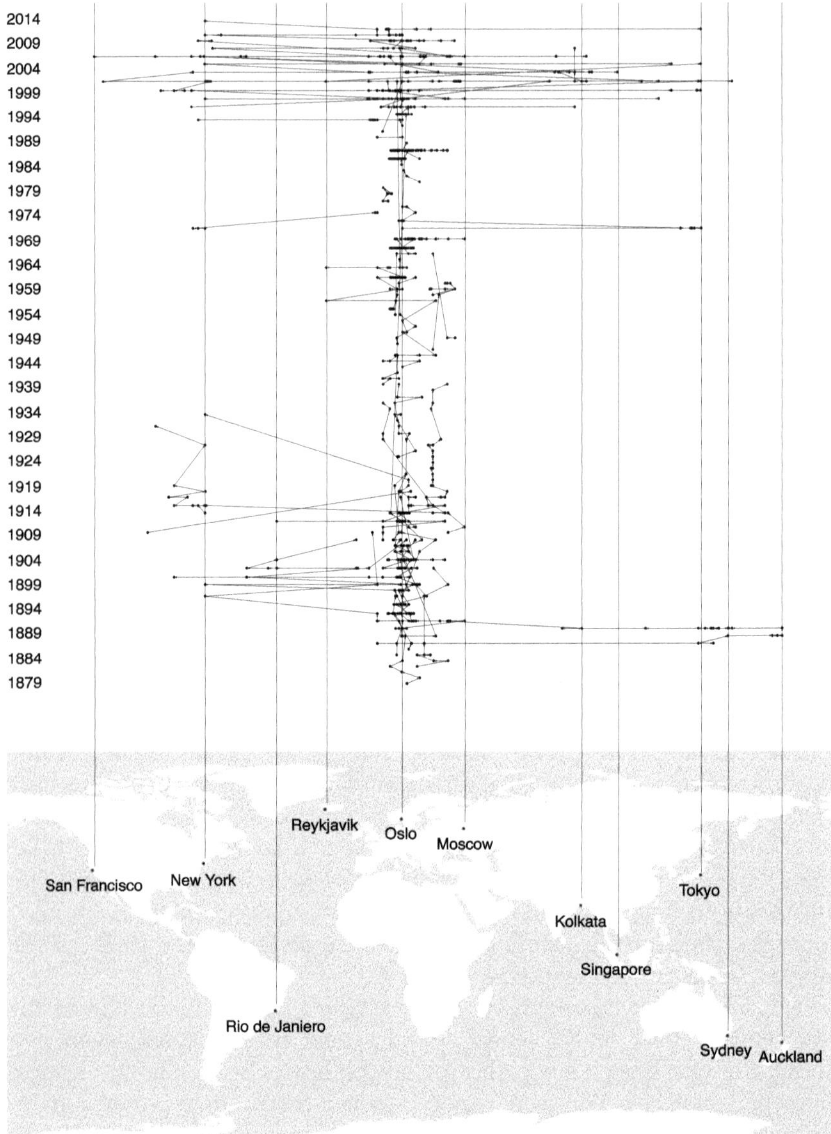

Fig. I.1 Touring *Et dukkehjem*, 1879–2014—a time-map depicting the trajectories of actresses playing Nora in three or more countries (Source: *IbsenStage*)

the database, there is still a clear indication that the global market for European productions of the play was severely disrupted during these years. From the middle to the late twentieth century, global touring makes a comeback. The artists driving this new wave come from Scandinavia, particularly Norway; the pattern they create begins with extensive touring in the Nordic region and expands south into thirteen European countries, before moving beyond the continent to East Asia and the USA. The final era, which sees a global explosion of activity, begins in 1990. It exceeds the boundaries of the first global wave with German and English as the dominant languages; in addition, there are a number of touring productions originating outside Europe, particularly in the Americas, and East and South Asia.

To analyse these touring maps, we have taken inspiration from two theoretical frameworks from the sociology of the arts. Pierre Bourdieu's theorisation of the European cultural field in the late nineteenth century is particularly apt for our study, given both the importance of his method of analysing cultural production and the coincidence in chronology in Bourdieu's survey and the first global wave of *Et dukkehjem* touring that is the subject of Chapter 2. Bourdieu identifies two oppositional poles or positions of power that are sought after by artists: dominance over the subfield of large-scale commercial production that attracted bourgeois artists seeking financial capital; and dominance over the subfield of alternative production that attracted bohemian artists in search of the prestige associated with informed critical acclaim, which he termed symbolic capital. He refers to works that are the focus of artistic competition as stakes in the game:

> [e]nrichment accompanies ageing when the work manages to enter the game, when it becomes a stake in the game and so incorporates some of the energy produced in the struggle of which it is the object. The struggle, which sends the work into the past, is also what ensures it a form of survival; lifting it from the state of a dead letter, a mere thing subject to the ordinary laws of ageing, the struggle at least ensures it has the sad eternity of academic debate. (1993, 111)

There is ample evidence that *Et dukkehjem* is a 'stake in the game' and has entered the 'sad eternity of academic debate' of which this book is a part. Artists have used the play for over a hundred years in their jostling for position in the cultural field. The struggle for financial and symbolic capital by female artists is of particular relevance to Chapter 2, as it concerns the competition between the early European Noras who toured the play around the globe at the end of the nineteenth century. Bourdieu contends that artists' successful accumulation of all forms of capital is influenced not only by their art practice, but also by their geographical location and their previous economic, cultural, and social capital. We add gender to this list of factors that are central to the workings of the cultural field. Given the subject matter of *Et dukkehjem*, controversy over the stage representation of sex and gender is to be expected; less visible are the competitive struggles between female and male artists over the cultural ownership of the work. The activities of the early European Noras have received little attention in comparison with the more familiar story of the struggle for symbolic power waged by Ibsen's male 'brokers' in the independent theatres of Paris, Berlin, and London. Yet the cultural diversity and sheer size of the audiences reached by these actress-managers far exceeded the numbers of spectators attending the limited seasons of the play presented by European avant-garde theatres.

From the struggle of the early Noras for a commercial share in the global theatre market, we move in Chapter 3 to examine the institutional forces at work in *Et dukkehjem*. To negotiate the shift from artists to institutions, we draw on the work of Régis Debray, who has theorised the role of the powerful institutional players in the process of cultural transmission. According to Debray, competition between artists will not ensure the duration of any work without additional institutional support. He suggests that every idea, religion, or text that survives through time has behind it an 'institution' (2004, 11). The maps of the last two eras covering the period from the middle of the twentieth century until today reveal the importance of major Norwegian theatre institutions and the Norwegian state. The patterns created by their activity at home and abroad reveal the historical importance of the play in the creation of a national imaginary for domestic consumption and the making of a national icon for export. If there is a single institution that has worked to promote *Et dukkehjem* as a major text in world theatre, it is the Norwegian government. In 2001, it was invited to lodge six documents in the United Nations Educational, Scientific, and Cultural Organisation (UNESCO) Memory of the World digital repository: one of the documents chosen was the original manuscript of *Et dukkehjem* by Henrik Ibsen. Norway was the first country to choose the manuscript of a play to represent its national culture. The nomination cited the importance of the play in Asia and the Third World, 'where its form became symbolic of modern Western drama and its content symbolic of values such as human rights and existential freedom' (UNESCO 2015).

CHAPTER 2

Mapping the Early Noras

Et dukkehjem was an international success by the early twentieth century, with performances in forty-six countries across five continents. Maps showing this first wave of globalisation of the play are the ***distant visions*** that structure this chapter; the patterns on these maps challenge conventional narratives of Ibsen's career by revealing an early commercial history of his most popular play.[1]

The maps that shape this chapter follow the trajectories of the artists who were responsible for this first global transmission of *Et dukkehjem*. To find them we listed all the contributors in IbsenStage who were connected with performances in three or more countries before 1914; by checking the production records, we found the twenty-two Noras responsible for spreading the play around the world. Yet who were these women, where did they come from, and what were the market conditions they met on their travels? This chapter follows these pioneering Noras on their journeys to Asia, Australasia, and the Americas, and examines the critical reception of their performances. While their productions account for 281 events out of a total of 825 recorded for these years, their transnational touring is crucial to an understanding of the global success of *Et dukkehjem*. Wherever they went, they left behind a legacy that informed the ongoing production history of the play. It was their persistence that secured *Et dukkehjem* a place in the repertoire of world theatre.

J. Holledge et al., *A Global Doll's House*, Palgrave Studies in Performance and Technology, DOI 10.1057/978-1-137-43899-7_2

While maps visualise this first global transmission of *Et dukkehjem*, there is a major question that they prompt but cannot answer: why did these early Noras devote so much of their creative energy to the international dissemination of this play? To answer this question, we shift from the distancing provided by maps to the close-ups of biographies to examine the lives of eight early Noras where the relationships between the role and lived experience were particularly entangled. All eight were remarkable women, but there are extraordinary similarities in their personal lives that help to elucidate this attachment to Ibsen's character. The transition from maps to biography, from distance to close up, is central to our methodology. Distant visions guide us to new sites of critical enquiry; when we reach these sites, we zoom in to consider the specifics of people and performances to answer the new questions stimulated by this research methodology. Combining these two approaches in this chapter uncovers a major social force behind the first global success of the play. Although discernible in multiple and sometimes contradictory ways, this force is the European women's rights movements of the late nineteenth and early twentieth centuries.

To cite these women's movements as one of the *forces of constraint* that we suggest in Chapter 1 are responsible for the global success of *Et dukkehjem* may seem like a contradiction, particularly as the social context they created made it possible for the early Noras to manage their own theatre companies. Yet these movements did function as an aesthetic constraint because they influenced women to make identical choices in their theatrical repertoires, thus limiting the diversity of world drama while simultaneously increasing the global success of *Et dukkehjem*. There are still fierce disagreements in academic circles about Ibsen's views on the political activism of his female contemporaries and his intentions in writing the play, which we address in the volume's conclusion, but this chapter provides incontrovertible evidence that the play was *used* by artists, publicists, and critics at the turn of the nineteenth and twentieth centuries to promote debates on the gender and sexuality issues of their day.[2]

Mapping the Trajectories of the Early Noras

The *Et dukkehjem* maps show that the Noras carved up the world's theatre markets according to the established spheres of European political influence. With the exception of one Japanese production, all the tours originated in Europe and followed global flows of European migration; they used the shipping, rail, and road networks to traverse the trade routes that linked European nations with their colonial settlements and diasporas. The English-speaking touring circuit extended across the globe, embracing Australasia and North America; German-speaking productions dominated central Europe and toured as far as Chicago in the west, Istanbul in the east, Tartu (Latvia) in the north, and Athens in the south; the Scandinavian productions circulated within the Nordic region, only venturing as far as Russia and Germany; the French productions travelled as far east as Turkey, west to Uruguay, and north to Norway; the Italian productions went north to Russia via Switzerland and the Austro-Hungarian Empire, and west across to Spain, to Uruguay, and to Mexico; the Portuguese and Greek productions were slightly more geographically contained, the former touring to Brazil and Uruguay, and the latter to Egypt and Turkey. A separate touring circuit emerged in Japan and expanded into East Asia.[3] By 1920, these global touring circuits reached their geographical limits. The only overlaps between these tours happened in cosmopolitan cities where performances were given in three or more languages: New York, St Petersburg, Montevideo, Rio de Janeiro, and Istanbul. That the world theatre market of the late nineteenth century was divided according to geo-political and language boundaries is understandable, but the successful integration of a play written in Dano-Norwegian into all these theatre markets is still remarkable.

Touring circuits for commercial theatre were well established by the late nineteenth century; they had produced the first truly international stars, including Sarah Bernhardt and Tomasso Salvini. Transnational touring was also a financial necessity for managers with expensive theatres in major cities: for instance, Henry Irving and Charles Kean both toured to America and Australia to support their activities in London (Davis 1985, 21). While the touring circuits that carried *Et dukkehjem* may not in themselves be remarkable, the fact that the twenty-two Noras used them to successfully export Ibsen's play challenges the conventional historical account of Ibsen's first international breakthrough. This is usually attributed to the efforts of his famous advocates: the major translators Wilhelm Lange, William Archer, and Moritz Prozor; the critics Georg Brandes, George Bernard Shaw, and Edmund Gosse; and the avant-garde producers Otto Brahm at Freie Bühne in Berlin, André Antoine at Théâtre Libre, Aurélien-Marie Lugné-Poë at Théâtre de l'Oeuvre in Paris, and Jacob Grein at the Independent Theatre in Britain. Pascale Casanova has argued that it was the collective foreign adoption of Ibsen in Britain, Ireland, and France that made him 'universally recognised as universal' (2007, 229).

Yet the *Et dukkehjem* maps suggest that it was the early Noras from Germany, Denmark, Norway, France, Italy, Portugal, Russia, Japan, the UK, and Greece who secured Ibsen's first international successes. These women are the artists who lie behind the trajectory patterns that crisscross the maps. The lack of historical importance accorded to them in the Ibsen story is symptomatic of what Bourdieu has termed the constant struggle over the relative value placed on symbolic and financial capital. A scholar must be able to 'proclaim the value of the author he defends' (Bourdieu 1993, 77). It is easier to defend Ibsen's value by highlighting his connections with the men of the European avant-garde than by his association with the actress-managers of the nineteenth-century commercial touring circuits; after all, the European avant-garde was to have a profound influence on the development of twentieth-century theatre.[4] The symbolic value attributed to Ibsen as a playwright associated with the early years of this aesthetic movement has been considerable. In contrast, the extraordinary power and authority attained by the late nineteenth-century actress-managers were short-lived. Their influence was a product of the social changes in the education and employment of women that emerged with the first wave of women's rights movements that swept through Europe and its diaspora cultures, colonies, and settlements, but disappeared with the outbreak of the First World War in 1914.

In explaining the early global success of *Et dukkehjem*, we cannot underestimate the fact that Ibsen wrote his play at precisely the time that these actress-managers reached the peak of their influence within the European theatre industry. They used the role of Nora to define their professional identities, to display their virtuosity as performers, and to justify their unconventional lives off stage. It was for all these reasons that Nora became a character of great importance to the women managing their own theatre companies at the end of the nineteenth century.[5] George Bernard Shaw, writing about the four major Ibsenite actresses in Britain—Janet Achurch, Florence Farr, Marion Lea, and Elizabeth Robins—described the differences between these new women of the British theatre and their predecessors in the following terms:

> [a]ll four were products of the modern movement for the higher education of women, literate, in touch with advanced thought, and coming by natural predilection on the stage from outside the theatrical class, in contradistinction to the senior generation of inveterately sentimental actresses, schooled in the old fashion if at all, born into their profession, quite out of the political and social movement around them—in short, intellectually naïve to the last degree. (1891, 140)

To distance themselves from a previous era dominated by the sentimental character *and* the sentimental actress, these new women of the theatre embraced Ibsen's plays and his complex female characters. In Britain, Elizabeth Robins claimed Ibsen as part of the women's struggle for an independent voice in an industry where

> freedom in the practice of our art, how the bare opportunity to practise it at all, depended for the actress, on considerations humiliatingly different from those that confronted the actor. The stage career of an actress was inextricably involved in the fact that she was a woman and that those who were the masters of the theatre were men. These considerations did not belong to art; they stultified art. (1932b, 33)

In Japan, the first performance of *Et dukkehjem* coincided with the appearance of the first modern actress on the stage in a theatre culture that had relied on female impersonators for centuries; the production was extensively reviewed by the feminist magazine *Seito*, named after the British feminist group the Bluestockings (Reich and Fukuda 1976, 281). Wherever the new women of the theatre gained influence, Nora became a site of commercial and artistic rivalry. When an actress succeeded in knocking out her national competition and had exhausted the local market, her next step was to embark on a transnational circuit in search of new audiences. Yet it was language and not distance that limited the touring trajectories of these actress-managers: they were performing in their mother tongues and, although they travelled great distances, they were playing to migrants from their own cultural backgrounds. *Et dukkehjem* became a valuable commodity in an age where gender issues were being hotly debated, and the actress-managers kept Nora in their personal repertoires for an average of fifteen years.

Europe: The Starting Point

Our first map, Fig. 2.1a, shows the dense web of touring trajectories of the Noras who dominated the European market. The Polish actress Gabriela Zapolska had the distinction of being the first transnational European Nora. From 1882, her touring circuit covered the ghost country of Poland, which had been partitioned between Prussia, Austria, and Russia during the late eighteenth century. She performed in all three territories and in the capital of the most repressive of the Polish colonisers, St Petersburg, where there was a migrant community of approximately 60,000 Poles.[6] It was not unusual to find performances produced in the Russian colonies touring to the capital, and

a

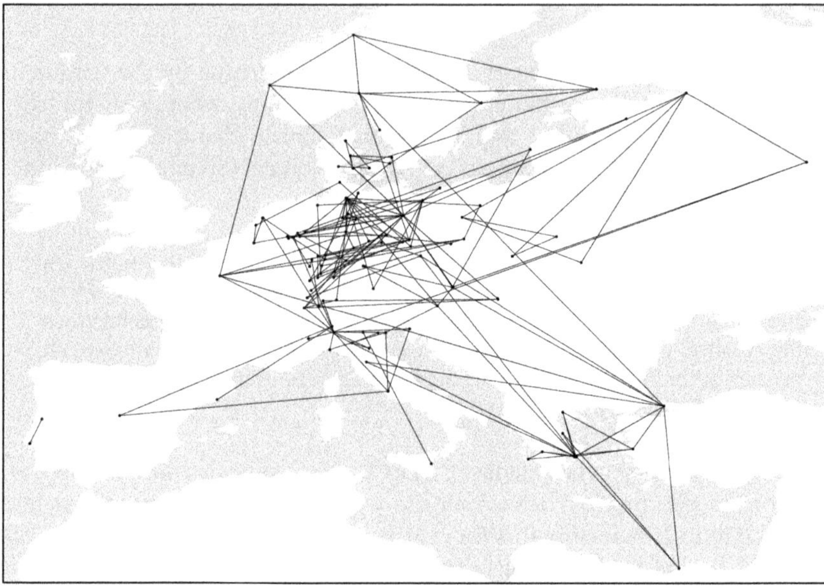

b

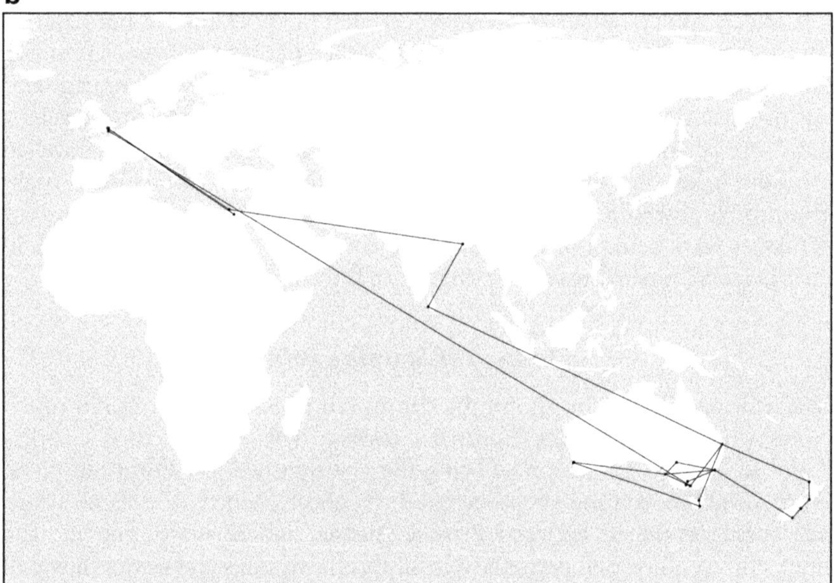

Fig. 2.1 (**a**) European tours by Agnes Sorma, Auguste Prasch-Grevenberg, Betty Hennings, Eleonora Duse, Emma Gramatica, Gabriela Zapolska, Irene Triesch, Johanne Dybwad, Kyveli Adrianou, Lilli Petri, Lucinda Simões, Suzanne Després, Teresa Mariani Zampieri (also known as Teresa Mariani), Thessa Klinkhammer, and Vera Komissarzhevskaya, 1879–1930 (Source: IbsenStage). (**b**) Janet Achurch tours to Australia, New Zealand, Colombo, Calcutta, and Cairo, 1889–92 (Source: IbsenStage)

Finnish actors were also regular visitors to Russia in the late nineteenth century; Ida Aalberg was the first Nora to play there in 1894 to an audience drawn from the 20,000 Finns living in the city.[7] As a city on the periphery of Europe, St Petersburg hosted Noras from Italy, Poland, Finland, and Germany. Although the Italian Noras, Eleonora Duse and Emma Gramatica, were frequent visitors to the Austro-Hungarian Empire, central Europe was dominated by five German Noras who toured the play as well as giving guest performances in the productions of resident companies: Agnes Sorma,[8] Thessa Klinkhammer,[9] Irene Triesch,[10] Auguste Prasch-Grevenberg,[11] and Lilli Petri.[12] Istanbul was the only city on the south-eastern border of Europe where the European Noras competed for audiences. The power struggles for influence over the Ottoman Empire, the 'sick man of Europe' prior to 1914, were reflected in the competition for audiences in this city. The documentation suggests that the first Nora to play Istanbul was the German actress Agnes Sorma.[13] Her company had toured extensively in Europe, visiting Italy, Austria, Belgium, Greece, and the Netherlands; she wrote the dates and places of all her performances on a tambourine given to her by Ibsen with his inscription 'To the most beautiful Nora'. Sorma was followed in Istanbul by the French actress Suzanne Després, who played there in 1906.[14] When Kyveli Adrianou[15] and Eleonora Lorandou[16] arrived a year later, they initiated what was to become the dominant pattern of Greek productions touring to Turkey and Egypt.

To provide coherence to the convoluted history of the global transmission of *Et dukkehjem* beyond the borders of Europe, we follow the trajectory of the Nora who covered the greatest distance, the British actress Janet Achurch. She performed the role in Australia, New Zealand, Ceylon, India, and Egypt in 1889–92; and three years later she made a brief appearance in the USA.[17] When Achurch went east she was a lone Nora following the trade and cultural routes of the British Empire, but when she went west she found herself in the congested market formed by European migration to North America. Not only was she absent from continental Europe, she also never ventured to South America, where the artists from southern Europe held sway. Achurch's trajectory provides the core narrative to the global flows of the play, as her geographical presence and absence speak to the competing European forces within the world theatre market at the turn of the century.

Going East

In 1889, Janet Achurch and her business partner and husband, Charles Charrington, signed a contract to perform a fairly standard repertoire of commercial plays in Australia and New Zealand. Figure 2.1b shows their touring circuit, which was typical of the one-way traffic of theatre from Britain to Australasia in the late nineteenth century. Before embarking on their journey, Achurch and Charrington used their advance from the Australian tour to mount a production of William Archer's translation of *A Doll's House*.[18] They booked the Novelty Theatre in London for seven performances; this was the first professional production of the play in Britain, and it created such a furore that it ran for a further seventeen nights.[19] Achurch and Charrington wanted to capitalise on their London success and offered to pay the Australian management group Williamson, Garner, and Musgrove five hundred pounds in compensation to break their contract, but their offer—equivalent to five months' touring (Charrington 1916)—was rejected. By the time they arrived in Melbourne, the reviews from the Novelty season had reached Australia, and the management insisted that the tour open with a performance of *A Doll's House*.[20] The play had not been mentioned in the original contract and the prompt copy from the production was in London.[21] As Charrington explained in a letter to George Bernard Shaw, they had no alternative but to reconstruct the performance from Achurch's memory: '[w]e wrote the play from memory, her memory mainly, there was nothing else to do. Archer had kept the script of his printed Edition de Luxe' (1916). Herbert Fleming, who had played Krogstad in London, was a member of their touring company, but Charrington had to take over the role of the absent Torvald. As the rehearsals for the local actors playing the remaining parts were minimal, the premiere of *A Doll's House* in Australia must have been heavily biased towards the scenes involving Nora, Helmer, and Krogstad.

After the Melbourne season, Achurch and Charrington ended their contract with their Australian management, but they remained in Australia and New Zealand for two years, performing in major cities and 'bush towns' (Charrington 1892). They presented a repertoire of twenty-five plays and gave a total of three hundred and sixty performances in Australia. *A Doll's House* was their most popular play with fifty-three performances, closely followed by forty-four performances of *Forget-Me-Not*, written by Florence Crauford Grove and Herman Merivale.[22] They toured to Adelaide, Sydney, Brisbane, Perth, and Hobart as well as Melbourne, and visited key regional agricultural and mining towns: Ballarat, Bendigo, Warrnambool, Broken Hill, Freemantle, and Launceston. From October 1890 to January 1891, they visited New Zealand and performed in Auckland, Christchurch, and Wellington. On returning to London, Achurch described her antipodean audiences as naïve colonials:

> [w]e visited a dozen of the smaller towns of the Australian continent, playing for a night at a time to the bush population [...]. I am glad to say that the piece held them wonderfully from beginning to end. Our chief difficulty was in getting them out of the theatre after the final fall of the curtain. They did not, or could not, appreciate the 'note of interrogation'. They continued to sit in their seats, saying that it was impossible that the play could be over, and adding that they intended to wait patiently until it came to an end. (Achurch 1892, 1–2)

In a detailed survey of the press reception of the Australian performances of *A Doll's House*, Christine Judith Angel analyses over 700 articles and reviews and evaluates them in four categories: Achurch's performances; reactions to the character of Nora; critiques of the play; and assessments of Ibsen's skill as a dramatist. She concludes that all the reviews of Achurch's performance were positive, while there were two positive reviews for every negative review dealing with the character of Nora, the play, and the dramatist. When the play toured New Zealand for three months, the response of the press was even more favourable (Angel 2014).

Homeward Bound

Although Achurch's tour was dominated by her experiences in Australia and New Zealand, she was also the first actress to perform Nora in Asia.[23]

> [w]e travelled by the British India line to Java, and played at Batavia for one night, much to the delight of the Dutch residents. Thence we proceeded to Ceylon, where the planters took *A Doll's House* very well. From Ceylon we went to Calcutta—still by the British India line—arriving there just about Christmas; indeed we spent Christmas night on board the steamer, and gave an entertainment for the benefit of our fellow passengers. We opened in Calcutta on Boxing Day. (Achurch 1892, 1–2)[24]

Charrington was not happy with the response of the expatriate audience in Calcutta and complained of the difficulties involved in 'changing plays constantly as is necessary in a town of small population' (1892, 2). The parochialism of their Calcutta audience can be surmised from Charrington's farewell speech: he told the spectators that he had visited the offices of the local English newspaper, spat in the face of the editor, and accused him of publishing 'a gross, cowardly and clumsy libel' (Charrington 1892, 2). He was referring to an article insinuating that Achurch's addiction to opium was responsible for a backstage disturbance that had delayed one of their performances. Achurch's description of the Calcutta audience was also suitably vitriolic; when asked by a London journalist how its members had responded to *A Doll's House*, she replied:

> [n]ot very much, I'm afraid. They are a great deal too tired and frivolous for anything but the lightest of comedy. Their constant complaint is that they are tired out. They work as hard as they possibly can in order to get back to England at the earliest moment, and half of them are invalids. Obviously, therefore, they are not in a condition to appreciate the work of a serious dramatist like Ibsen. (Achurch 1892, 1–2)

There is no evidence that the Calcutta audience included anyone other than members of the expatriate British community. The play might have found a new audience when Achurch and Charrington moved to Bombay and performed for the Parsee community, but they did not include *A Doll's House* in their repertoire. As Achurch explained with a tone of unquestioning cultural superiority, 'we gave the Parsees a little Shakespeare—they are very fond of Shakespeare' (1892, 1–2). There are no records of Indian productions of *Et dukkehjem* between the brief appearance of Achurch in Calcutta and the Utpal Dutt adaptation *Putuler Sansar* in 1951. Seven years later in 1958, the play became a phenomenal success with Sambhu Mitra's adaptation, *Putul Khela*, and entered the dramatic canon of Indian theatre. This production ran for twenty years and is the best documented example of a post-colonial adaptation of the play (Ahsanuzzaman 2012; Gupta 2006). Apart from the Calcutta location, the only connection between this production and the earlier Achurch colonial performance is the William Archer version that Mitra used as the basis of his translation into Bengali.

The last stop between India and London on the Achurch and Charrington touring map was Cairo, and it was here that they began to encounter some resistance. Arriving at the Cairo Khedivial Theatre, Achurch was met with cultural hostility from the French and Italian communities: 'I don't believe they dreamt of the possibility of such a thing as an English artist; to their minds it seemed incomprehensible, incredible, beyond the nature of things' (Achurch 1892, 1–2). Eventually the French residents were persuaded to join the British audiences at performances of *A Doll's House*, but the Italians stayed away despite the fact that there were no competing productions on offer from other European Noras. It was to take another twenty years before the first Greek Nora, Kyveli Adrianou, reached Alexandria.[25] The Cairo experience confirmed two important factors about the Achurch Charrington tour: firstly, they may have covered vast distances but they were performing to a very limited cultural demographic of British emigrants and colonial expatriates; and secondly, the sphere of British influence over the theatrical market to the East of Egypt was vast. Achurch was confronted by a far more competitive market when she travelled west, as is clear from the next maps (Fig. 2.2), which show the multiple trajectories of European Noras across the Atlantic. They were drawn to this New World by the fifty million Europeans who had emigrated to the Americas during the nineteenth century.

Going West

German, Russian, French, and British Noras all crossed the North Atlantic with productions of *Et dukkehjem*, but none of them could claim to have introduced the play to North America (Fig. 2.2a). By the end of the nineteenth century, 300,000 Norwegians had settled in the Midwest, and Ibsen's writings had travelled with them to the Americas. From the 1870s, his plays were part of the curriculum at the University of Wisconsin and the Luther College in Iowa. In 1882, an adaptation of the play *The Child Wife* was staged by amateurs in Milwaukee, where the German speakers were familiar with Ibsen's work; the source text for this adaptation into English was Wilhelm Lange's German translation (Haugen 1934, 396). The polish actress Helena Modjeska made the first abortive attempt at mounting a professional production in Louisville, Kentucky in 1883.[26] Although she performed in English, the interpretation was based on her productions from Warsaw and the Polish Theatre in St Petersburg. After a single night, Modjeska removed the play from her repertoire: 'The public was not yet ripe for Ibsen' (qtd in Schanke 1988, 7). Public readings of the play were given by the professional actress Kate Reignolds in Washington and New York in 1890 (Schanke 1988, 9), and Minnie Maddern Fiske, a successful child actress and musical comedy soubrette, presented a second full production of the play at the New York Empire Theatre in 1894. Fiske acquired a reputation as a formidable American Ibsenite, but this first performance was only a tentative venture that took the form of a benefit matinee for a local maternity hospital.[27]

To unravel the complex impact of European actress-managers on this fledgling market for *Et dukkehjem* in North America, we begin by examining the final episode of Janet Achurch's global tour as Nora. She arrived

a

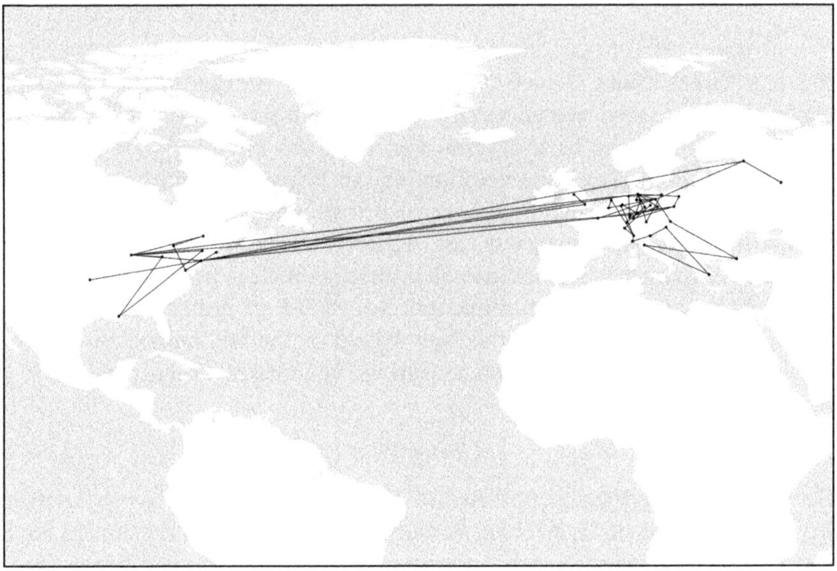

b

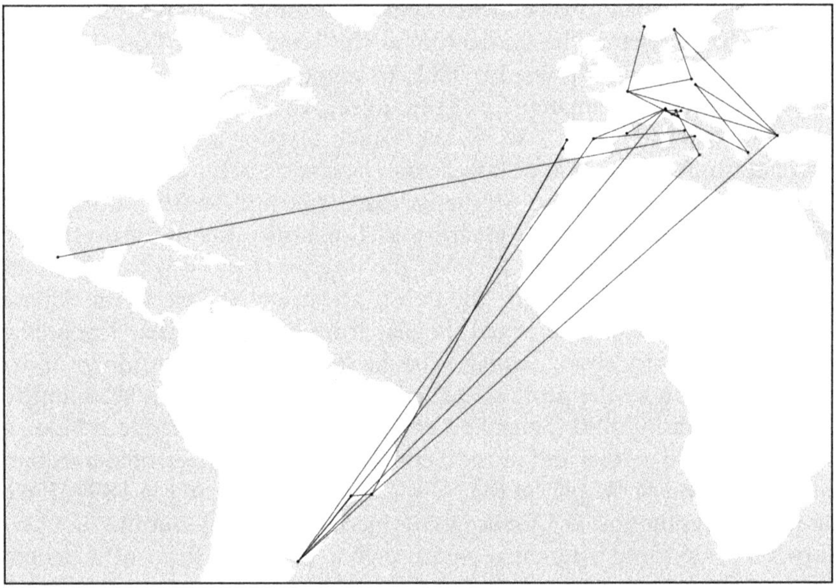

Fig. 2.2 (**a**) North American tours by Gabrielle Réjane, Minnie Maddern Fiske, Janet Achurch (in America), Beatrice Cameron, Agnes Sorma, Vera Komissarzhevskaya, and Alla Nazimova (Source*:* IbsenStage). (**b**) South American tours by Teresa Mariani Zampieri (also known as Teresa Mariani), Lucinda Simões, and Suzanne Després (Source*:* IbsenStage)

in New York in March 1895 within days of a performance by the French Nora, Gabrielle Réjane, at that city's Abbey Theatre.[28] If this performance in French, together with the scattered local productions in English, had been her only competition, Achurch's Nora might have attracted an audience. But in 1889 a serious American rival had begun a tour that lasted for almost as long as Achurch's tour in Australia. Beatrice Cameron opened in Boston and played occasional matinees in New York, Philadelphia, Washington, Baltimore, Chicago, and St Louis.[29] The same week that Achurch appeared as Nora at the Novelty Theatre in London, Cameron's husband and theatrical partner, the actor-manager Richard Mansfield, had been there performing *Richard III*. He returned to New York with a copy of William Archer's *A Doll's House*; Beatrice Cameron read the play and persuaded her husband to include it in their company's touring repertoire. Despite the vitriol with which the theatre critics greeted the play, Cameron's performance was not without praise and she continued to give special matinees as Nora on tour: when she played Philadelphia, women queued for seats with their children, assuming from the title that the play was a family entertainment (Schanke 1988, 9).

Ironically, it was Richard Mansfield who was responsible for bringing Janet Achurch to the United States. He had contracted her to join his new theatrical venture at the Garrick Theatre; she was to play the lead in George Bernard Shaw's *Candida*.[30] When Achurch arrived in New York with the manuscript, Mansfield read the play and wrote to Shaw: 'three long acts of talk—talk—talk—no matter how clever that talk is—it is talk—talk—talk'. He also found Achurch impossible: 'I couldn't make love to your Candida [...] if I had taken ether' (Mansfield (1895) 1965, 523–24). Achurch used the New York press to publicise her predicament: her employer would not produce *Candida* and none of the plays he suggested as substitutes had roles that appealed to her. In a major article in the *New York Dramatic Mirror*, she explained that her contract had been cancelled and she would return to England, but first she would give her New York debut at the Hoyt's Theatre under the management of Frederick C. Whitney. The season would open with *Forget-Me-Not*, followed by *A Doll's House*; the differences between the roles 'are very marked and should certainly show whether I have any claim as an actress' (Achurch 1895).[31] Her next press release stated that the manager F.C. Whitney had been replaced by Thomas Namack and the season at the Hoyt's Theatre would be shortened to a week. With all the confusion, it is not surprising that the first-night audience for *A Doll's House* was small and the *New York Times* found 'the acting of the support company was not competent' ('Ibsen in English Again' 1895).[32] The review challenged the statement in the programme that Nora was Achurch's 'original character' by pointing out that numerous productions in Germany and Scandinavia had preceded the Novelty Theatre season in London. Modjeska was mentioned, and Beatrice Cameron praised, but Achurch's Nora was condemned: 'She enlisted not a bit of sympathy for the heroine last night, though she held the attention of her audience closely, partly because of the variety of her means of expression, partly because of her extreme oddity' ('Ibsen in English Again' 1895). Two days later a further review in the same paper contained a damning critique of her performance: 'her acting did not suggest a possible future for her as a "star" in this country' ('Notes of the Stage' 1895).

Achurch set sail for London and never returned to the USA. Considering the commotion surrounding the season at the Hoyt's Theatre, the hastily formed company of local actors, and her history of increasing drug addiction, it is not surprising that Achurch's Nora was panned in New York. Yet despite the retrospective praise given to previous English-speaking Noras, the play was not well received by American critics in the 1890s; even the popular French diva Réjane had been informed by the *New York Times* that her single performance as Nora was her 'least satisfying portrayal' ('The Theatrical Week: Mme Rejane's' 1895) and that 'New-Yorkers do not care much for Ibsen in any language' ('The Theatrical Week: Dullness' 1895). In retrospect, perhaps Eleonora Duse was the most astute of the European visitors; she listed the play in her advance publicity, but dropped it from her repertoire on arrival in New York, choosing instead to thrill audiences with performances of *La Dame aux Camellias.*

Achurch was not the last European Nora to try her luck on the stages of New York. Agnes Sorma, the famous German Nora, was the next arrival in 1897. She had performed the play in St Petersburg, Berlin, and Hanover, and her first tour across the Atlantic was organised by the New York Deutsches Theater.[33] Her German-speaking audience gave her 'earnest, and breathless attention' and the *New York Times* reviewer described her as 'soberly toned and harmonious as to seem like nature itself' ('Dramatic and Musical' 1898).[34] But when she reached Chicago her performance, to a largely German-speaking audience at the McVicker's Theatre, was described in the *Chicago Tribune* as technically accomplished with a 'wonderful mastery of detail', but lacking in the natural qualities of Minnie Maddern Fiske ('Sorma at M'Vicker's' 1898). In comparison to the English-language versions of the play, these German performances were marginalised in the press because of the language of performance. A similar fate befell Vera Komissarzhevskaya nearly ten years later when she performed Nora for Russian speakers in New York: her audience was drawn from the 700,000 Jewish immigrants to the USA who had escaped pogroms in Russia between 1899 and 1907.[35]

By the turn of the century, New York critics were suggesting that it was passé for foreign actresses to display their talents by playing Nora:

> [a]lthough the role, for some unknown reason has come to be regarded as a text, it involves no difficulties which any actress of proper technical proficiency and experience should not be able to overcome, and comparatively unknown actresses have been able to give interesting performances of it. ('Russian Actress Appears as Nora' 1908)

The market was drying up, but a year earlier the Russian actress Alla Nazimova had appeared in New York, and her Nora was to take the USA by storm.[36] She switched from performing in Russian to English and even though her accent was considered impossible to understand, the *New York Times* reviewer could 'recall no such illumination of the role, and incidentally of the play' ('Looking Forward to a Week of Serious Drama' 1907). She was praised as a genius: 'Sympathy oozed for this Nora as it has never done for any other' (qtd in Schanke 1988, 44). Nazimova broke through the critical resistance to the play and Nora stayed in her repertoire until 1918. She performed the role in Chicago, Cleveland, Washington, New Orleans, Toronto, Montreal, and repeatedly in New York.[37] In 1922, she produced a silent film of *A Doll's House* in Hollywood and added her own optimistic ending. The film has not survived, but the final image finds Nora on the street in a winter snow storm: 'She stands for a moment hesitant and then steps out into the world and with arms outstretched and a great air of invincibleness, she exultantly breasts the elements' (Arthur Denison qtd in Hanssen 2015). Five silent films based on *Et dukkehjem* were made in the USA between 1911 and 1922. The marketing strategy used by Edwin Thanhouser, the producer of the 1911 version, relied on the fact that all the Noras, from Kate Reignolds to Alla Nazimova, had cemented the play into the nation's theatrical repertoire: 'You cannot go wrong if you rig up some special advertising display for this very fine feature. Simply the words "A Doll's House," by Ibsen, will do, outside the show, but paint 'em in big letters with the name "Thanhouser" underneath, as a guarantee of merit' (1911). The *Et dukkehjem* legacy left by early Noras in North America was an absorption of the play into the silent film industry. The play may have been imported as theatre, but it was exported as film.

South America

While Modjeska, Réjane, Achurch, Sorma, Komissarzhevskaya, and Nazimova were competing for audiences in the North American theatre market, the famous Noras of Italy, France, and Portugal were performing for their diaspora audiences in South America (Fig. 2.2b). Between 1880 and 1900, over a million Italians arrived in Brazil. Italians were also a significant community in Montevideo, where Garibaldi, the great Risorgimento hero, had led an Italian legion in the Uruguayan war of independence. Argentina had absorbed two and a half million migrants in the second half of the nineteenth century, mostly from Spain and Italy. The realities of performing Ibsen in South America at the beginning of the twentieth century can be glimpsed from a fascinating diary written by the actor Guido Noccioli, who was employed by Eleanora Duse on her 1906–07 tours to Brazil, Uruguay, and Argentina. At her farewell performance of *Rosmersholm* in Rio de Janeiro, the stage door of the theatre was stormed by a group of students demanding (and obtaining) free tickets to the performance on the grounds that 'there are likely to be few opportunities of seeing this play being performed again in Brazil in the near future, it would be unfair to deprive us of this rare privilege' (qtd in Pontiero 1982, 102).[38] Duse had played Nora with great success, particularly in London and Moscow, but on this tour her Ibsen repertoire was confined to *Hedda Gabler* and *Rosmersholm*. It was the Italian actress Teresa Mariani Zampieri who first performed Nora in Uruguay in 1898 (von Bergen 2006, 108).[39] In Montevideo, her company was touring with fifteen plays in repertoire and *Casa di bambola* was only seen once in a double bill with the one-act farce *La Bustaja* (*The Corset Maker*). The performance took place in a 600-seat theatre, but only a third of the tickets were sold and the play was presented for a single night. The text was Moritz Prozor's French version translated into Italian by Luigi Capuana, which Eleonora Duse had used in Milan in 1891. The newspapers had been following the Ibsen phenomenon in Europe and the performance attracted media attention, but according to the reviewer from *El Siglo* the audience was perplexed at this new style of theatre and somewhat shaken by the ending of the play. The critic went on to question whether Ibsen was 'deeply mentally disturbed or just a bitter and irredeemable skeptic when it comes to the truth and morality of our social institutions' (qtd in von Bergen 2006, 109).

Just over a year later in 1899, a Portuguese production arrived in Montevideo.[40] The famous actress Lucinda Simões was the manager of the company and played Mrs Linde; the role of Nora was taken by her daughter, Lucília Simões; and Christiano de Souza, who played Torvald, was responsible for adapting the play from the French translation by Moritz Prozor.[41] A review of Simões's production of *A casa da boneca* appeared in *El Siglo*; the reviewer again focused on the ending of the play, questioning why it had not been changed and arguing that the ideas it contained, while appropriate for Nordic audiences, had no relevance in Latin countries (von Bergen 2006, 110). As the performance had been advertised as a gala for Lucília Simões, the audience was still appreciative, applauding at the end of every act, throwing flowers onto the stage, and presenting the young Nora with flower baskets at the final curtain. After Montevideo, Simões's company travelled to Brazil, premiering the play in Rio de Janeiro. Lucinda was known in this city where she had performed, married, and given birth to Lucília. Her daughter had spent her early childhood in Brazil before rejoining her mother in Portugal.

Although the Simõeses gave the first performance of *A casa da boneca* in Rio, the Italian actress Clara Della Guardia was the first Nora in São Paulo. The articles in the press about both Brazilian performances mirrored the Uruguayan responses. The ending was criticised on aesthetic grounds by Artur Azevedo, the major theatre critic in Rio, because of the implausible speed of Nora's transformation; and on moral grounds by Carlo Parlagreco, a professor of art history, because it encouraged women to abandon their homes. The critic Oscar Guanabarino analysed the mental health of Ibsen and his central character; he quoted the Italian physician Cesare Lombroso, who had achieved notoriety by suggesting that artistic genius was a form of hereditary insanity and that all women were subject to a latent immorality. Even the critics who were impressed by Ibsen's Nora believed that they were watching a depiction of mental instability. Journalist Luiz Guimarães Filho, an advocate for women's rights, described Nora as a 'unique lunatic' and claimed that the play 'cruelly demonstrates the falsity of female education in modern society' (qtd in Silva 2007, 40).

Although the French translation by Prozor was the source text for these early South American performances, and French theatre companies (including those of Sarah Bernhardt and Réjane) were regular summer visitors to Brazil, it was not until 1906 that the first French Nora arrived in Rio (Magaldi 2005, 291).[42] Suzanne Després had created the role for the symbolist Théâtre de l'Oeuvre in Paris, where her husband, Aurélien-Marie Lugné-Poë, had played the role of Torvald. As Ibsen was no longer a novelty to Brazilian audiences, the critics concentrated on the symbolist techniques used in the production, praising Després for being less histrionic than the Noras of Lucília Simões and Clara Della Guardia.

With the exception of Teresa Mariani Zampieri, who became the first Nora to play Mexico in 1904, none of the European Noras ventured beyond the established theatrical touring circuit of Brazil, Argentina, and Uruguay. In contrast to the legacy of the Noras to the north of the continent, where *Et dukkehjem* was being adapted into silent films, the legacy of the Noras to the south was limited to critical commentaries on Ibsen's play, which peaked, particularly in Brazil, around the centenary celebrations of his birth in 1928. The first South American film version, *Casa de Muñecas* directed by Ernesto Arancibia, was made in Argentina and released in 1943, but the next wave of theatre productions had to wait until the 1950s.

East Asia

The complexities of the rivalries between the European Noras in the Americas, fuelled by theatre reviews comparing their performances, provides a sharp contrast to the East Asian history of the play, where the Japanese actress Matsui was the only early Nora.[43] She travelled on a circuit that reflected her country's growing military influence following the Sino- and Russo-Japanese wars. The cultural transmission of *Et dukkehjem* from Europe to Japan was negotiated with ease by both artists and critics; they successfully utilised the text to fit their national context. Originally translated into Japanese in 1901, the play was first performed in September 1911 by the Association of Literature and Arts at Bungei Kyokai Shenjyo in Waseda, directed by Shimamura Hogetsu (Sato 1981, 278). In 1907, 'new woman' had become a popular expression in Japan; when Nora walked onto the Tokyo stage four years later, she immediately became the quintessential 'new woman' from the 'West' (Sato 1981, 278). 'Of course, the success of Nora had no little influence on the world of drama', the critic Akiba Taro wrote in 1937, 'but more than that, it considerably stimulated the world of thought in that age. It was this age when a group of "new women," the Bluestockings, advocated Noraism for the emancipation of women' (qtd in Sato 1981, 279). The male critics who attended the first Tokyo performance conflated the 'new woman' as represented by Nora and the 'new woman' as personified by the actress Matsui Sumako. 'Without reservation or exaggeration', wrote Kusuyama Masao, 'I believe that the Nora played by this actress Matsui Sumako must be remembered as a monument which resolved for the first time problems of using actresses in Japan, and which, on stage, emancipated women for the first time' (qtd in Sato 1981, 278).[44] Matsui Sumako performed Nora in Taiwan (occupied by Japan in 1895) and Korea (a Japanese protectorate from 1910); unfortunately, the details about these performances are vague. She also toured to Manchuria and Vladivostok, which were under increasing Japanese influence from 1904 to 1905, but there is no documentation indicating that she included Nora in her repertoire. Although she never played Nora in China, news of her performance travelled by word of mouth to Shanghai through two students studying in Tokyo in 1911. When they returned home to Shanghai they established the New Play Group and in 1914 presented *Nora* in a theatre on the Nanjing Road (Kano 2001, 130). This was probably an improvised performance reconstructed from memory by an all-male theatre troupe; it initiated one of the richest and most complex cultural assimilations of a play in world theatre (Tam 1985; Eide 1987; He 2004). Social drama, in the form of realist texts, was one of the many features of European modernity imported into East Asia in the early years of the twentieth century, and the most popular foreign play prior to 1941 was *Et dukkehjem.*

Mapping Audiences

By following the trajectories of early Noras, we have traced the cultural transmission of *Et dukkehjem* across five continents via touring circuits created by nineteenth-century European theatre companies. The combined performances of actress-managers familiarised global audiences with *Et dukkehjem* and the play was successfully absorbed into the repertoires of emerging theatre cultures, where it still has a place in the twenty-first century. With the exception of Matsui's East Asian tours, all the performance locations were tied to Europe through histories of migration and colonisation; nevertheless, the bush town audience in rural Australia had little in common with the fervent Ibsenite students of Rio de Janeiro, or the audience Achurch called invalid English in Calcutta. If there is a common pattern in the reception of all the touring productions, it can be found in the marketing of the play as a reflection of the changing gender politics of Europe and the controversy it had caused 'back home' in that continent's cities. Yet the reviewers stressed their cultural distance from Europe and Ibsen's depiction of gender inequalities; many of them insisted that the power relations depicted in the play were *foreign* to their local culture. To this extent, the women's emancipation movements in Europe not only produced the actress-managers who exercised their influence over the repertoire of world theatre, they also affected the global reception of *Et dukkehjem*.

In 1889, a reviewer of Beatrice Cameron's performance exclaimed that 'Norway must be at least a thousand years behind the times' in the area of women's rights if works like *A Doll's House* could 'shake it to its foundations' (Schanke 1988, 8). In New Zealand a review of Achurch condemned the treatment of women in Germany and Norway from a position of superiority typical of a society perceiving itself to be the world leader over women's suffrage:

> German women are still to a considerable extent looked upon and treated by their 'lords and masters' as inferior creatures. They are also bound down by many conventional ideas from which their English and American sisters have long since emancipated themselves. [...] Norway, it seems, is in the same backward condition. (Review of Janet Achurch in *A Doll's House*, *New Zealand Herald* 1891, 5)[45]

Bizarre as the idea of a unique psychopathology of Nordic women may sound, it was a common theme in the early reception of Ibsen's women in the Americas. The Rio de Janeiro critic João do Rio interpreted the 'foreignness' of Nora in the Simõeses' production as an illustration of an insanity peculiar to women living in the North. He praised the actress's performance for its scientific accuracy: 'Lucília perfectly incarnates this complex type of hysteria with the nervous insanity of Nordic women' (qtd in Silva 2007, 40). Mrs Maddern Fiske received a similar response in Chicago for performing Nora in a 'Norwegian madhouse for melancholia' (Schanke 1988, 16). In East Asia, the foreignness of the text was visually enhanced in the early productions of the play by the actors' use of prosthetic noses and hair dye to represent Caucasians. This cross-ethnic make-up was still being used in Japanese performances of Ibsen as late as the 1980s. In the first performance of the play in 1912, the distance between the character of Nora and the women in the audience was evident in reviews written by three female critics for the feminist magazine *Seito*.

One of them addressed the character directly: 'Nora, Japanese women find it incredible that you could be such a thoroughly instinctive and blind woman' ('H' 1912, 133). Emphasising the *foreignness* of *Et dukkehjem* thus created a public space for debates about the relative social position of women inside and outside Europe. It suited critics, audiences, and artists to present Ibsen's play as a foreign world. It allowed audiences to feel an imaginary superiority to the outdated gender inequalities of Europe, and it avoided any direct criticism of the gender inequalities within the social milieu of the audience.

Even if Ibsen's first international success can be linked directly and indirectly to the social changes tied to the European women's movements, this does not explain why so many of the actress-managers selected *Et dukkehjem* for their repertoire. There were plenty of 'new woman' plays written in the 1890s, not to mention other female parts written by Ibsen, but the most popular role with actress-managers was Nora. What was it about the character that they found so attractive? While the *Et dukkehjem* maps provoke these questions, they cannot answer them. A different kind of mapping is required to chart the internal life-worlds of the early Noras. To investigate whether there are any similarities between the lived experiences of these women that could explain their decision to perform *Et dukkehjem*, we have delved into the biographical histories of the early Noras from three continents. Five of them are familiar figures from the *Et dukkehjem* map: Alla Nazimova, Matsui Sumako, Gabriela Zapolska, Janet Achurch, and Eleonora Duse. The remaining three are significant early Noras who stayed at home: Eleanor Marx, Lan Ping, and Olga Chekhova.

Internal Maps

All eight actresses expressed an identification with Ibsen's character. As they had escaped from unsuccessful marriages prior to performing *Et dukkehjem* and had been subjected to social condemnation for transgressing the bounds of conventional bourgeois morality, it is likely that the force pulling them towards Nora was personal in nature. Nora figures in their autobiographies and in private and public correspondence, and ambiguities abound over the boundaries between character and actress, fiction and lived reality. Assuming an identification with Nora allowed these actresses to claim an identity space as 'new women'.[46] This did not necessarily translate into public advocacy for women's rights, but it did allow them to demand a social status as professional artists and theatre entrepreneurs to counteract their labelling as immoral women of the theatre.[47]

Their personal histories demonstrate the degree to which they had digressed from the life-worlds of the women in their audiences. Their female spectators did not have the same divorce rights as the men sitting next to them in the auditorium, and if they did leave their husbands they could expect to be excluded from polite theatre-going society. Any identification with Nora for the female spectator was probably limited to fantasies of an existence beyond the confines of dependent wife and dutiful mother, though Nazimova believed that a process of identification was also at work in her audiences: 'You may have met Nora on the street or taken Hedda Gabler to dinner. But you did not recognise them because Ibsen was not at hand to introduce them to you. That is why you have to go to the theatre to see them [...] and often see something of yourself too' (Nazimova qtd in Lambert 1997, 132). Whether Nazimova was right about her audiences' familiarity with living Noras is impossible to ascertain, but there is no doubt that the women on the stage had lived the social consequences of Nora's decisions. The similarities in their personal lives, with regard to broken marriages and lost or deserted children, suggest possible common motivations regarding their choice of Nora as a vehicle for self-expression.

Alla Nazimova

Alla Nazimova (Fig. 2.3b) was twenty-eight when she performed Nora in New York. Born in Yalta, in the Crimea, she supported herself while studying acting in Moscow, first through prostitution, and later by assuming the role of mistress to a wealthy older man whom she called her millionaire. In 1899, she fell in love with Alexander Sanin, assistant to the Russian director Konstantin Stanislavski. When he rejected her, she reacted by marrying one of her fellow actors, Seryozha Golovin. It is possible that this marriage was never consummated. Within a year, Nazimova had begun an affair with the prominent actor-manager Pavel Orlenev. In 1905, Orlenev's company travelled to London and New York in an attempt to break into the international theatre touring circuit that crossed northern Europe and the East Coast of the USA. While the company was in New York, Emma Goldman became Orlenev's patron and lover. When Orlenev returned to Russia, Nazimova remained in the USA and signed a contract with Shubert theatre management. Her first role as an American actress was

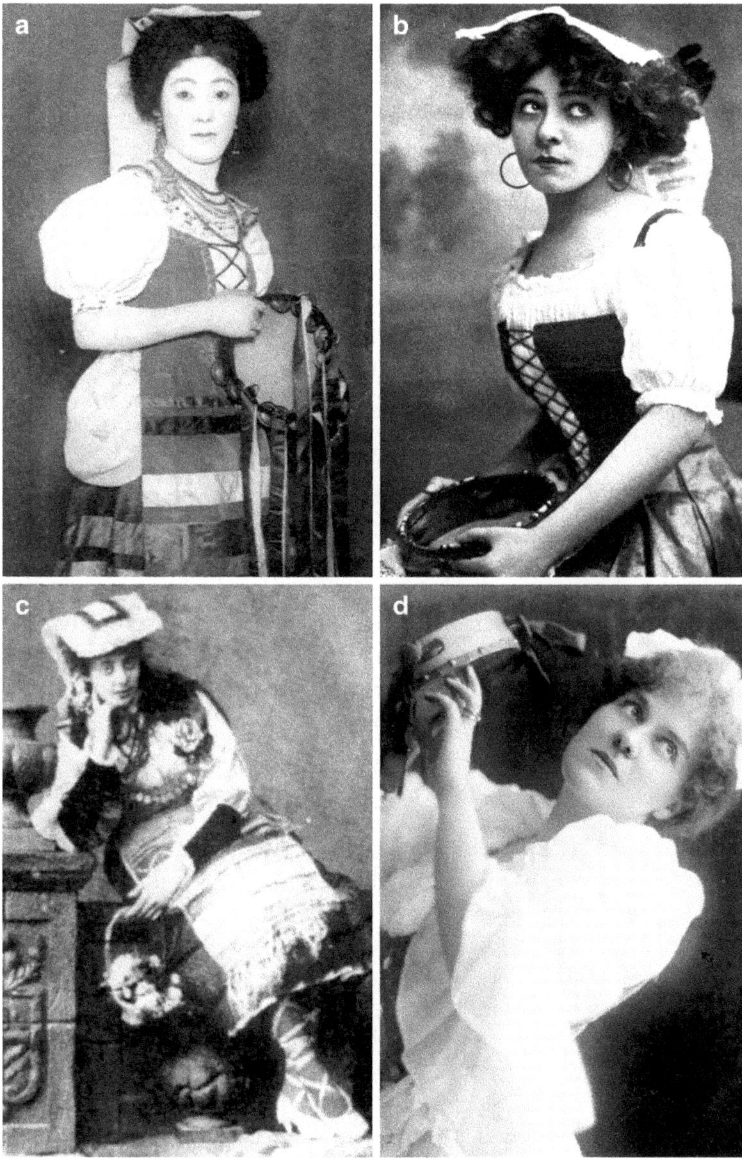

Fig. 2.3 (**a**) Matsui Sumako as Nora (Source: Tsubouchi Memorial Museum, Waseda University). (**b**) Alla Nazimova as Nora (Source: Wikipedia). (**c**) Gabriela Zapolska as Nora (Source: Wikipedia). (**d**) Janet Achurch as Nora (Source: State Library of New South Wales)

Nora; Nazimova is believed to have provided the intellectual and aesthetic leadership for the production.

Matsui Sumako

Matsui Sumako (Fig. 2.3a) had been married and divorced twice by the time she played Nora at the age of twenty-five. Born in 1886, she was the youngest of eight children of a prosperous provincial family in Japan. When her father died and the family lost its financial security, she moved to Tokyo to live with her sister and train as a seamstress. Her first marriage to an innkeeper lasted three months; it has been suggested that she contracted venereal disease from her husband, became infertile, and was rejected by his family (Kano 2001, 124). It was her second husband Maezawa Seisuke, a history teacher, who introduced Matsui to the theatre. He persuaded Tsubouchi Shoyo, the founder of the Theatre Institute of the Literary Society (Bungei Kyokai Engeki Kenkyuko), to accept her into the new acting course at the Institute. She was one of only four women students, and became the first major female star of the Japanese new theatre, or *Shingeki*. Shortly before her first public performance as Ophelia in *Hamlet*, she divorced her second husband. Her next role was as Nora, which she performed (without the second act) on a small stage built by Tsubouchi Shoyo in his garden. The production was remounted in a full version at the Imperial Theatre, Tokyo.

Janet Achurch and Eleanor Marx

Janet Achurch (Fig. 2.3d) joined a touring theatre company in her late teens and soon married St Aubyn Miller, a little-known playwright. By the time she was nineteen, the marriage was over and she was living with the actor Charles Charrington. They married six years later to add respectability to their partnership for the Australian tour. While Achurch was the first professional actress to perform Nora in Britain, the first public reading of William Archer's translation of *A Doll's House* was held at the London home of Eleanor Marx and her lover, Edward Aveling, in 1886 (Kapp 1972–1976, 103). Marx played Nora, Aveling played Torvald, and George Bernard Shaw read the part of Krogstad. Eleanor was the sixth child and youngest daughter of Karl Marx. At seventeen, while working as her father's secretary, she met and fell in love with Hippolyte Lissagaray, a thirty-four-year-old journalist and member of the Paris Commune.

Her father disapproved of the relationship and refused to give his permission for the marriage until she was twenty-five years old. Within two years of their eventual marriage, the couple had separated. In 1884, she met Edward Aveling through her membership of the Social Democratic Federation. At the time that she produced the first public reading of *A Doll's House* in London, she was building a career as an author and activist, and was contemplating training as an actor.

Lan Ping

Lan Ping was twenty-one when she was asked to play Nora at the Golden Gate Theatre, in a production mounted by the Shanghai Amateur Drama Association in 1935. The political struggle between the communist underground and the nationalist government was particularly intense in Shanghai, and this conflict was taken to be analogous with the confrontation between Nora and Torvald. The production played for two months in the middle of 1935; it closed when the director, Zhang Min, refused to accept changes demanded by the official government censors. Within months of playing Nora, Lan Ping was arrested as a suspected communist sympathiser while working as a night school teacher in a tobacco factory. She was released after a few weeks and, although the exact details are obscure, it appears that she signed a document denouncing the Communist Party. Yu Qiwei, whom she had married four years earlier in 1931, had introduced her to the Party. This was her second marriage, her grandparents having arranged a marriage for her to a businessman in Jinan the previous year. That arrangement lasted only a few months before she moved to Qingdao and began the affair with Yu Qiwei; the marriage with Yu Qiwei was similarly short-lived. He was arrested and imprisoned, and when he was released he rejected Lan Ping, supposedly because she had taken a lover during his absence.

Gabriela Zapolska

In addition to broken marriages and multiple affairs, many of the early Noras had abandoned their children, either because of the social condemnation of illegitimacy or because of the demands associated with their professional lives. Collectively, they had one miscarriage; two children who died in infancy (one while in the care of a wet nurse); and two daughters who were raised by surrogate parents. Gabriela Zapolska (Fig. 2.3c) was twenty-four when she performed Nora in 1882. At seventeen, she married Konstanty Eliasz Śnieżko-Blocki, an officer in the Russian army. According to Zapolska, in this marriage she 'lost everything, beginning with (her) girlish delusions and ending in (her) fortune' (qtd in Murjas 2007, xl). It is also possible that she had a miscarriage. At the age of twenty, she joined an amateur theatre troupe in Warsaw. The director, Marian Gawalewicz, was a journalist; they had an affair and Zapolska became pregnant. As Gawalewicz was already married, she had no alternative but to enter the Convent of Visitants in Warsaw, where unmarried mothers were confined until the birth of their illegitimate children. Zapolska found the convent intolerable, and travelled in secret to Vienna where she gave birth to Gawalewicz's child. She named the child Maria and left her with a foster family, where she died, supposedly from neglect. Zapolska had no other children.

Eleonora Duse

Eleonora Duse added the role of Nora to her repertoire when she was thirty-three years old, by which time she was already an experienced actress-manager with a professional history of touring productions across Europe and South America. As the child of a theatrical family, her sexual relationships never conformed to conventional bourgeois morality. Her first affair, with the editor and writer Martino Cafiero, was short-lived. He left her when she became pregnant, and she gave birth to a son who died within months. A year later, she had an affair with Tebaldo Checchi, a fellow actor in the Cesare Rossi Theatre. Again she became pregnant, but this time she married her lover and gave birth to a girl, whom she named Enrichetta (Fig. 2.4). The baby was left with a wet nurse in Turin, the first of the many surrogate mothers and professional educators whom Duse employed to raise her daughter. The marriage with Checchi did not last, and Duse divorced him four years later when she began an affair with another actor, Flavio Andò. At the time that she performed the role of Nora, she had discarded Andò and was having an affair with the poet Arrigo Boito.

Olga Chekhova

Olga Chekhova was twenty-five when she played Nora in a silent film version of *Et dukkehjem* produced by UFA (Universum-Film AG) movie

Fig. 2.4 Eleonora Duse with her daughter, Enrichetta (Source: Fondazione Giorgio Cini di Venezia)

studio at Babelsberg, near Berlin (*Nora* 1922).[48] Under the leadership of the producer Erich Pommer, this studio became the largest film complex in Europe. Chekhova moved to Berlin from Moscow in 1921 with her lover Ferenc Jaroszi, an officer in the Austro-Hungarian army. She was escaping from the poverty of post-revolutionary Russia, and from a failed marriage with Anton Chekhov's nephew Mikhail. The families of the couple were related: her aunt, Olga Knipper, was the actress wife of Anton Chekhov. Mikhail Chekhov was to become famous in American theatre as an actor-teacher, but as a young man he was obsessive and an alcoholic; the marriage was a disaster. Chekhova gave birth to a girl, known within the family as Ada; when she left Mikhail she took her daughter with her. It was the winter of 1917, and according to Chekhova her daughter would have died from starvation but for the milk supplied from the family cow of the great Russian singer Feodor Chaliapin. In desperation, Chekhova asked her parents to take Ada with them to Siberia. Three years later, when the family met again in Moscow, Ada did not recognise her mother.

Breaking Social Convention

As these short biographical studies of marriage and motherhood graphically illustrate, all these women broke the social conventions of their diverse cultures. Eleanor Marx took Aveling's name even though they never married, and Achurch married Charrington to avoid social embarrassment on the Australian tour. Lan Ping hid her first marriage from the censorious eyes of the early Chinese Communist Party, and Matsui Sumako was publicly denounced for neglecting her second husband while studying to be an actor. When it came to motherhood, the actresses were subjected to exactly the same humiliation as their contemporaries who had illegitimate children. In Italy, if an unmarried mother wanted to give up her child, she had to take it either to a foundling home or the local church; if she tried to leave it anywhere else, she could be imprisoned for five years and publicly flogged. When Duse gave birth to Cafiero's son, she sent him a picture of his child; he returned it with a message implying that she was a whore. These actresses' past lives fitted the negative identity spaces of whore, adulteress, and fallen woman. By identifying with the fictional character of Nora, they could reimagine the incidents in their lives that had attracted criticism as fierce struggles for personal freedom. This manipulation of a fictional identity was aided by a contemporary theatre discourse that saw great acting as synonymous with the submerging of the actor's self within the frame of the performed character. Apparently, in her private life Alla Nazimova 'actually became the character of her current play' (qtd in Schanke 1998, 133), while Duse 'lived her role with such truth that there seemed no distance between the soul of the heroine she was playing and the deepest part of her own soul' (qtd in Sheehy 2003, 116).

The contemporary rhetoric that merged actresses with their characters adds weight to the suggestion that the actress-managers chose Nora to counter social ostracism. It could be said that the common force influencing their choice of the role was the growing social opposition, associated with the women's rights movements, to sexual double standards in bourgeois cultures that ostracised divorced women but not men, held women exclusively to blame if they bore illegitimate children, and denied women any significant public role outside motherhood. Their attachment to Nora would seem to reflect the contemporary social forces seeking to redefine the social and sexual lives of professional women. It explains why the actress-managers added *Et dukkehjem* to their repertoire, but it does not account for their continued attachment to the play in the face of negative or ambivalent criticism. As our mapping of the touring productions has shown, the early Noras were not greeted with unequivocal critical success, yet their commitment to performing the play did not waiver. Not only did they perform *Et dukkehjem* for extraordinary lengths of time, they reworked the play in multiple forms: dramatic parody, a short story, and a silent film. To understand their ongoing attachment to the play, we need to continue our investigations into their lives past the point of their first performances in the role.

Nora and Women's Subjective Autonomy

Speculation about the fate of Nora after the curtain falls has always been a feature of *Et dukkehjem*, and dramatic sequels to the play have been created in multiple cultures exploring the destiny of women who dare to challenge conventions associated with marriage and motherhood. The lives of the early Noras are flesh-and-blood sequels from which we can glean something about the subjective autonomy available to women in Europe and East Asia during the late nineteenth and early twentieth centuries. Traces of Nora are visible in their lives in their attempts at sexual relationships of equality as pre-shadowed in the final lines of the play; the difficulty of combining motherhood with professional autonomy; and finally feelings of self-worth.

Gabriela Zapolska attempted suicide in 1888; she survived, continued to perform Nora for seventeen years, and became the first modernist playwright of the Polish Theatre. She wrote forty-one plays, twenty-three novels, one hundred and seventy-seven short stories, and a single film script. Her short story 'Malaszka' (1883) begins where *Et dukkehjem* ends. It is the story of a Ukrainian peasant who abandons her husband and child; when she returns home, she finds her child dead and her husband mad. She dies trying to save a red skirt from her burning home; the garment symbolises her sexual desire. After the death of her illegitimate daughter, Zapolska never had another child, though she did have a further short-lived marriage to a painter.

Eleanor Marx demonstrated her political will and autonomy in her work as an author, socialist activist, and translator. She translated two of Ibsen's plays and wrote a satirical version of *Et dukkehjem* that she composed with Israel Zangwill to rebuff the critics who considered Nora an unwomanly woman (Zangwill and Marx 1891). The end of *A Doll's House Revisited* is rewritten in the style of a contemporary melodrama, with Nora falling to her knees and begging forgiveness. Unfortunately, Marx's personal life also took on an air of melodrama with her suicide in 1898, which was popularly believed to be a response to the discovery that her lover, Edward Aveling, had secretly married a young actress. The inquest into her death cleared Aveling of criminal liability, but he was widely believed to have provided her with the hydrogen cyanide that killed her. An alternative rationale offered by the eminent English historian E.P. Thompson suggests that she killed herself for fear of a public scandal that would expose her father as an adulterer and suggest that Freddie Demuth, the son of the Marx's maid, Helene Demuth, was her half-brother (Thompson [1976] 1994).[49] Whichever version is to be believed, clearly she was trapped within the patriarchal structures of her age.

Nora was 'the great event' of Janet Achurch's life, according to her second husband Charles Charrington. Her obituary in *The Times* referred to her 'wonderful performance as Nora Helmer', which 'was the talk of London for many a day' (qtd in Charrington 1916). She identified strongly with the role, constantly returning to it when her career was in trouble. When she was touring the play in Australia, she gave birth to Nora, her only daughter. Ironically, it was this second Nora in her life who inadvertently caused her death: while giving birth to her daughter in a Melbourne hospital, Achurch was given morphine, which triggered a life-long addiction. The shock of her daughter's death in 1914 after a long-term illness led to her own death from an overdose in 1916. Her death certificate stated that the primary cause of death was her morphia and cocaine habit. Charrington was with her to the end.

One of the greatest actresses of her generation, Duse played Nora for fifteen years, and claimed a special connection to Ibsen's heroines. While working on the role of Nora, all her pet names—'piccoletta', 'cheirichetto', 'bumba'—disappeared from the correspondence with her lover Arrigo Boito. Eventually, she broke off the correspondence, having told him 'I work—I think of nothing but working' (qtd in Sheehy 2003, 100). Duse did not include *Casa di bambola* in her repertoire for the 1907 South American tour; apparently she had seen Suzanne Després play the role, and afterwards 'sent Després her own costume for the role, vowing never again to play Nora' (qtd in Pontiero 1982, 158). Her motivation for this decision may have been more complex than it appears; her tour manager in South America was Lugné-Poë, the director of the Théâtre l'Oeuvre in Paris and Suzanne Després's husband. He claimed that Duse asked his wife, 'If, once, your lover or your husband, if I possessed him… once… just once… [y]ou wouldn't bear me ill will, would you? It's the golden hinge of friendship' (qtd in Sheehy 2003, 222). If, as some biographers claim, Lugné-Poë and Duse were lovers, it is possible that she relinquished the role of Nora in return for the loan of a husband and as a bizarre form of apology to Després.[50] Duse's personal relationships, both with her lovers and with her daughter, were disastrous. Enrichetta was brought up in boarding schools and by professional carers. Duse wanted to give her daughter an education away from the world of the theatre. The fraught separation between mother and child haunted the next generation: Enrichetta placed both her children in religious orders when they were teenagers. Duse died of influenza on tour in Pittsburgh, aged sixty-five.

The role of Nora launched Nazimova's American career, and by 1910 a theatre had been named after her in New York: Nazimova's 39th Street Theatre. In 1918, she moved to Hollywood and became a major silent movie star. After three years, her popularity began to fade and she used her own capital to produce two films: *A Doll's House*, and a version of Oscar Wilde's *Salome*. She was notorious within Hollywood as the leading figure in the lesbian film community; her magnificent estate on Sunset Boulevard was known as the Garden of Alla, and she owned a lesbian bar on sunset strip (Lambert 1997). In her film production of *Salome*, all the actors she cast were either gay or lesbian. In 1925, when her marriage of convenience with Charles Bryant collapsed and he made public the nature of their relationship, Nazimova is rumoured to have contemplated suicide. For the last seventeen years of her life, she lived in a small apartment above the garage of her former Hollywood estate, with her partner, Glesca Marshall.

At some stage in the rehearsals or performances of *Et dukkehjem*, Matsui Sumako fell in love with her director, Shimamura Hogetsu. He was fifteen years older than she, a respected theatre critic, and a teacher at the Theatre Institute. He was also married, with children. Their relationship provoked a major scandal and ultimately resulted in the demise of the Institute. To dispel popular prejudice that all actors were immoral, and that actresses in particular were glorified prostitutes, Tsubouchi Shoyo insisted that members of the Institute should not have affairs. Matsui was dismissed and Shimamura resigned. Together they established the Art Theatre (Geijutsuka). With Matsui as its star performer, the theatre became commercially successful and toured cities in Taiwan, Korea, and Manchuria, and the Russian port of Vladivostok. In 1918, Shimamura died from influenza, aged forty-seven, and within two months Matsui committed suicide. Despite her popularity as an actor, she was vilified in numerous publications on Japanese theatre. Shimamura was depicted as the victim of Matsui's manipulations: his death was attributed to her neglect, while her suicide was seen as indicative of 'her "perverse sexual desire" (***hentai sei-yoko***) for Hogetsu's corpse' (qtd in Kano 2001, 130; emphasis in original).

Chekhova's performance in *Nora* launched her film career, but it is difficult to find traces of an empathetic identification with Nora in her life choices because they are veiled in political intrigue. Chekhova was one of Hitler's favourite actresses (Fig. 2.5b). There were rumours that Chekhova was one of his mistresses, but this is highly unlikely. She married again to a wealthy businessman, but this did not last, and she had a succession of young lovers. Chekhova is the second of the Noras who was known to have spied for the Russians. Her brother, Lev Knipper, recruited her as a Soviet spy because of her association with Hitler, Goebbels, and Goering. In exchange for her cooperation, Stalin allowed her mother and daughter to move to Berlin.

Lan Ping's career was secured by playing Nora in 1935, and the production gave her the entrée she needed to the Diantong Film Company in Shanghai. She claimed that *Et dukkehjem* had been her favourite play ever since she had studied Ibsen at the Arts Academy in Jinan. She felt she had discovered the 'woman-rebel' in the play, and had gone far 'beyond Ibsen's original conception of the character' (qtd in Terrill 1984, 67). Her association with the character was played out in her relationship with her lover, the critic Tang Na, whom she met while performing Nora. When

a

b

Fig. 2.5 (**a**) Jiang Qing and Mao Zedong, c. 1945 (Source: RA/Lebrecht Music & Arts). (**b**) Olga Chekhova with Adolf Hitler at a reception given by Joachim von Ribbentrop, Minister of Foreign Affairs, May 1939 (Source: Ullstein Bild/ Lebrecht Music & Arts)

the relationship broke down, Lan Ping published two open letters to Tang Na, explaining why she had to follow her own path of self-realisation. While the traces of an empathetic identification with Nora are palpable in Lan Ping's career, her life as Jiang Qing, wife of Mao Zedong, is shrouded in political intrigue. She is alleged to have committed suicide in 1991 by hanging herself in a hospital bathroom. At the time of her death, she was estranged from her only child (Fig. 2.5a).[51]

What conclusions can be drawn from this biographical information, aside from saying that these women lived extraordinarily interesting lives? All of them succeeded in claiming civil space to exercise self-autonomy as artists or political activists, in some cases attaining enormous social, political, or cultural power. Yet in the private sphere they were less successful in achieving the objective embedded in Nora's last line of the play: 'At samliv mellom oss to kunne bli et ekteskap', translated literally into English as 'That cohabitation/daily life together between us could become a marriage'.[52] Ibsen uses 'samliv' elsewhere in his plays to suggest the easy companionship of friendship, but this quality was not typical of the marriages and affairs of the Noras. Janet Achurch's second marriage to Charles Charrington is a possible exception, while Nazimova removed herself from the problem by choosing same-sex partners. None of these actresses succeeded in incorporating motherhood into their working lives except for Achurch, but it is difficult to gauge the impact of her morphine addiction on the relationship with her daughter. The most disturbing similarity in the lives of these actors is the difficulty they had in maintaining an ongoing sense of self-worth. Three of them committed suicide, two of them attempted suicide and failed, and one died of drug addiction. While the character of Nora lays claim to the identity space of subjective freedom, these women attempted to embody it, and they encountered enormous difficulties.

There is one further astonishing aspect to the lives of these actresses. It is connected to that other identity space represented by the character of Nora, the one that has nothing to do with modernist subjectivity, but everything to do with subaltern femininity. It is dependent on disguise, secrets, and masquerade. Just as Nora survives in her fictional domestic world through masquerade, these women used the same mechanisms to survive in their public worlds, and not just in their work as actors, though nearly all of them were extraordinary exponents of this art. All except for Eleanor Marx survived by living double lives, either in the world of political intrigue or in the eyes of the public. Nazimova passed as heterosexual, and Achurch hid her addiction. Zapolska had close contacts within the Russian secret service, and it has been suggested that she gave them information about the Polish

Socialist Party. Chekhova and Jiang Qing played the far more dangerous game of political masquerade with three of the most powerful men of the twentieth century: Josef Stalin, Adolf Hitler, and Mao Zedong. Ibsen wrote the visionary possibilities of a new identity space for women in modernity into the final scene of *Et dukkehjem*, but in the rest of the play he represents the complexities and subtleties of subaltern femininity. Nora survives in the patriarchal family through masquerade, but there are no clues regarding the skills she will need to survive in the world outside the home. It would appear that these actors who played Nora applied the lessons of masquerade contained in the first three acts of the play to survive in the 'fourth acts' lived within their chosen political and public worlds.

Whichever strategies the early Noras used to turn the aspirations of a fictional character into a lived reality, it took all their physical strength, intellectual acumen, and emotional determination. As Matsui Sumako explained in her autobiography, *Peony Brush*, 'Nora's self-awakening was but the first step in her journey. She must go on. A self-awakening that is not the result of much floundering and fumbling through the cold, dark world is not a true, very powerful self-awakening' (qtd in Birnbaum 1999, 30). Perhaps it was the indeterminacy of the ending of the play and the need to 'go on' in their attempts to create theatrical representations of 'new women' that cemented their attachment to *Et dukkehjem*. What is certain is that all their 'floundering and fumbling through the cold' in both their personal and professional lives was inextricably linked to the desire for change in their lives both on and off the theatrical stage.

Conclusion

The *Et dukkehjem* touring maps are the distant visions that have shaped this chapter with their patterns of intersecting trajectories of European actress-managers. To uncover the forces behind these patterns we have examined the touring circuits that followed the flows of colonisation and migration, looked for similarities in the critical reception of the performances, and zoomed in for close-ups on the private worlds, or internal maps, of significant early Noras. Maps to biography, distance to close up, digital visualisation to qualitative interpretation: these are the movements that inform the methodology of this chapter. By combining these different perspectives, we now have an answer to one of the central questions for our study: what accounts for the *initial* global success of *Et dukkehjem*? It lies in the actions and motivations, animated through changes in the social organisation of gender, of a group of women who attained an unprecedented influence in world theatre at the end of the nineteenth century.

We have challenged one of the conventional narratives of Ibsen's career: *Et dukkehjem*, his most popular play, had an early commercial success more significant in its global impact than the performances staged by the European avant-garde. Following our assumption that all the patterns displayed on the maps are created by social, aesthetic, economic, or political forces, we have investigated the underlying dynamics shaping these patterns. The most obvious commonalities exist in the marketing and reception of this first global dissemination of *Et dukkehjem* and can be attributed to forces associated with changes in the social position of women. These changes not only opened up career opportunities for female artists, they were also used by critics to contextualise the reception of Ibsen's play outside Europe. In an indirect way, these social changes were also responsible for a repetitive pattern in these actress-managers' repertoire choices that resulted in so many productions of Ibsen's play, thus limiting the diversity of plays available on the global touring circuit.

The professional and personal stories of the women responsible for the first international distribution of *Et dukkehjem* challenge the accepted view that Ibsen's success was ensured by his male 'brokers'. The Noras marketed Ibsen on the commercial theatre touring circuits associated with colonisation and migration, and eighteen of them managed or co-managed their own theatre companies. Nora allowed them to display their virtuosity as performers and to redefine the public image of personal lives. She gave them a new identity space to inhabit at a time when women in diverse cultures were demanding changes in the social organisation of gender. The success of actress-managers in challenging the male dominance of the theatre industry was short-lived, as is clear from this title of a *New York Times* article published in 1896: 'High Salaries are Doomed: English Actresses Out of Work Because They Demand Too Much'. But it was not just high wages that brought the reign of these theatrical divas to an end: the outbreak of war radically changed the global theatrical market place; the touring companies disappeared; the power structures within the theatre industry were transformed through the emergence of directors from avant-garde theatres; and actresses were once again incorporated within a theatre industry dominated by men. It was not until the 1970s that female theatre artists regained some control over theatre repertoires, but they used their influence to programme plays written by women, not plays written by men about women.

Bourdieu warns against the dangers of 'disregarding the social conditions underlying the production of the work and those determining its function' (1993, 140). If there are social conditions that underpin the first international spread of *Et dukkehjem*, they are the movements for women's emancipation that began in late nineteenth-century Europe. This is the force that made a phenomenal success out of *Et dukkehjem*, as there can be no other play from that era that was kept in repertoire by so many actresses for so many years. The conditions that supported the promotion and dissemination of *Et dukkehjem* during this first wave of international success disappeared with the outbreak of war in Europe in 1914, but the connections between the play and other sexual vectors of social change have never disappeared. The character of Nora has continued to attract artists who are intent on challenging social discrimination on the grounds of sex and gender, but the precise combination of forces that empowered women performers and gave them such strong managerial influence over the global theatre industry has long disappeared.

While the intensity of international touring that characterises the early *Et dukkehjem* maps reappears in the late twentieth century, the forces behind these new trajectories have radically changed. Instead of utilising the land and sea trade routes of a European diaspora, the tours travel by air from one heavily subsidised international festival to another. The productions are directed and managed primarily by men and the audiences tend to be the elite consumers of global cultural products. The city that sits at the centre of the pattern is Oslo. It is for this reason that the next chapter investigates the power of the Norwegian state in the story of *Et dukkehjem* and asks: is it responsible for the continuing presence of the play in the repertoire of world theatre?

Notes

1. See Koht (1971), originally published in Norwegian in 1928–29, for a biography that influenced the dominant critical tradition and overlooked this first global dissemination of the play; and Frederick Marker and Lise-Lone Marker (1989) for a symptomatic selection of productions dating before 1914.
2. The academic debates surrounding the interpretation of Ibsen's female characters were triggered by the publication of Joan Templeton's *Ibsen's Women* (1997).
3. The East Asian touring circuit is not marked on the *Et dukkehjem* maps because of the present lack of detailed information on the venues and performance dates.
4. We have followed the nineteenth-century convention of using 'actress' in this chapter to refer to actresses and actress-managers, but use the non-gender-specific 'actor' in subsequent chapters.

5. Ibsen's Nora, Hedda Gabler, Ellida (*Lady from the Sea*), and Rebecca (*Rosmersholm*) signalled a major representational shift from the heroines of the sentimental comedies and melodramas written by the commercial French dramatists and popularised through the international tours of Sarah Bernhardt: *Fédora* (Sardou), *Frou-Frou* (Meilhac and Halévy), *Adrienne Lecouvreur* (Scribe), and *La Dame aux Camellias* (Dumas *fils*).
6. For Gabriela Zapolska performances see: 'Gabriela Zapolska'. *IbsenStage*, Contributor 434385. https://ibsenstage.hf.uio.no/pages/contributor/434385.
7. See 'Ida Aalberg'. *IbsenStage*, Contributor 427513. https://ibsenstage.hf.uio.no/pages/contributor/427513.
8. See 'Agnes Sorma'. *IbsenStage*, Contributor 427367. https://ibsenstage.hf.uio.no/pages/contributor/427367.
9. See 'Thessa Klinkhammer'. *IbsenStage*, Contributor 439040. https://ibsenstage.hf.uio.no/pages/contributor/439040.
10. See 'Irene Triesch'. *IbsenStage*, Contributor 427219. https://ibsenstage.hf.uio.no/pages/contributor/427219.
11. See 'Auguste Prasch-Grevenberg'. *IbsenStage*, Contributor 437638. https://ibsenstage.hf.uio.no/pages/contributor/437638.
12. See 'Lilli Petri'. *IbsenStage*, Contributor 432284. https://ibsenstage.hf.uio.no/pages/contributor/432284.
13. '*Nora*'. Date Unknown. Performed by Agnes Sorma as Nora. Agnes Sorma Ensemble, Istanbul, Turkey. *IbsenStage*, 79125. https://ibsenstage.hf.uio.no/pages/event/79125.
14. *'Maison de Poupée'*. 1906. Performed by Suzanne Després as Nora. Suzanne Després Company, Theatro Mnimatakion, Istanbul, Turkey. January 24. *IbsenStage*, Event 80493. https://ibsenstage.hf.uio.no/pages/event/80493. Després's success in the city was closely tied to the support of the theatre impresario Muhsin Ertuğrul, who admired the Théâtre de l'Oeuvre and had seen her play Hamlet in Paris. In accordance with IbsenStage, we have used Després as opposed to the alternative spelling, Desprès.
15. *'Nora I Kouklospito'*. 1907. Performed by Kyveli Adrianou as Nora. Thiasos Kyveli Adrianou, Theatro Mnimatakion, Istanbul, Turkey. October 30. *IbsenStage*, Event 80685. https://ibsenstage.hf.uio.no/pages/event/80685.
16. *'To spiti tis kouklas'*. 1907. Performed by Eleonora Lorandou. Ellinikos Dramatikos Thiasos Dionysis Tavoularis-Tilemachos, Theatre Variete, Istanbul, Turkey. November 21. *IbsenStage*, Event 80697. https://ibsenstage.hf.uio.no/pages/event/80697. The Suzanne Després Company did a return season of *Maison de Poupée* to the same theatre in 1908.
17. For records of Achurch performances see 'Janet Achurch'. *IbsenStage*, Contributor 427547. https://ibsenstage.hf.uio.no/pages/contributor/427547.

18. Janet Achurch also used a hundred pounds from Henry Irving to mount *A Doll's House*; he had given it to her as a gift to present a light comedy called *Clever Alice*.
19. '*A Doll's House*'. 1889. Directed by Charles Charrington. Performed by Janet Achurch as Nora. Novelty Theatre, Great Queen's Street, London, England. June 7. *IbsenStage*, Event 75649. https://ibsenstage.hf.uio.no/pages/event/75649.
20. '*A Doll's House*'. 1889. Directed by Charles Charrington. Performed by Janet Achurch as Nora. Princess Theatre, Melbourne, Australia. September 14. *IbsenStage*, Event 76249. https://ibsenstage.hf.uio.no/pages/event/76249.
21. Archer kept the prompt copy in London where he was preparing an Edition de Luxe of his translations of plays by Ibsen.
22. The latter play was written in the same year as *Et dukkehjem*, and it provided a contrasting role for Achurch of a high-society French woman.
23. '*A Doll's House*'. 1892. Directed by Charles Charrington. Performed by Janet Achurch as Nora. Colombo, Ceylon. December 1. *IbsenStage*, Event 75684. https://ibsenstage.hf.uio.no/pages/event/75684.
    '*A Doll's House*'. 1891. Directed by Charles Charrington. Performed by Janet Achurch as Nora. Corinthian Theatre, Calcutta, West Bengal, India. December 26. *IbsenStage*, Event 75683. https://ibsenstage.hf.uio.no/pages/event/75683.
24. Batavia is not marked on the Achurch touring map because it is unclear from her interview whether the company performed *A Doll's House* or another play from its repertoire. We have not been able to find any other records of this performance.
25. '*Nora*'. 1910. Performed by Kyveli Adrianou as Nora. Thiasos Kyveli Adrianou, Theatro Alampra, Alexandria, Egypt. October 12. *IbsenStage*, Event 80783. https://ibsenstage.hf.uio.no/pages/event/80783. For Kyveli Adrianou performances see 'Kyveli Adrianou'. *IbsenStage*, Contributor 448958. https://ibsenstage.hf.uio.no/pages/contributor/448958.
26. '*Thora*'. 1883. Performed by Helena Modjeska. Macauleys Theatre, Louisville, Kentucky, United States. December 7. *IbsenStage*, Event 76558. https://ibsenstage.hf.uio.no/pages/event/76558. It was based on the following production: '*Nora*'. 1882. Directed by Jan Tatarkiewicz. Performed by Helena Modrzejewska as Nora. Teatr Wielki, Plac Teatralny 1, Warsaw, Poland. March 10. *IbsenStage*, Event 76996. https://ibsenstage.hf.uio.no/pages/event/76996.
27. '*A Doll's House*'. 1894. Performed by Minnie Maddern Fiske as Nora. Empire Theatre, Broadway, New York, United States. February 15. *IbsenStage*, Event 76446. https://ibsenstage.hf.uio.no/pages/event/76446. For Minnie Maddern Fiske performances see 'Minnie Maddern Fiske'. *IbsenStage*, Contributor 435193. https://ibsenstage.hf.uio.no/pages/contributor/435193.

28. See 'Gabrielle Réjane'. *IbsenStage*, Contributor 432582. https://ibsenstage.hf.uio.no/pages/contributor/432582. The New York production is not listed in IbsenStage, but it is referenced in Schanke (1988, 18).
29. *'A Doll's House'*. 1889. Directed by Richard Mansfield. Performed by Beatrice Cameron as Nora. Richard Mansfield Company, Globe Theatre, Boston, Massachusetts, United States. October 30 *IbsenStage*, Event 76967. https://ibsenstage.hf.uio.no/pages/event/76967. For Beatrice Cameron performances see 'Beatrice Cameron'. *IbsenStage*, Contributor 436132. https://ibsenstage.hf.uio.no/pages/contributor/436132.
30. There was no place for Ibsen in Mansfield's repertoire, although he was responsible for the first North American production of *Peer Gynt*. He wrote to his friend the critic William Winter about the contracting of Achurch: 'I have seen Janet act, and I fancy that, after Ellen Terry perhaps a long way after she is, by far, the cleverest actress in London. Any leaning she may have toward Ibsen and cult I will straighten swiftly' (Winter 1910, 223).
31. The repertoire also contained a curtain-raiser, *In the Season*. Written by Langdon Elwyn Mitchell, son of Dr Weir Mitchell, the famous American physician associated with treating Charlotte Perkins Gilman and Virginia Woolf, it had been running for four months in London.
32. *'A Doll's House'*. 1895. Performed by Janet Achurch as Nora. Hoyt's Madison Square Theatre, Broadway and W. 24th St, New York, United States. June 6. *IbsenStage*, Event 75681. https://ibsenstage.hf.uio.no/pages/event/75681.
33. *'Nora'*. 1897. Directed by Mathieu Pfeil. Performed by Agnes Sorma. Deutsches Theater, Irving Place Theatre, New York, United States. April 12. *IbsenStage*, Event 77304. https://ibsenstage.hf.uio.no/pages/event/77304.
34. *'Nora'*. 1898. Directed by Emil Marx. Performed by Agnes Sorma as Nora. Agnes Sorma und die Irving Place Theatergesellschaft, N.Y., McVicker's Theatre, Chicago, Illinois, United States. April 3. *IbsenStage*, Event 78968. https://ibsenstage.hf.uio.no/pages/event/78968.
35. *'A Doll's House'*. 1908. Performed by Vera F. Komissarzhevskaya as Nora. Mme Vera F Komissarzhevskaya Repertory, Daly's Theatre, 1221 Broadway (30th St.), New York, United States. March 15. *IbsenStage*, Event 75362. https://ibsenstage.hf.uio.no/pages/event/75362. See 'Vera. F. Komissarzhevskaya'. *IbsenStage*, Contributor 449852. https://ibsenstage.hf.uio.no/pages/contributor/449852.
36. *'A Doll's House'*. 1907. Directed by Henry Miller. Performed by Alla Nazimova as Nora. Princess Theatre, 29th St. (Broadway), New York, United States. January 14. *IbsenStage*, Event 76968. https://ibsenstage.hf.uio.no/pages/event/76968. See 'Alla Nazimova'. *IbsenStage*, Contributor 427384. https://ibsenstage.hf.uio.no/pages/contributor/427384.

37. She also played Nora on stage in Oakland, California, but the play had been introduced with considerable success to San Francisco by a very young Blanche Bates in 1898: '[s]he has broken the ice and there is no further reason why we should not have an intelligent, human play now and then' (qtd. in Stevens 1898, 29).
38. *'Rosmersholm'*. 1907. Designed by Edward Gordon Craig. Performed by Eleonora Duse as Nora. Compagnia Eleonora Duse, Teatro Lírico, Rio De Janeiro, Brazil. July 16. *IbsenStage*, Event 80483. https://ibsenstage.hf.uio.no/pages/event/80483.
39. *'Casa di bambola'*. 1898. Directed by Ettore Paladini. Performed by Teresa Mariani Zampieri as Nora. Compagnia Paladini-Zampieri, Teatro Solís, Ciudad Vieja, Montevideo, Uruguay. September 27. *IbsenStage*, Event 77462. https://ibsenstage.hf.uio.no/pages/event/77462. See 'Teresa Mariani Zampieri'. *IbsenStage*, Contributor 434718. https://ibsenstage.hf.uio.no/pages/contributor/434718.
40. *'A casa da boneca'*. 1899. Directed by Lucinda Simões. Performed by Lucília Simões as Nora. Companhia Lucinda Simões, Teatro Solís, Ciudad Vieja, Montevideo, Uruguay. December 29. *IbsenStage*, Event 75457. https://ibsenstage.hf.uio.no/pages/event/75457. See 'Lucília Simões'. *IbsenStage*, Contributor 433220. https://ibsenstage.hf.uio.no/pages/contributor/433220.
41. Originally performed in Coimbra, it was the first production of an Ibsen play in Portuguese, although Eleonora Duse had played Hedda Gabler in Italian as part of her Lisbon repertoire in 1898.
42. *'Maison de Poupée'*. 1906. Performed by Suzanne Després as Nora. Suzanne Després Company, Rio de Janeiro, Brazil. *IbsenStage*, Event 76064. https://ibsenstage.hf.uio.no/pages/event/76064.
43. 'Matsui Sumako'. *IbsenStage*, Contributor 431469. https://ibsenstage.hf.uio.no/pages/contributor/431469. There is still more research that needs to be done on the details of the Matsui tour; for this reason the only records on her contributor page relate to the Tokyo performances.
44. This conflation reflected the emergence of the arts as an attractive arena for middle-class women looking for new roles outside the home; actresses had also recently reappeared on the Japanese stage after an absence of 300 years (Rodd 1991, 175).
45. The first attempt to pass a women's suffrage bill in New Zealand had occurred three years earlier in 1887 and women won the vote in 1893.
46. Our use of the phrase 'identity space' in this chapter refers to the concept as defined by Jonathan Friedman: 'culture is about the products of a more complex and specific substrate of cathected identity spaces embedded in hierarchical processes of socialization. Identity spaces [...] are about the construction of selfhood and worldhood. The two are aspects of the same process' (1994, 76). For further discussion of the application of this concept to intercultural theatre, see Holledge and Tompkins (2000).

47. Biographical criticism has, on its own, long been discredited in critical circles, but, when combined with the other forms of analysis we provide here, it offers a fuller picture of the attraction that these actresses had to the role of Nora. As this chapter demonstrates, these actresses broke with social conventions and found an echo in the fictional character of Nora.
48. Two versions of the film were made, the first following the original text and the second working from the revision provided by Ibsen for the first stage production in Germany.
49. See the review of Yvonne Kapp's biography of Eleanor Marx by E.P. Thompson, first published in New Society in 1976 and later in Thompson (1976) 1994.
50. The connection between Duse and Després is just one of the international associations that form the French *Et dukkehjem* network; it reached as far as Maurice Tourneur, the director of a silent film version of *A Doll's House* made in the USA in 1918, and Gabriela Zapolska, the Polish actress who began this story of the European touring Noras.
51. Jiang Qing was arrested in 1976; in 1981 she was condemned to death, but this sentence was commuted to life. She was released to hospital on medical grounds in 1991.
52. May-Brit Akerholt, the major translator of Ibsen for the Australian theatre, provided the following notes on this line: 'If you put "ekteskapelig" in front of "samliv," you get "married life," and "samliv" in Ibsen's time would be read as a couple who live together, married or not. There is an untranslatable twist or subtext in the last word "ekteskap," which is the Norwegian word for "marriage." However, the word "ekte" on its own means "true, genuine, real"' (Akerholt 2015).

CHAPTER 3

'Peddling' *Et dukkehjem*: The Role of the State

> [T]he truly national author is the one who knows how to impart to his work those undertones which ring out to us from mountain and valley, from meadow and shore, and above all from our own inner minds. (Ibsen [1851] 2010, 83)

According to Régis Debray, an idea or artefact can only survive if there is an institution committed to its preservation: it works like 'a kind of registry or patent office, but rather than passively conserving its charges, it is never done sifting, revising, censuring, interpreting, and peddling them' (2004, 11). It is hard to find a successful text in world theatre that does not hold a central position within its culture of origin, and it should come as no surprise that all the major institutions committed to the global transmission of *Et dukkehjem* are based in Norway, but the degree of involvement of the state in the promotion of the play is unusual even in world drama. The nation's major theatre institutions and public broadcasters, together with significant twentieth-century Norwegian theatrical families and an array of government departments, have successfully 'peddled' *Et dukkehjem* and maintained its position within cultural markets for more than a century. They are the force behind the repeated theatrical signs and symbols that we refer to as the dominant *Et dukkehjem* performance tradition. Nora, tambourine in her hand, is the iconic image of this tradition, shown later in Chapter 5, Fig. 5.2, with examples from performances covering one hundred and thirty-five years and five continents. How was this tradition created and transmitted between

J. Holledge et al., *A Global Doll's House*, Palgrave Studies in Performance and Technology, DOI 10.1057/978-1-137-43899-7_3

productions? We may guess that the Norwegian institutions are implicated in the story, but which institutions, and how have they managed to peddle the play so successfully for over a century?

The distant visions that structure this investigation into the Norwegian institutional forces contributing to the global success of *Et dukkehjem* are maps and network graphics that show the movements of Nordic artists performing in multiple productions. The first pattern we consider is a map of the touring trajectories of the early Nordic Noras. Although they had very little involvement in the first global dissemination of the play, these women were responsible for creating a major interpretative tradition in performing *Et dukkehjem*. The institutional force at the centre of this tradition is the Christiania Theatre, Kristiania (Oslo), which becomes the Norwegian Nationaltheatret in 1899. The second set of patterns we analyse shows the regional and global flows of Nordic artists and productions from 1914 to 1990. Unbroken lines of artists link these tours back to the premiere of the play in Copenhagen in 1879. The discovery of this degree of artistic interconnection, based on 825 records of productions in the Nordic countries, is unprecedented in the study of a single play.[1] The Norwegian institutions behind this extraordinary continuity of aesthetic transmission include not only Nationaltheatret, but also regional theatres, national broadcasters, dominant theatrical families, and government cultural bodies. The content of this transmission creates the third set of patterns, consisting of repetitive tropes sourced from illustrations, marketing images, and photographic traces. The fourth group of patterns comes from maps showing the post-1990 global distribution of the play. These touring circuits are as extensive as those used by the nineteenth-century actress-managers, but they are heavily subsidised. Following the money trail reveals that the presence of *Et dukkehjem* in the twenty-first-century theatre markets is heavily reliant on Norwegian government funding initiatives that stimulate new productions and support international touring. Together, these patterns divulge a complex story of the relationship between a play and a nation state.

Before embarking on our analysis, we briefly consider the context in which the play acquired its national significance. Pascale Casanova has argued that an international classic presupposes a national classic, particularly in 'small' countries where the emergence of new literatures can be crucial to establishing a national identity (2004). Norway declared independence in 1814 and was unusual in nineteenth-century Europe in privileging theatre above other forms of literature in the formation of national culture. In 1854, Marcus Jacob Monrad, the prominent

Norwegian philosopher, insisted that within the newly constituted country, '[n]o other artistic institution is of such great importance to the development of nationality as the national theatre' (qtd in Schmiesing 2006, 31). Yet from its inception, the modern public theatre in Norway was in foreign hands. Established in 1827 by the Swede Johan P. Strömberg, the Christiania Theatre, the major Norwegian theatre in what is now Oslo, was completely dominated by foreign managers and artists, who came primarily from Denmark until the 1860s. This made it an ideological and political battlefield. An authentic Norwegian theatre, with Norwegian actors speaking Norwegian, was championed by the early romantic poets, the nationalists, and, significantly, the playwrights Henrik Ibsen and Bjørnstjerne Bjørnson, both of whom were active in the struggle to create new Norwegian theatres (Hansen 1888; Blanc 1899, 1906; Schmiesing 2006). The first performance of *Et dukkehjem* at the Christiania Theatre in January 1880 was held a month after the premiere in Copenhagen, Denmark, the capital of the colonising power responsible for the 'four hundred year night' that had removed all social, cultural, economic, and political power from Norway. Although the Christiania Theatre was no longer in the hands of Danish directors, actors, and dramatists, the images of the production show that it was deeply influenced by the Copenhagen performance (Caretti 2002; Hov 2010).

Pattern One: The Building of an Aesthetic Tradition

Our first pattern shows the trajectories of five significant early Nordic Noras who toured the region between 1879 and 1937: Betty Hennings,[2] Adelaide Johannesen,[3] Ida Aalberg,[4] Johanne Dybwad,[5] and Tore Segelcke.[6] While the early European Noras were circling the globe, these Nordic Noras were creating a performance tradition that would last until the late twentieth century.

In the years immediately following its world premiere in Copenhagen, the play spread rapidly over the region, with performances in all the major cities of the Nordic countries. Most of the trajectories in Fig. 3.1a represent the movement of individuals who were invited to give guest performances as Nora in productions tied to resident theatres. This practice of guesting was atypical in the careers of the early European Noras; in the UK, Italy, Russia, and France, the actress-managers toured with their companies performing *Et dukkehjem* as part of their standard repertoire. The only other country with a similar guesting practice was Germany,

a

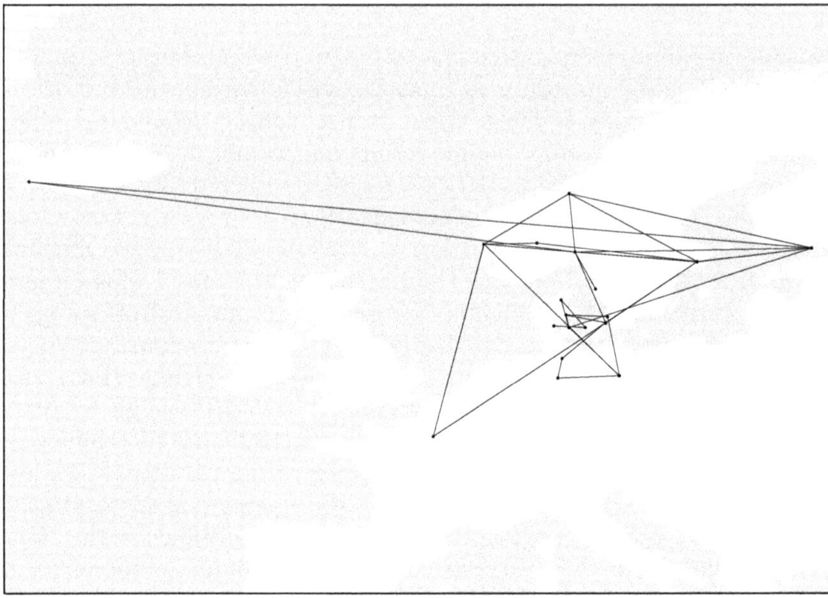

b

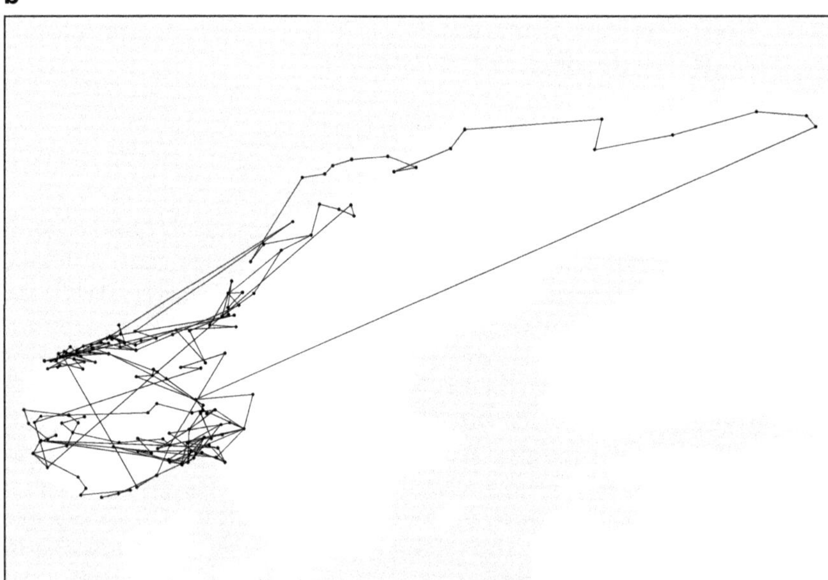

Fig. 3.1 (**a**) Touring trajectories of major Nordic Noras 1879–1937: Betty Hennings, Adelaide Johannesen, Ida Aalberg, Johanne Dybwad, and Tore Segelcke (Source: IbsenStage). (**b**) Touring trajectories of major Norwegian productions 1966–90 (Source: IbsenStage)

the major difference being that in the Nordic map a single theatre, the Christiania Theatre, dominates the touring circuit. The first Norwegian performance of the play took place in this theatre in 1880; it was directed by Johannes Brun and starred Johanne Juell. In comparison with the premiere of the play a month earlier at the Royal Theatre in Copenhagen, this Norwegian production had little regional prestige. Juell performed the role twenty-five times in the first season and another three times in a return season later that year (Blanc 1906, 44).[7] And then something happened that was profoundly to influence the production history of *Et dukkehjem*: Johanne Juell died on 29 April 1882. Rather than lose a box-office success from its repertoire, the theatre invited three actors who had played Nora in other cities to give guest performances in the role: Adelaide Johannesen, the first to play the role at Den Nationale Scene in Bergen; Betty Hennings, the Danish actor who premiered the role in Copenhagen; and the first Finnish Nora, Ida Aalberg. These Kristiania guests performed over a two-year period (June 1883, September–December 1883, and May 1885). The adoption of this guesting practice, triggered by the early death of Johanne Juell, resulted in a blending of interpretative approaches to the play that made the Kristiania production a major site for aesthetic exchange within Nordic theatre. As the touring map drew attention to this otherwise overlooked site, we examine in detail this process of aesthetic blending that gave birth to a performance tradition that spread as far as China and Japan.

Our argument that the dominant tradition of performing *Et dukkehjem* was derived from a process of aesthetic blending is based on the collaborative nature of theatre production. The Nordic Noras were invited to give guest performances in different theatres because of the originality of their characterisations, but to succeed in new surroundings they had to fit their interpretations to the performances of the acting ensembles at the host theatres. This was a two-way process, with the supporting casts in the different cities also readjusting their roles to the new interpretation of the guesting Nora. All the actors involved, whatever their status, were left with performance memories of the effect of this process. If innovations in the playing found favour with local audiences, they were likely to be incorporated into future performances. Potentially this was occurring at all levels of the acting: the emotional interactions between characters, the playing of physical actions, the prioritising of elements within the plot as significant for character development, and the timing and pacing of the performance. While reviewers and audiences focused on the diversity in the interpretations of Noras, the performances of the actors in the local productions were simultaneously being homogenised. This theatrical practice gathered together production knowledge from rehearsal rooms and stages from across the whole of the Nordic region.

Every time the Kristiania production was remounted to accommodate a guest, there were alterations in the cast, but the director together with the three actors playing Dr Rank, Helene, and the Porter were always present. Johanne Juell's interpretation of Nora 'struck to their hearts with angst and stifling tears for all the thousands of women in a similar situation' (Review of *Et dukkehjem* at Christiania Theater 1880). The reviews attributed a balanced palate of negative and positive emotions to Juell: she combined childishness, naivety, frivolity, warmth, sweetness, and heaven-aspiring joy with angst, despair, and an abyss of pain. The resolution of these mood swings was described as a persona who is defiant, cold, proud, and stoically calm. In the final scene with Torvald, she became 'a flaming accuser, who on behalf of all womanhood threw him and society a gauntlet in the face. Her Nora was an organ for women's struggle for independence, and she acted as a preacher' (*Christiania Intelligentssedler* 1885). The reviewers concentrated on the differences in the guests' characterisations of Nora. Betty Hennings, the original Nora, was perceived as a quintessential late nineteenth-century stage ingénue: this archetype combined the sexual innocence of a pre-pubescent girl with the exhibitionist display of the mature female body. The adjectives used to describe Hennings's Nora read like a checklist of emotions for the successful portrayal of the role: innocent, lively, beautiful, young, naïve, captivating, nimble, graceful, childish, frivolous, joyful, fluttering, and inexperienced. The dominant image of this Nora was 'the little fluttering butterfly-like child-wife' (Bøgh [1879] 1980). Ida Aalberg, the first Finnish Nora, embodied the romantic idealism of a generation of artists and intellectuals. Aalberg's reviews were full of references to Nora's inner states: inner distress, inner torment, and inner moral struggle. Her emotions were described as extreme: madness, desperation, hysteria, horror, agony, angst, terror, and passion. Together they were considered symptomatic of spiritual suffering and transformation. The Kristiania production successfully absorbed and incorporated elements from all of these radically different interpretative approaches: the 'flaming accuser', the romantic and tragic idealist, and the 'child wife'. The critics were in general agreement that no one could match Hennings's first-act child-woman; Juell's strident feminism was passé; and Aalberg's tarantella too excessive for Scandinavian tastes (*Christiania Intelligentssedler* 1885; Review of *Et dukkehjem*, *Dagbladet* 1885; and Review of *Et dukkehjem*, *Aftenposten* 1885). As Adelaide Johannesen was an unknown actor from Bergen, her interpretation went unrecorded in the comparative reviews of the Kristiania Noras.

In September 1890, after a five-year gap, a new Nora appeared on the stage of the Christiania Theatre: Johanne Juell's daughter Johanne Dybwad. The story of this mother and daughter echoes that of other early European Noras (see Chapter 2). Juell married a fellow actor at nineteen and gave birth to her daughter, also Johanne, a year later. The marriage did not last and when she moved to Kristiania, her daughter was left with relatives in Bergen. Johanne Dybwad inherited the role of Nora from her mother, but it carried a blending of the rich diversity of interpretative influences absorbed in the previous years by all the actors at the Christiania Theatre. It was as if the theatre had been marking time for eight years until the daughter could step, quite literally, into her mother's costume. Dybwad's performance was mercurial: gay, wild, untamed, capricious, trembling, and anguished.[8] The reviews contained echoes of the earlier reports of Juell's physical presence, Aalberg's idealism, and the softness of Hennings's ingénue. Dybwad must have been schooled in the playing of the role in the rehearsal room: she was a young performer working with her mother's director, Johannes Brun; her Torvald was Olaf Mørch Hansson, who had played the part of Nils Krogstad with her mother; and in the rest of the cast there were actors who had performed alongside one or more of the previous guesting Noras.

Dybwad played Nora for seventeen years. Her claim to being *the* Norwegian Nora was fully legitimised in 1899 when the Christiania Theatre became the Norwegian Nationaltheatret. By this time, the Nordic guesting practice was being replaced by company touring: in 1890, Betty Hennings toured a complete Danish production to Kristiania, followed in 1904 by Ida Aalberg's Finnish company. There were also competing productions from actors breaking away from Nationaltheatret for commercial or personal reasons. Despite these rivals, Dybwad reinforced her ownership of the role by performing the play with a new Nationaltheatret production that marked Ibsen's death in 1906. Her own theatre company remounted this production as one of four Ibsen plays that toured to Denmark and Germany the following year. The Copenhagen reviews found the production surprisingly familiar, no doubt because it represented an amalgamation of so many Nordic influences, but in Berlin it was identified as unpalatably Norwegian (Waal 1967, 116). This would suggest that the aesthetic blending of interpretative influences that had begun at the Christiania Theatre in the 1880s had matured into a recognisably Nordic approach to performing the play.

Although the Christiania Theatre was the institutional force behind the consolidation of this performance tradition, the move from domestic to international distribution required the intervention of the Norwegian state. Dybwad officially handed the role to Tore Segelcke in 1936.[9] She had dropped Nora from her professional repertoire after the disappointments of the German tour, but did not relinquish the role at Nationaltheatret for another thirty years. The occasion that triggered this casting change was the company's tour to Paris for the International Exposition Dedicated to Art and Technology in Modern Life in 1937. The significance of this Paris performance as an assertion of national culture is reflected in the Norwegian programme for the Exposition, which describes the production of *Et dukkehjem* as an 'authentic expression of the Norwegian way to interpret Ibsen [...]. [T]he ideas it holds have played a decisive role in the intellectual development in Norway' (*Catalogue du pavillion de la Norvège à l'exposition internationale de Paris* 1937, 53). This tour is the last trajectory to appear on the map of the early Nordic Noras, but three years after the Paris Exposition, the figure of Nora is directly identified with the nation itself. In 1940, a few weeks after Germany invaded Norway, *Et dukkehjem* was performed as a signifier of national resistance. German censorship opened a field of coded messages and symbolism in which Norwegian reviewers interpreted Nora (performed by Tore Segelcke) as 'Mother Norway [...] bursting with pain, and yet full of strength' (Ringdal 2000, 237).

Our first pattern reveals how the Christiania Theatre, a minor institution in a theatre culture dominated by Denmark, harnessed production knowledge from several Nordic countries to create an interpretation of *Et dukkehjem* that was exported to Paris as uniquely Norwegian. In the next part of this story, we look at another pattern showing the role that *Et dukkehjem* played in building national culture within Norway. We analyse the network of artists who transmitted knowledge from the 'Norwegian' interpretation of *Et dukkehjem*, in a process that had a global influence on approaches to performing the play.

Pattern Two: The Transmission of a Tradition

In the years following the Second World War, there was little touring of *Et dukkehjem*, aside from some exports of Tore Segelcke's Nationaltheatret production to Vienna, the USA, Mexico, and the Nordic region. A sudden expansion of touring occurred in the 1960s with international productions from European countries: two Swedish productions toured Scandinavia, one of which also went south to Italy; Greece resumed touring to its pre-1914 circuit of Egypt and Turkey, with the addition of Cyprus; an English tour travelled to North America; the Germans toured twice to Austria and Switzerland; while the French did a single tour to Belgium and Luxembourg. The most concentrated activity came from within Norway: in addition to four international tours, there was extensive regional touring across the country to community venues (Fig. 3.1b). The theatre institutions behind these Norwegian tours were all subsidised by the government: Det Norske Teatret and Riksteatret (1966, 1974), Riksteatret (1989), and Teatret Vårt (1990).[10] These touring circuits were reflective of the cultural policies that swept Western Europe in the 1960s and 1970s that aimed at democratising the consumption of national culture by taking art to the people. This regional map illustrates not only the extensive reach of these cultural policies, but also the significance of the play in building national culture from Farsund to Vadsø. This new pattern of activity raised an obvious question: did it represent a departure from, or a continuation of, the pre-war aesthetic tradition that had been created and consolidated in Oslo and exported to the Paris Exposition?

To establish whether a connection existed between these touring productions and the pre-war tradition, we created another distant vision of the production data as a network graphic. We took the whole of the Nordic *Et dukkehjem* production history, with its 825 events and 2268 participating artists, and searched for productions that were linked by these artists.[11] We knew that the guesting Noras had created links between productions in the early Nordic history of the play, but we had no idea whether there were any connections in the post-war period. As theatre is a collaborative art form, complex interconnections between artists working on diverse projects are commonplace, but artists connected to multiple productions of the same play are harder to find. We hoped to find a director or designer who had worked on two productions, or actors who had moved from younger to older roles in the course of their careers, but we were astounded to discover that of the 2268 participating artists, 1236 (54%) were connected across a core cluster of 556 events. This was an extraordinary degree of interconnection to discover within the production history of a *single* play. We had stumbled on a fascinating discovery: all the major Nordic touring productions of the post-war period were interconnected through a chain of artists that reached right back through the blending years of the play's early history to the original Norwegian production at the Christiania Theatre in 1880. In all the linked productions, at least one artist in the rehearsal room could claim to be the custodian of a direct line of descent from this early production of the play.

Since our search was focusing solely on the Nordic productions, we were not sure whether this degree of artistic interconnection was a common feature within the production history of *Et dukkehjem*. For instance, in Germany the Thalia Theater had produced the play twenty-three times over a period of one hundred and thirty-three years, and the Düsseldorfer Schauspielhaus had produced the play fifteen times over one hundred and eight years, so there was every chance that there were other lines of aesthetic transmission.[12] We repeated the network analysis with the whole *Et dukkehjem* production history and found that of the 15,571 participating artists, 6133 (39%) were connected to clusters of ten or more events. There was one other major cluster, apart from the Nordic, and this centred on German-language performances; although both clusters included productions from beyond Europe, they were not connected by any participating artists, as is shown in Fig. 3.2.

The uncovering of such rich artistic interconnections in the history of *Et dukkehjem* implied that the cultural transmission of specific knowledge regarding the production history of a play based on lived experience of previous performances was widespread in rehearsal rooms; it further suggested that other canonical works of modern drama might be subject to a similar form of theatrical inheritance.

Having established that the degree of interconnection between artists in the Nordic production history of *Et dukkehjem* was not an isolated phenomenon, we returned to the line of cultural transmission that began with the Christiania Theatre production in 1880, and traced it to the final performances of major Norwegian tours in Bergen and Eidsvåg in Norway, and Hallunda in Sweden in 1990, and to the 1991 Nationaltheatret production (Fig. 3.3). Eighteen key individuals were responsible for holding this network of productions together. The touring Noras were clearly important, but so were four directors from Nationaltheatret, two of whom had acted in earlier productions.[13] Some of the most important linking figures were directors, designers, and actors with very simple trajectories bridging two productions that were separated by several years. Geographically, the places where the transmission was particularly significant included Oslo, Trondheim, and Bergen, and the capital cities Copenhagen, Stockholm, Reykjavik, and Helsinki. We took the 1991 Nationaltheatret production as an endpoint because of the importance of this institution to the history of the dominant performance tradition, though the network analysis showed that this line of transmission continued into the twenty-first century. An offshoot of the network in the USA ended in San Francisco in 2010; a performance connected to the 1991 Nationaltheatret production was staged

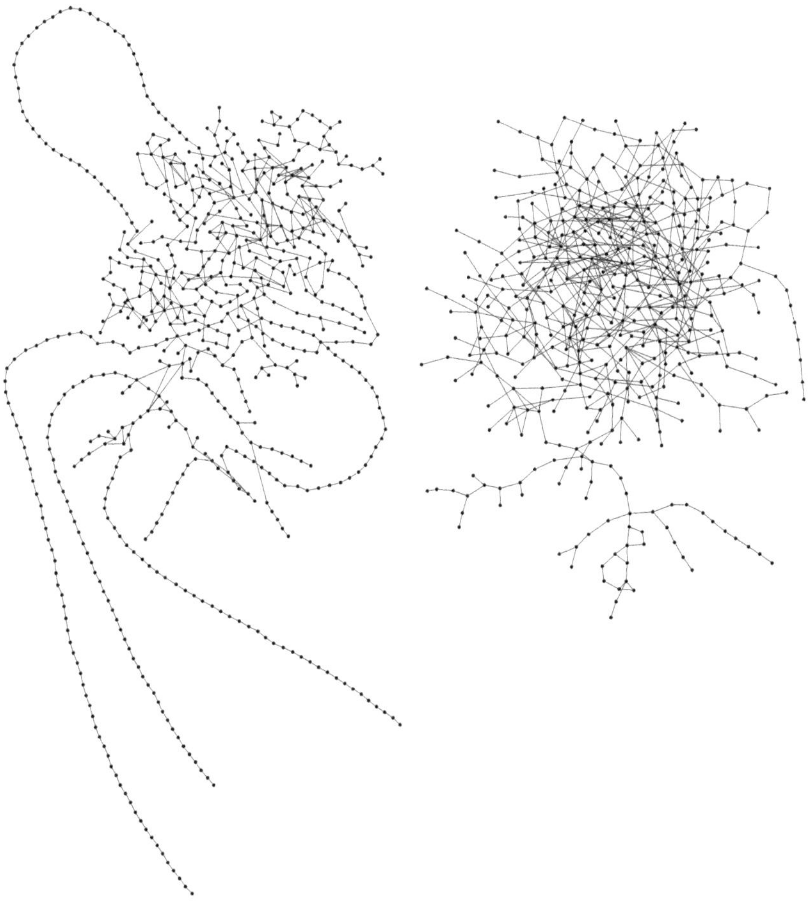

Fig. 3.2 'Nordic' (*left*) and 'German' (*right*) clusters in the network of *Et dukkehjem* events linked by participating artists (Source: IbsenStage)

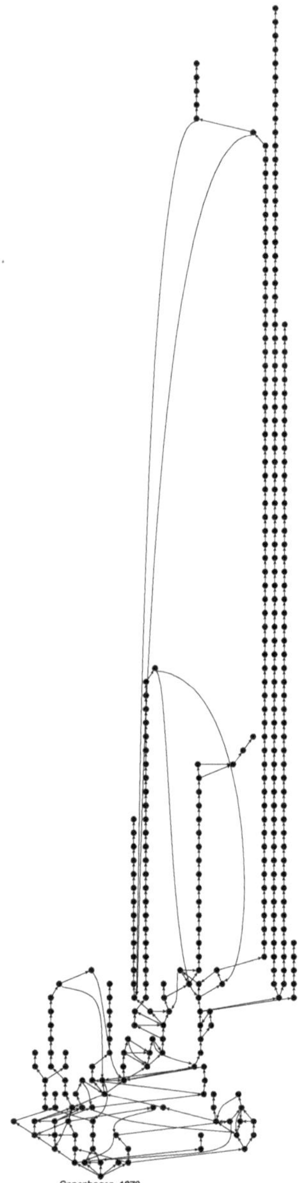

Fig. 3.3 Network of artist-to-artist transmission through the 'Nordic' cluster of *Et dukkehjem* events from the premiere production in Copenhagen, 1879 (Source: IbsenStage)

in Oslo in 2008; and a production linked to the Eidsvåg performance was mounted in Skien, Ibsen's birthplace, in 2014.

Our network analysis posed some compelling questions: who were the key artists linking this network of productions and, most importantly, was there evidence of aesthetic transmission in the performance traces? Could we find artists who were the surviving custodians of this tradition and ask them to share their experiences? We traced the links between the artists in this network of productions from the point at which Dybwad relinquished the role of Nora to the 1991 Nationaltheatret performance. A simplified diagram of this network is reproduced in (Fig. 3.4). The productions are identified through the actors playing Nora, and the names of key artists linking the productions are marked on the connecting lines that create four main branches. Two radio productions played a significant function as meeting points where artists from the different branches came together. This diagram, with its fifteen Noras and fourteen additional artists (some of whom duplicate links), indicates the importance of interpersonal connections within the field of theatre in the consolidation, maintenance, and transmission of a performance tradition.

The major institutions that are the force behind the productions linked by the artists are NRK, the Norwegian national broadcaster, and seven major theatre companies. All of these institutions, except for the wartime Bærum Studiescene—an alternative theatre run by young artists in occupied Oslo—were and are subsidised cultural bodies supported by the Norwegian state.[14] As funding is given to all these institutions to promote the national culture, it is not surprising that they are instrumental in disseminating the work of *the* major Norwegian playwright. Nationaltheatret created five separate productions; Det Norske Teatret created two; while Riksteatret toured three versions, one of which it also produced. Through the activities of these publicly funded theatres, the state (or even the Nation in nationalist ideology) and regional authorities were instrumental in holding the network together. After the Paris tour in 1937, the Norwegian government continued to support the dissemination of this 'authentically' Norwegian *Et dukkehjem* through funding to public broadcasters, the attachment of Norwegian artists to overseas productions, and international touring productions to the Czech Republic, Finland, Germany, Hungary, Norway, Poland, Russia, Sweden, Denmark, France, Iceland, Belgium, the UK, Austria, and Japan.

While there was nothing particularly remarkable about the list of institutions associated with the network of productions, identifying the individual artists drew attention to another institution that was also playing a significant linking role, and that institution was the family.

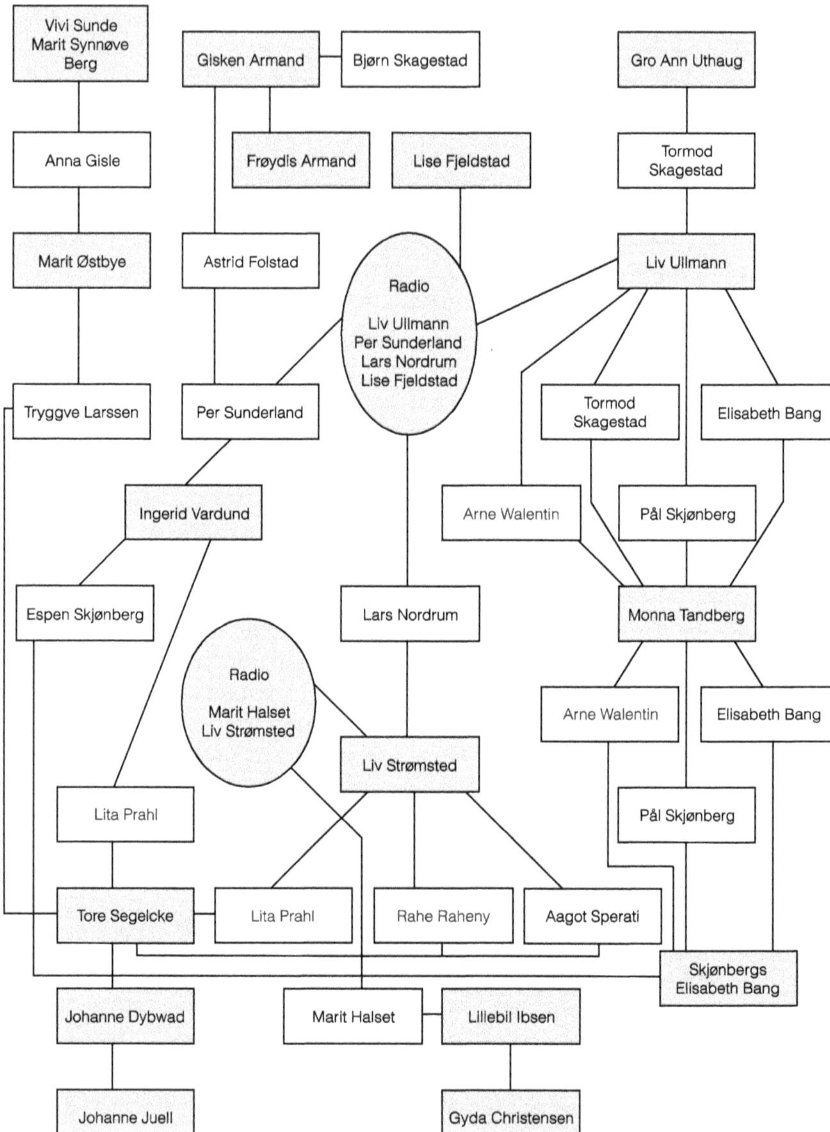

Fig. 3.4 Norwegian artistic network: productions with Noras marked in grey, radio versions as circles, remaining names indicate linking artists (Source: IbsenStage)

Family Stories: Cultural Inheritance as Aesthetic Constraint

It is a great irony that a play so famous for critiquing the family should be dependent on this very institution for its success within Norwegian theatre. Of the twenty-nine artists in the line of transmission, fifteen had significant family connections within the network. Theatre historians have tended to minimise the importance of the generational transmission of aesthetic knowledge via theatrical families since the late nineteenth-century European theatre, and have tended to concentrate on the influence of prestige artists and training systems. This shift in scholarly emphasis reflects the decline in importance of dominant theatrical families in the established European theatre cultures; a decline that was caused by the sudden influx of middle-class actors associated with the growing professional status of the art form. But it does not take account of the mechanisms that underpinned the creation of younger theatre cultures within the region. As we have already mentioned, the Norwegian theatre was a comparative latecomer to European culture, the first Norwegian actor appearing on the main stage in 1850. Theatrical families played a significant role within the Norwegian productions of *Et dukkehjem*, while during this same period theatrical families were losing their influence in the older European theatre cultures.

It is difficult to gauge the effect of the ubiquitous personal relationships between the Noras and Torvalds that characterised the first eighty years of the production history. The more persuasive argument that demonstrates the influence of the personal lives of the network artists on the performance tradition comes not from the marriages or affairs between actors playing these central roles, but from the divorces emanating from within Nationaltheatret. On two occasions they were the catalyst for rival productions of *Et dukkehjem* mounted by artists breaking away from the network.[15] The more significant of the two occurred in 1922, when the director of Nationaltheatret, Halfdan Christensen, who had played Torvald for Johanne Dybwad and later directed the Tore Segelcke production, divorced his second wife, Gyda Christensen. That same year, she appeared in a modern-dress production of *Et dukkehjem* at Centraltheatret in Oslo.[16] This production challenged the received wisdom regarding the period staging of the play and it also threatened to create an alternative Norwegian aesthetic tradition founded on family ties. Just as Dybwad had derived her claim to the role of Nora through her mother, Gyda Christensen handed the role to her daughter (and Halfdan's stepdaughter), Lillebil Ibsen.[17] In 1956, when Lillebil performed Nora, she was already married to Ibsen's grandson Tancred. The contested claims of the extended Christensen theatrical family to the interpretative control of *Et dukkehjem* were further complicated after Halfdan's death. His third wife, Gerda Ring, took over his role as the director of the Segelcke production in 1954, directed a new production of the play in Copenhagen in 1955, and advised on another in Beijing in 1956.

Yet the most obvious example of a theatrical family's cementing of the aesthetic tradition associated with *Et dukkehjem* comes from the post-war history of the Skjønberg family. In 1944 Espen and Pål Skjønberg were members of Bærum Studiescene. They persuaded their mother Henny Skjønberg to direct a play; she chose *Et dukkehjem*. The production was a family affair, with Espen playing Torvald and designing, Pål playing Dr Rank, and Elisabeth Bang, who married Pål, playing Nora.[18] Bang and the Skjønberg brothers had a close connection with the play for the next thirty years: between them, they produced, acted, and directed in the three major post-war productions starring Ingerid Vardund, Monna Tandberg, and Liv Ullmann.[19] The theatrical dynasties appearing in this story constitute the elite within the history of Norwegian theatre. They were also an important force in securing the success of the play in the national repertoire, making the play an important 'stake in the game' of Norwegian theatre.

Pattern Three: Aesthetic Transmission

Uncovering a line of artists who linked the major Norwegian touring productions of the twentieth century to the first performance by Johanne Juell opened up the possibility of tracing 'through time (diachronically), [a] developing and changing' transmission of performance knowledge (Debray 2004, 3). The challenge is to identify the aesthetic content of this transmission. By following the sequence of productions linked by artists, we have found traces of repetitive interpretative tropes in performance that are a clear indication of constraint over creative diversity in the staging of *Et dukkehjem*. We have termed this transmission the dominant tradition of performance, because it was promoted for over a hundred years by the combined institutional forces of the Norwegian state and its theatres.

We investigated the content of the aesthetic transmission by collecting production drawings and photographs. Since theatre companies did not adopt the practice of taking photographs during dress rehearsals until the 1970s, performance photos are available for only the final productions in our sequence; images from the earlier period consist either of artists' impressions or tableaux staged during photo calls organised for publicity purposes. We began by analysing the visual sign systems of the sets and costumes. We knew that there would be inevitable echoes within the *mise-en-scène* because four of the designers had worked on multiple productions over a twenty-year period: Rahe Raheny (Segelcke and Liv Strømsted productions); Arne Walentin (Strømsted, Tandberg, and Liv Ullmann productions); Lita Prahl (Segelcke and Ingerid Vardund productions); and Anna Gisle (Marit Østbye, and Vivi Sunde/Marit Synnøve Berg productions).[20]

Live Hov has drawn attention to similarities between the pictorial representations of the first performance in Kristiania and the Copenhagen premiere, the Danish image being 'created from cutting and pasting various photos of the four characters, which were glued on to the background showing the set' (2010, 30). This photomontage significantly influenced the composition of production photographs of later performances. Laura Caretti has written at some length about the image of the Madonna, reproduced from a painting by Raphael, that appeared in the original design in 1879 (2002, 82). It was not in Ibsen's stage directions, yet it appears again in the Segelcke production in 1936. We searched for the Raphael Madonna image in the post-war designs and found it again in the Liv Strømsted production in 1956. As Rahe Raheny designed both productions, it is understandable that the image repeats, but it is surprising that it is the same painting by the same scenic artist. As a design element in the Nordic production of *Et dukkehjem*, Raphael's Madonna had a life of seventy-seven years.

The most obvious similarity between the production designs of the performances that hold the sequence of productions together is placing the dramatic action within a domestic interior signifying a late nineteenth-century bourgeois household. There are also numerous echoes in the costume designs, all of which reference the 1880s. Most of the production photographs are in black and white, but similarities in texture and pattern are visible. While the photographs provide ample evidence of a naturalistic aesthetic in the settings and costumes, they also reveal clues about the actors' playing of the text.[21]

To discover a physical gesture repeated by actors in productions separated by more than a hundred years is incontrovertible evidence of a performance tradition inhibiting creative innovation. Debray suggests that '[n]o tradition has come about without being an invention or recirculation of expressive marks and gestures' (2004, 2). One vivid example comes from the *mise-en-scène* of the tarantella rehearsal that echoes through production after production, from Copenhagen in 1879 to Bergen in 1990. While the ubiquitous image of Nora with the tambourine raised in her left hand could be said merely to represent the original Italian dance, the figure of Torvald instructing her has no referent other than the playing of the scene. In the photomontage from the Danish production in 1879, the figure of Emil Poulsen is conducting Nora's performance (Fig. 3.5a); Noralv Teigen repeats these gestures in the production photograph of the Gro Ann Uthaug performance in 1990 (Fig. 3.5b).[22] This archetypical Torvald pose can be traced back through photographs taken in 1957, 1955, and 1880.[23]

Another performance moment is repeated in images of Nora decorating the Christmas tree. In each case, the actor's facial expression invites the viewer to interpret the emotional content of her unspoken thought. The emotions represented by the actors are all slightly different: Tore Segelcke communicates a melancholic sadness in 1936 (Fig. 3.6a); Monna Tandberg is transfixed by a combination of shock and fear in 1966 (Fig. 3.6b); Liv Ullmann mixes sadness with disgust in 1971 (Fig. 3.6c); and Gro Ann Uthaug seems fixated on some shocking revelation in 1990 (Fig. 3.6d).[24] Despite these differences in emotional colouring, the actors are all using the same performance technique used in psychological realism to elicit an empathetic response from spectators: they are dropping the character's social mask to reveal a supposedly truthful interiority to the audience. These repetitive images are another example of the dominant aesthetic tradition of performing *Et dukkehjem* that lasted for over a hundred years, traces of which can still be found in productions of the play around the world.

Unconscious Assumptions or Conscious Constraints

We wanted to talk with actors who had been part of the tradition. Were they aware of their role within the network that we had uncovered? Did they have a subjective sense of being part of this tradition while rehearsing and performing the play? We were hopeful that they would provide anecdotal accounts of aesthetic transmission in rehearsal rooms, green rooms, and dressing rooms. When actors, directors, and designers begin work on a play-script, the task of embodying the characters involves multiple decisions that take aural, physical, and visual forms. Rehearsal rooms

Fig. 3.5 (**a**) Detail of Emil Poulsen (Torvald), Det Kongelige Teater, 21 December 1879, Copenhagen (Source: The Royal Library in Copenhagen). (**b**) Detail of Noralv Teigen (Torvald), Sogn og Fjordane Teater, 8 March 1990 (Source: Trygve Schønfelder)

Fig. 3.6 (**a**) Tore Segelcke, Nationaltheatret, Oslo, 13 October 1936 (Source: photographer Ernest Rude, photo archive of National Theatre, National Library, Oslo). (**b**) Monna Tandberg, Det Norske Teatret, Oslo, 26 February 1966 (Source: Svein Sturlason). (**c**) Liv Ullmann, Det Norske Teatret, Oslo, 24 January 1974 (Source: Svein Sturlason). (**d**) Gro Ann Uthaug, Sogn og Fjordane Teater, 8 March 1990 (Source: Trygve Schønfelder)

are experimental laboratories for this process: what feelings, actions, and character relationships does the dialogue suggest? In this creative process, directors, designers, and actors, particularly if the latter have status within the field of cultural production, will explicitly or implicitly share their knowledge of past rehearsals, performances, and productions from other relevant plays. This knowledge is rarely committed to paper; it is transmitted orally, often anecdotally. More importantly, it can be transmitted from body to body through the use of images, gestures, actions, and the representation of emotional states. The replication of these body states is frequently justified by actors' preconceived assumptions about the correct interpretative approach for a particular text or specific role. The network of the Nordic production history of *Et dukkehjem* posed an intriguing hypothesis that a unique tradition of embodiment, transmitted through a chain of artists over more than a century, could have imposed a set of unexamined normative assumptions about the performance of this single dramatic text in Norway. It was this hypothesis that the interviews were designed to explore.

We interviewed six of the nine surviving Noras within the network, and three of the most prominent figures of the older generation of artists within the tradition.[25] The actors acknowledged the influence of key linking network artists, such as Tryggve Larssen or Astrid Folstad, but denied having heard anecdotes about earlier performances during rehearsals. As a general rule, it seems that the artists linking the network avoided citing information about past productions as part of the creative process. Although Monna Tandberg performed with Elisabeth Bang as Mrs Linde in productions that toured to sixty-nine venues in eight countries, she was surprised to discover in our interview that Bang had played Nora in 1944. While the interviews did not support our hypothesis that there was an explicit oral tradition of anecdotes about previous productions transmitted in the rehearsal room, all our interviewees except one told us that they had seen previous versions of the play and heard stories about other productions from their contemporaries.

Since the production photographs we had uncovered revealed striking similarities in the gestures the actors used, we were interested to know more about the physical techniques employed in rehearsals. Marit Østbye recalled that the actor Tryggve Larssen gave her precise instructions on how to loosen a long strand of hair from her wig while dancing the tarantella. Some actors recalled being given instructions by directors about where and when to move on stage; others remembered having interpretative control over the initial patterns of movement that directors refined later in rehearsal. Whereas Monna Tandberg remembers being given freedom to explore Nora's physicality by the director Tormod Skagestad in 1971, Gro Ann Uthaug remembers the same director giving her the exact sequence of gestures to use when showing the silk stockings to Dr Rank. All the actors agreed that standard rehearsal-room protocol in the 1970s and 1980s gave directors control of the physical dynamics in a scene, the creation of tableaux, and even specific character gestures; they were not required to provide actors with a rationale for these decisions. Perhaps the directors were responsible for some of the bodily transmissions visible in production photographs. Olaf Mørch Hansson and Halfdan Christensen, two of the major directors in the network, had originally played Torvald; Elisabeth Bang and Pål Skjønberg directed and acted in three productions over ten years; Tormod Skagestad was responsible for four productions over twenty-five years; and Gerda Christensen, Halfdan's wife, restaged her husband's earlier production. Unfortunately, none of the directors who created this spine of connection through the network is alive today.

Even if the directors were instrumental in transmitting certain physical tropes from one actor to another, the gestural repetition in the Norwegian tradition of performance cannot be attributed to this single cause. It probably relies on *many* forms of conservation; it is the overdetermined character of tradition that keeps it alive. Marit Østbye said it was her impression that many of 'the gestures come from Johanne Dybwad. Everyone has seen the photos of her doing it. You do it the same way. I have only seen photos from the performance with Tore Segelcke' (Østbye 2011). These visual images have a form of authority and have a role to play in the forces of cultural transmission; some of the theatre programmes, particularly at Nationaltheatret, have made a point of reproducing a pictorial production history of the play that emphasises an interpretative consistency.

Our interviews raised challenging questions about the subjective perceptions of actors regarding the consolidation and imposition of an aesthetic tradition. We were confronted by the contradiction that the actors believed their interpretations were unique and original, while the visual evidence showed numerous points of repetition not only in the physical tableaux and set and costume designs, but also in gestural tropes. Perhaps this is not surprising, since critical acclaim for European theatre practitioners has been associated with interpretative originality for most of the twentieth century; to deliberately replicate the performance of a famous predecessor can be viewed as a form of theatrical plagiarism. It was clear that the possibility of repetition was repressed within the rehearsal room, but the fact that the actors were acutely aware of the play's canonical importance may have confused fidelity to the written text with fidelity to a particular tradition of staging the play. Alternatively, the answer to this conundrum may lie within the practices of psychologically realistic acting, whereby performers feel in total control of the characters' inner thoughts and feelings, but accept the necessity of physical constraints imposed by external forces, whether these are the theatre architecture, set and costume designs, or the director's conceptual control.

The Noras interviewed all shared a consciousness of having been part of a tradition, a fact that they valorised very differently. The last two Noras illustrate this beautifully. Gro Ann Uthaug, who played Nora in a very successful performance in 1990 at Sogn og Fjordane Teater, expressed satisfaction and pride in a performance that she herself (and a few critics) characterised as 'traditional'. However, Gisken Armand at Nationaltheatret, who first played the role in 1990, recalls feeling trapped in a 'room too small' during the performance, and claims that she wished for something different and more radical. We encountered one major difference in the group interview we conducted with Edith Roger, Joachim Calmeyer, and Espen Skjønberg: they interpreted the network links and family connections as arbitrary coincidences and not as a line of aesthetic transmission. While they agreed that there was a strong Ibsen tradition, they felt that it resided in the practice of textual analysis within the rehearsal room and in the *authority* of the text. This, they said, has changed today, since now 'anything goes'. All interviewees were fascinated to find themselves part of a theatrical network, even if they were sceptical about its influence over their creative choices. When the actors who played Nora referred to a performance tradition, it was described as an 'unconscious' influence (Sunde 2011), or as something that 'left a mark without our being aware of it' (Armand 2011). Perhaps this only added to its effectiveness and, as Debray suggests, '[*o*]*ptimal transmission is transmission forgotten*' (2004, 15; emphasis in original). The last production in the network sequence that we investigated took place at Nationaltheatret in 1991. It was presented as part of the programme of the first International Ibsen Stage Festival. This is not to imply that the creation of this festival was responsible for the death of the tradition, rather that Gisken Armand's feeling of being trapped in 'a room too small' was a theatrical zeitgeist.

None of the artists was surprised that the dominant performance tradition weakened in the 1990s. They attributed the radical shift in the Norwegian staging of *Et dukkehjem* over the past twenty years to multiple influences: inspiration from other European theatres, the globalisation of the theatre industry, a new generation of artists for whom 'anything goes', and the rise in a conceptual theatre dominated by directors. Norwegian productions since the 1990s have incorporated temporal and spatial relocations; genre experimentation, including site-specific, expressionist, magical realist, and postdramatic versions; and interpretative decisions embracing cross-gender and cross-ethnic casting.[26] Yet if the dominant tradition was supported for so long by major Norwegian institutions, why did they fail to preserve it; or, conversely, what were the conditions that made it advantageous for these institutions to remove aesthetic constraints and encourage creative innovation? In the hope of answering this question, we returned to our touring maps to look for traces of the influence of Norwegian institutions in the post-1990 world of *Et dukkehjem*.

Pattern Four: *A Doll Home* in the Ibsen Industry

The centre of the recent explosion of international touring is Oslo, which has become the major destination for global performances of *Et dukkehjem*, but not a production site for new Norwegian international tours. When the map showing artists' trajectories in the post-1990 era is compared with the actress-managers' maps, the invisible boundaries that restricted artists' movements in the earlier period have gone. The pattern of languages has also shifted: German and English are the dominant European languages; the Scandinavian languages, French, and Japanese have a modest presence, while Portuguese, Russian, Polish, and Greek have disappeared; the new languages that have taken their places include Arabic, Bengali, Bosnian, Dutch, Spanish (an Argentinian production), Kurdish, Hindi, Urdu, and Nepalese. Three major German theatres have mounted international tours: Thalia Theatre in Hamburg; Schaubühne am Lehniner Platz, the theatre responsible for the most extensive tour of the play having visited twenty-two countries; and Theater Oberhausen, which has visited five countries since its premiere in 2011. The English-language circuit has expanded primarily because of the Mabou Mines production from New York, which has visited sixteen countries over eight years; but there have also been three minor tours from the UK and one from Malawi. English is used in performances from India, as well as in a recent production by a company based in Belgium. The Scandinavian countries, together with France and Spain, have undertaken small tours. New activity has emerged in the most unlikely places where there was no previous history of Ibsen productions, which begs the question: why are artists from Malawi, Zimbabwe, Zambia, Palestine, Turkey, Egypt, Nepal, Bangladesh, and Pakistan so attracted to *Et dukkehjem* in the early twenty-first century?

The presence on the map of new activity in theatre cultures outside Europe prompted us to investigate the contexts of these productions. We could find no similarities in the social or aesthetic rationales provided by the participating artists to explain their choice of *Et dukkehjem*, but there was a pattern of financial subsidy from the Norwegian government, usually administered through a local embassy. Cultural aid provided by the Norwegian government was responsible for introducing *Et dukkehjem* into these diverse twenty-first-century theatre markets. IbsenStage holds 1295 records of productions presented in 68 countries since 2000; although the Norwegian government has been directly involved in only a fraction of these productions, its indirect influence has been immense. In the final part of this chapter, we consider a new phenomenon in the cultural transmission of *Et dukkehjem*: the 'Ibsen Industry'.

In 2006, the then Norwegian Foreign Minister Jonas Gahr Støre wrote a newspaper article reflecting on the coming year-long official celebration of the Ibsen centenary:

> Ibsen has had a central place in our cultural activities for many years, and now we are concentrating our efforts. We will support traditional and innovative Ibsen events in a large number of countries. We will highlight the relevance of Ibsen's writings to our own time, in all continents and in different cultural settings. [...] Altogether, these efforts will promote Norway as a modern nation and highlight and revitalise an important part of our cultural heritage. [...] Ibsen puts Norway on the map. He is clear and he is bold. He puts important issues on the agenda. He evokes associations with Norway and Norwegian art. All this is giving Norway a more distinct image. (Støre 2006)

Under Støre's leadership, the Ministry of Foreign Affairs promoted Ibsen as a national symbol of arguably universal *and* 'Norwegian' values, such as gender equality, accountability in governance, democracy, and protection of the environment. At the end of the twentieth century, and particularly in the years following the events of 11 September 2001, Norwegian soft diplomacy began to increase its use of cultural aid in the area of public diplomacy; the goal was to promote the image of Norway as a benevolent force in global politics. The origin of this international branding of the country as a force for 'global good' dates from the establishment of the Nobel Peace Prize in 1901, but it takes on greater significance after 1993 when Norway's efforts at peace mediation between the Israelis and the Palestinians resulted in the Oslo Accord. In the following two decades, the Norwegian government engaged in peace and reconciliation processes in the Philippines, the Balkans, Guatemala, Colombia, Sri Lanka, Cyprus, Somalia, and the Sudan; *New York Times* correspondent Frank Bruni describes this activity as 'a frenzy of Norwegian peacemaking, or at least peacetrying, that has put peace somewhere alongside oil and timber as one of this country's signature exports' (2002). Alongside these signature exports sits Ibsen. Large amounts of taxpayers' money have been invested in Ibsen-related events by the Ministries for Culture, Education, Research, and Foreign Affairs, primarily through festivals, prizes, scholarship, and awards.

Major government initiatives promoting *Et dukkehjem* include the International Ibsen Stage Festival in Oslo and discrete Ibsen festivals in major Asian cities, particularly Delhi and Dhaka; seminars and conferences on gender equality that include local productions of the play; the Ibsen Awards Scholarships, which fund a variety of artist-led projects using the play as the source material; new translations of the play into Arabic (Classical Arabic and Egyptian Arabic), Hindi, Spanish, Persian, Chinese, Japanese, and Russian; and scholarships for international students to write theses on Ibsen, many of whom choose to concentrate on adaptations of the play in their local theatre cultures. These programmes all help to secure a place for *Et dukkehjem* in world theatre.

International Ibsen Festival

The establishment of the International Ibsen Festival was a Nationaltheatret initiative. Stein Winge, the first director of the Festival, formulated a strategy to revitalise the Ibsen tradition through the introduction of new influences from international sources; as he was also the director of Nationaltheatret, he evidently had no desire to perpetuate a single dominant aesthetic tradition. Corporate sponsorship, particularly from the DNB Norwegian bank and Telenor, Norway's leading telecommunications operator, played a significant role in building the event. The Festival received a major contribution from the Ministry of Culture to build momentum for the 2006 Festival to commemorate the centenary of Ibsen's death. Apart from this single initiative, state subsidy comes to the Festival indirectly through the annual budget of Nationaltheatret.

Controlling the interpretative strategies in the performance of *Et dukkehjem* and exporting productions as the expression of a national ethos are no longer a Norwegian priority. Productions echoing the interpretative tropes associated with the dominant performance tradition had faded by the twenty-first century, only lingering on in the Anglo theatre world of North America, Britain, and Australia. In the 2010 Festival brochure, Keld Hyldig argued that the international productions presented since 1990 had shifted the Norwegian tradition of producing Ibsen from an actor-based to a director-based theatre. He concluded by saying, '[i]t is hard to tell how the performance of Ibsen in Norwegian theatre will develop in future' (Nationaltheatret 2010). Hanne Tømta, the current director of both the Festival and Nationaltheatret, believes that the Festival 'has opened our eyes to new possibilities of staging Ibsen, giving us totally different viewpoints, and deepening our understanding of his dramas' (Tømta 2015). Winge's aim of revitalising the Norwegian Ibsen tradition proved to be a phenomenal success, but ironically this new creativity is kept within the country. The Norwegian government is no longer interested in exporting productions from Nationaltheatret and a private foundation has been established to help the company respond to overseas invitations. As a consequence, the global market for productions of *Et dukkehjem* in the twenty-first century has been dominated by German- and English-speaking productions.

What began as an artistic push to revitalise an aesthetic tradition has escalated into a second international touring explosion equalling the impact of the actress-managers at the turn of the nineteenth and twentieth centuries. The Festival is not the only mechanism at work, but the lure of an invitation acts as a force constraining the diversity of the global repertoire to favour Ibsen's plays while simultaneously encouraging artists to be innovative within the adaptation process. The roads to Oslo have become paved with symbolic and financial capital, as long as productions can surprise with their aesthetic originality, the novelty of their cultural interpretations, or their iconoclasm. The map showing the trajectories of *Et dukkehjem* productions invited to the Festival between 1990 and 2014 reveals that most of the invitees come from countries with a history of importing past Norwegian productions (Fig. 3.7a). The USA, Western Europe, Russia, and Japan were the touring destinations of Johanne Dybwad, Tore Segelcke, and Monna Tandberg. Now the prestigious state and contemporary theatre companies from these countries are invitees to Oslo; the only new countries in the *Et dukkehjem* trade are Pakistan,

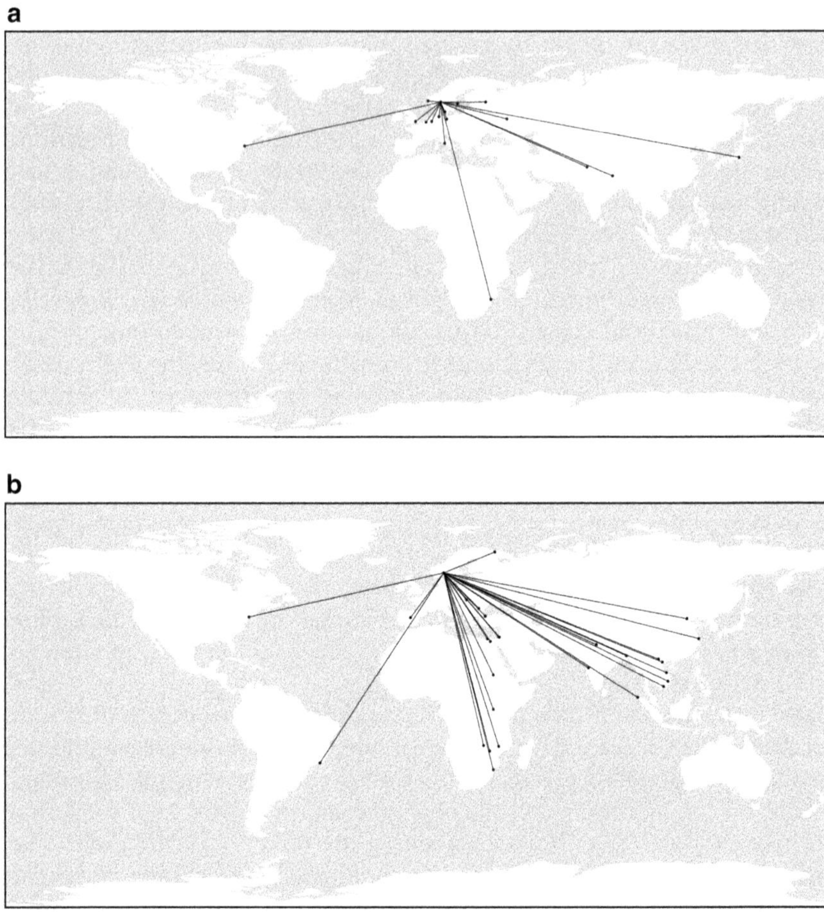

Fig. 3.7 (**a**) Adaptations of *Et dukkehjem* (including *Nora's Daughters* from Mozambique) imported to the International Ibsen Festival, from 1990 to 2014 (Source: *IbsenStage*). (**b**) International distribution of Norwegian government funds promoting *Et dukkehjem* through the Nora's Sisters programme, the Ibsen Award Scholarships, and grants from the Ministry of Foreign Affairs (Source: *IbsenStage*)

Nepal, and Mozambique.[27] An invitation to Norway offers financial benefits as well as increased regional prestige, which for the smaller theatre companies outside Europe translate into increased regional touring after the performance in Oslo.

The International Ibsen Festival is one of the many new international arts festivals that emerged in the 1990s.[28] Two major productions of *Et dukkehjem* broke into this global market at the beginning of the twenty-first century: the Schaubühne am Lehniner Platz production directed by Thomas Ostermeier, and the Mabou Mines production directed by Lee Breuer. These productions cornered a new market because they represented not only a European heritage, but also a contemporary aesthetic based on innovative performance techniques and theatre technology. Both productions were invited to the International Ibsen Festival. Mabou Mines opened in New York in 2003 and played in Oslo the following year; it continued to tour the world until 2011. The Schaubühne production opened in 2002, and also played Oslo in 2004, by which time it had toured extensively in Europe. It continued to tour Europe for the following five years as well as playing in Australia, Japan, South Korea, Taiwan, and North America. The highly visible success of these Ibsen products in the international arts market, combined with the possibility of an invitation to a major European festival dedicated to presenting productions based on Ibsen's dramas, contributed to a significant increase in global productions of the Ibsen repertoire.[29]

While the International Ibsen Festival was becoming established in Oslo, the Norwegian Foreign Ministry began to fund Ibsen events outside Norway, particularly in Asia. One long and highly successful association was with the Centre for Asian Theatre (CAT) in Dhaka, where a conference entitled 'Gender Issues in Ibsen's Plays' was held in 1997, followed by 'The Relevance of *A Doll's House*' in 2002, which included a festival of three Bangladeshi productions of the play. Another conference was held to commemorate the Ibsen centenary in 2006,[30] and CAT hosted a festival of twenty-one productions of Ibsen's plays from six countries in 2009. Building on the Dhaka success, funding was provided for a major Ibsen Festival in Delhi; four works based on *Et dukkehjem* were presented in the four festivals held between 2008 and 2012.[31] The subsidies for the Delhi event enabled attendance to be free, but there were issues surrounding financial accountability, which inadvertently opened up a space for Norwegian producers to act as cultural brokers. In 2010, Inger Buresund established the independent arts organisation Ibsen International, with an aim 'to contribute to international cooperation within the fields of art, culture, trade and industry and research' (Ibsen International 2010). Ibsen International received generous funding from the Norwegian government and mounted a series of events held annually in China since 2010, including a production of *Nuola* (*Wan'ou Zhi Jia*) directed by the Norwegian choreographer Un-Magritt Nordseth, and starring the famous Shanghai transsexual performer Jin Xing (2010), as well as *Nora—A Contemporary Opera*, a bicultural work composed by Du Wei with libretto by Jon Fosse entitled *Too Late*, directed by Victoria Meirik, which premiered in Tianjin in October 2014.[32]

Ibsen Awards Programme

A second programme sponsored by the Norwegian government and administered through Teater Ibsen in Skien, Ibsen's birthplace, involves an annual competition for Ibsen Award Scholarships and a small festival where previous winners are invited to present the productions funded through the scheme. Twenty-six scholarships were awarded to projects in twenty-one countries between 2008 and 2014 (Fig. 3.7b). Those connected to productions of *Et dukkehjem* included a translation of the play into Arabic; a Turkish performance in Kurdish, *Nora/Nûre*; the Egyptian dance work *Nora's Doors*; a Sudanese mixed-media work on the symbol of the hijab, *Nora's Cloth*; and *Me. A Doll's House*, an adaptation mixing live music and film noir by a Bucharest company, which was part of the project Hedda's Sisters: Empowering Women Artists from Romania and Eastern Europe.[33] In addition to these productions, the scheme also funded a symposium for *Et dukkehjem* artist/adaptors from sub-Saharan Africa. Participants from Kenya, Mozambique, Zimbabwe (Harare and Bulawayo), Zambia, South Africa, Eritrea, and Malawi met in Lusaka to discuss their adaptations of the play. Their motivations for using *Et dukkehjem* as source material for productions were context specific, but many of them had received financial assistance from local Norwegian embassies, particularly for performances in 2006. The Zambian and Malawian adaptations of *Et dukkehjem* were commissioned by embassy staff for the Ibsen centenary; the Kenyan Norwegian Embassy sponsored the Pioneer Players production of the same year; financial support for several Ibsen projects was given to the New Horizons Theatre in Harare; and close connections existed between Norway and the theatres in Eritrea and Mozambique as Helge Rønning, from the University of Oslo, was dramaturg on both productions. The only performances that did not directly or indirectly receive Norwegian funding were Johannesburg's Market Theatre production at the Baxter Studio in 1990, and the Amakhosi Theatre 'Women in Arts Project' adaptation in Bulawayo in 2003.[34]

Nora's Sisters

Festivals and scholarship awards have proved effective mechanisms for influencing the repertoire across a broad spectrum of theatre institutions, from the state theatres of Europe to theatres for social justice in southern Africa, but *Et dukkehjem* has also been used to further Norwegian diplomacy. In the field of public diplomacy, Norway and Canada are today's most successful exponents of niche branding based on association with what Joseph Nye calls 'attractive causes' (2004, 9): Canadians have used land-mine activism and the invention of the UN peacekeeper, the Norwegians peace initiatives and gender equality. *Et dukkehjem* has played a part in this international branding exercise (Fig. 3.7b).[35] The best funded of all the soft diplomacy cultural programmes run by the Ministry of Foreign Affairs was the Nora's Sisters project. Initiated as part of the 2006 Ibsen centenary, it proved such a popular programme that its life was extended to 2010.

Across the world, Norwegian embassies were funded to convene seminars on 'gender equality and the respective roles of today's women and men in different societies and cultural settings' (DECO 2011). Seminars were organised in sixteen countries between 2006 and 2010. Many of these events culminated in performances of *Et dukkehjem*. The official Nora's Sisters publication contained a chart showing the legislative history of Norway's journey towards gender equality. While the seminar programmes emphasised that each culture must define its own journey to this goal, the goal itself was defined through the pioneering efforts of Norway. The 'Norwegian-ness' of the seminars was emphasised by opening presentations from major Norwegian public figures: diplomats, leading politicians, including the prime minister in 2006, artists, and even royalty. A speech from Inga Marte Thorkildsen, a Norwegian politician, at the Ramallah seminar was typical of these presentations:

> In 1981 we got our first female prime minister, Gro Harlem Brundtland from the Labour Party [...]. Gro's cabinet was called the Women's Cabinet, and she opened the way for progress for Norwegian women. Kindergardens, the right to paid leave for the parents for up to one year, the right to be away from work when the children are ill, the right to get your job back after a parental leave, shelters all over Norway for battered women, separate places

> to take care of victims of violence, more women in the important positions in the private sector—all these rights and freedoms have been realized because women in the parliament, in the government and at the grassroots level have made a common cause. (Thorkildsen 2008)

While these legislative achievements are laudable, the reiteration of Norwegian milestones invited inevitable comparisons with the situation in Ramallah. Even though it was never stated explicitly in the policy documents relating to Nora's Sisters, over half of the seminars took place in low- and middle-income countries (LMICs), among them significant sites of recent violent conflict: Palestine, Banda Aceh, and Uganda.[36] The format of the seminars placed Norway as the country not only asking the questions but also living the answers. Norway was represented as a legislative utopia in the fight for gender equality.[37]

Mixing the objectives of public diplomacy (which focus on projecting a national imaginary of a benevolent progressive country) with the demand for sex and gender equality in other countries can be hazardous. There can be *unattractive* consequences to niche marketing *attractive* causes. To many Islamic cultures, Western feminism is seen as a facet of Western imperialism because of the history of colonial feminist discourse that has been used to justify policies of colonisation and military intervention. The essence of this discourse is that Europe has successfully eradicated discrimination on the grounds of sex and gender and therefore has a responsibility to intervene in countries where time-locked traditional practices oppress women and children. This discourse has a long history: it played a role in legitimising British colonial policy in the nineteenth century and was still in use as a justification for the recent war in Afghanistan. As Shaun Riordan points out in his critique of new foreign policy paradigms:

> Even where core western values are clearly in the interests of the individual, e.g. right to life, freedom of expression, and equality of the sexes or ethnic groups, the perceived need of a group or nation to identify itself in opposition to the west can lead to their rejection. (2005, 10)

The decision to name an interventionist programme after Ibsen's Nora invites rejection because it implies that the seminar participants, particularly in LMICs, are 'sisters' trapped in the social inequalities of nineteenth-century Europe. Yet despite this denial of coeval time, Nora's Sisters seminars proved successful with embassies and their local contacts. Every seminar was shaped by interactions between embassy staff and local non-government organisations committed to countering discrimination on the basis of sex or gender. While Norwegian progressive gender policies framed all the seminars, the involvement of local speakers ensured that debate was tied to the cultural context. One of the seminars with significant local impact was held in Malawi, where the key local organisation was the theatre company Nanzikambe. Melissa Eveleigh, the British director of the company, who also directed *Breaking the Pot*,[38] the adaptation of *Et dukkehjem* commissioned by the embassy, considered the Blantyre Nora's Sisters seminar a watershed event: she had never seen so many Malawian women attending a public meeting.

Eveleigh is just one of the many international artists who praise Norway for its cultural aid and non-prescriptive approach to funding. Her views are echoed across northern and southern Africa and South Asia. Few strings are attached to Norwegian cultural grants and there are no explicit restrictions on artists' interpretation of Ibsen's texts. Equally, the Nora's Sisters seminars provided a public space for important debates on gender and sexuality, regardless of their framing by the Norwegian experience. Encouraging creative diversity as an expression of individual freedom and freedom of speech are important platforms in Norway's public diplomacy, and this message is carried by the diversity of uses the government has made of *Et dukkehjem* in the twenty-first century.

Conclusion

We have unravelled the intertwined forces of major theatre companies, theatrical families, state departments, and state policy initiatives in producing *Et dukkehjem*. This has been made possible by visualising the Nordic production history as a series of touring maps and artistic networks. Over a period of 135 years, Norwegian institutions have 'peddled' the play so consistently that without their influence, it is difficult to imagine its global success. From the first performance in 1880, the play was seen, read, and discussed widely in Norway. Although the ideas within the play were criticised and ridiculed by many Norwegian conservatives, virtually no one questioned its importance as a dramatic text. The play answered deep national needs. As a young nation on the periphery of Europe, Norway longed for opportunities to project an image of itself as *modern*, and the theatrical modernity of *Et dukkehjem* outweighed the absence of a patina invested by age. By 1937, the Norwegian government was exporting the play to Paris for the International Exposition Dedicated to Art and Technology in Modern Life. That the Norwegian nation would use

Et dukkehjem to promote its national value and pride to the rest of the world less than sixty years after its publication says something about the play's position not only within the field of theatre, but also as a symbol of national culture. While criticising patriarchy, the text simultaneously fed into the nationalist ideology of Norway as a nation of strong, autonomous citizens. This heritage could be traced to the Middle Ages when, instead of nobility, Norway had independent and enlightened farmers who owned their own land. The extreme version of this ideology tries to construct a bridge all the way back to the Viking heroes of the Icelandic sagas.[39] Its relevance to *Et dukkehjem* lies in the representation of Norwegian women as independent and strong, which may explain why Norway was happy to promote itself officially through a text that implied criticism of its own gender politics. By the 1960s and 1970s the play was regularly toured across the whole of Norway as part of a movement for building national culture. When the oil revenues started to grow during the 1990s with the establishment of The Petroleum Fund (Government Pension Fund Global), it is not surprising to find that the play was co-opted into Norway's efforts to build an international profile. The success of the 2006 international programme to celebrate the centenary of Ibsen's death boosted the use of the national playwright as a key platform of the nation's soft diplomacy. By 2011 and 2012, the government budget for Ibsen-related activities had reached approximately fifty million kroner (€ 5.45 million).[40]

It is no longer a priority for Norwegian institutions to control the artistic interpretation of *Et dukkehjem* as part of a national imaginary: it is the discourses of individual freedom and gender equality, coupled with the encouragement of creative diversity, that best serve the country's interests today. Artists on every continent are being invited to improvise with Ibsen's drama and to make of it what they will: it is a container ready to be filled by any content deemed progressive by local producers and their Norwegian sponsors. Through its festivals, awards, cultural aid, and even occasional sponsorship through Statoil, the part-government-owned multinational oil and gas company, Norway has been the engine driving the global distribution and production of the play in the twenty-first century. Yet it would be a mistake to imagine that Norwegian financial and symbolic capital is being dispensed without reference to the country's values as a social democracy; Norwegian soft diplomacy promotes artistic freedom, but its funding is still predicated on an assumption that art must have a utilitarian function and social relevance.

The extraordinary diversity of cultural experience absorbed into recent global performances of the play implies that it has assumed a mantle of universality and transcended its connection with the European colonial expansion that first carried it around the world, unless the institutional forces maintaining its presence in the canon of world drama are acknowledged. This Norwegian success story suggests that we should be asking whether the public diplomacy of nation states, which openly seeks to gain political and economic advantage by influencing 'hearts and minds' abroad, is responsible for maintaining the current hierarchy of dramatic texts in the world theatre canon. Are the dominant (if constantly fluctuating) positions of Shakespeare, Goethe, Ibsen, Brecht, Chekhov, Lope de Vega, Molière, Beckett, and O'Neill reflecting the universal application of their plays within our changing world, or are they a reflection of the relative power and influence of the nation states using these writers as 'brand' names?

Notes

1. The Nordic countries are Denmark, Finland, Iceland, Norway, and Sweden.
2. See 'Betty Hennings'. *IbsenStage*, Contributor 427226. https://ibsenstage.hf.uio.no/pages/contributor/427226.
3. See 'Adelaide Johannesen'. *IbsenStage*, Contributor 427225. https://ibsenstage.hf.uio.no/pages/contributor/427225.
4. See 'Ida Aalberg'. *IbsenStage*, Contributor 427513. https://ibsenstage.hf.uio.no/pages/contributor/427513.
5. See 'Johanne Dybwad'. *IbsenStage*, Contributor 428957. https://ibsenstage.hf.uio.no/pages/contributor/428957.
6. See 'Tore Segelcke'. *IbsenStage*, Contributor 434592. https://ibsenstage.hf.uio.no/pages/contributor/434592.
7. See 'Johanne Juell'. *IbsenStage*, Contributor 430451. https://ibsenstage.hf.uio.no/pages/contributor/430451.
8. According to the critic Tor Hedberg, Johanne Dybwad embodied 'feminine idealism': in the third act she 'retains even now her feminine softness and weakness, tries to spare him, has a prayer for forgiveness in every hard word which must be said because it is the truth [...]. [S]he puts down the keys: she knows that they will be needed the next day. It is her last act of housewifely care and she slips softly away, humble but firm, so little, so weak, so touchingly helpless in all her strength' (see Tor Hedberg, *Svenska Dagbladet*, 8 May 1901, qtd in Waal 1967, 250).

9. See 'Tore Segelcke'. *IbsenStage*, Contributor 434592. https://ibsenstage.hf.uio.no/pages/contributor/434592.
10. 'Det Norske Teatret'. Norway. *IbsenStage*, Organisation 32463. https://ibsenstage.hf.uio.no/pages/organisation/32463; 'Riksteatret'. Norway. *IbsenStage*, Organisation 32426. https://ibsenstage.hf.uio.no/pages/organisation/32426; 'Teatret Vårt'. Norway. *IbsenStage*, Organisation 32466. https://ibsenstage.hf.uio.no/pages/organisation/32466.
11. For these calculations, participating artists are contributors to events with functions other than translator, playwright, composer, adaptation, and author.
12. 'Nationaltheatret'. Oslo, Norway. *IbsenStage*, Organisation 32424. https://ibsenstage.hf.uio.no/pages/organisation/32424; 'Thalia-Theater'. Hamburg. *IbsenStage*, Organisation 32407. https://ibsenstage.hf.uio.no/pages/organisation/32407; 'Düsseldorfer Schauspielhaus'. Düsseldorf, Germany. *IbsenStage*, Organisation 33230. https://ibsenstage.hf.uio.no/pages/organisation/33230; 'Den Nationale Scene'. Bergen, Germany. *IbsenStage*, Organisation 32409. https://ibsenstage.hf.uio.no/pages/organisation/32409.
13. These directors were 'Johannes Brun'. *IbsenStage*, Contributor 434631. https://ibsenstage.hf.uio.no/pages/contributor/434631; 'Olaf Mørch Hansson'. *IbsenStage*, Contributor 429818. https://ibsenstage.hf.uio.no/pages/contributor/429818; 'Halfdan Christensen'. *IbsenStage*, Contributor 428572. https://ibsenstage.hf.uio.no/pages/contributor/428572; 'Gerda Ring'. *IbsenStage*, Contributor 432652. https://ibsenstage.hf.uio.no/pages/contributor/432652.
14. Nationaltheatret was given an annual subsidy from the 1930s; NRK is a government-owned public broadcaster; Det Norske Teatret was established in 1912 to promote theatre in Nynorsk and is supported by the state; Riksteatret is the national touring theatre, fully financed by the Norwegian state with a duty to tour nationally; and Trøndelag Teater, Teatret Vårt, and Sogn og Fjordane Teater are important regional companies (with local touring responsibilities) subsidised by the national and regional authorities together. See 'Trøndelag Teater'. Norway. *IbsenStage*, Organisation 32978. https://ibsenstage.hf.uio.no/pages/organisation/32978; and 'Sogn og Fjordane Teater'. Norway. *IbsenStage*, Venue 13393. https://ibsenstage.hf.uio.no/pages/venue/13393.
15. Olaf Mørch Hansson (Dybwad's first Torvald) and Thora Hansson (Adelaide Johannesen's Mrs Linde) divorced in 1896, after sixteen years of marriage. When Thora Hansson found that her contract with Nationaltheatret had not been renewed, she leased the Tivoli Theatre in Kristiania and challenged her former employer by directing a rival production of *Et dukkehjem*, with herself as Nora. Her husband remained with

Nationaltheatret and, somewhat ironically, was promoted from Torvald to the director of the play when it was produced again in 1906. See 'Thora Hansson'. *IbsenStage*, Contributor 435100. https://ibsenstage.hf.uio.no/pages/contributor/435100.

16. 'Gyda Christensen'. *IbsenStage*, Contributor 428571. https://ibsenstage.hf.uio.no/pages/contributor/428571.
17. 'Lillebil Ibsen'. *IbsenStage*, Contributor 430253. https://ibsenstage.hf.uio.no/pages/contributor/430253.
18. 'Elisabeth Bang'. *IbsenStage*, Contributor 427853. https://ibsenstage.hf.uio.no/pages/contributor/427853: 'Bærum Studiescene'. Norway. *IbsenStage*, Organisation 32541. https://ibsenstage.hf.uio.no/pages/organisation/32541.
19. 'Ingerid Vardund'. *IbsenStage*, Contributor 433902. https://ibsenstage.hf.uio.no/pages/contributor/433902; 'Monna Tandberg'. *IbsenStage*, Contributor 433624. https://ibsenstage.hf.uio.no/pages/contributor/433624; 'Liv Ullmann'. *IbsenStage*, Contributor 433854. https://ibsenstage.hf.uio.no/pages/contributor/433854.
20. 'Liv Strømsted'. *IbsenStage*, Contributor 434647. https://ibsenstage.hf.uio.no/pages/contributor/434647; 'Marit Østbye'. *IbsenStage*, Contributor 433400. https://ibsenstage.hf.uio.no/pages/contributor/433400; 'Vivi Sunde'. *IbsenStage*, Contributor 433539. https://ibsenstage.hf.uio.no/pages/contributor/433539; 'Marit Synnøve Berg'. *IbsenStage*, Contributor 434705. https://ibsenstage.hf.uio.no/pages/contributor/434705.
21. As early as 1922, the Gyda Christensen production in Oslo had challenged this approach by using a contemporary setting, and there were any number of post-war international versions that relocated the time and place of the drama. The most significant innovation in set design that we uncovered in our sequence of productions was the design by Guy Krohg for the 1971 Vardund tour to Japan: the walls of the domestic interior were abstracted into a semi-circular wall surfaced like planked wood in shades of pink with a pink carpet and grey furniture. The closest network link to the Vardund performances is the Nationaltheatret 1990 production with Gisken Armand as Nora. For this production, Luboš Hrůza, the Czech designer, created a conventional domestic interior, but once again controlled his colour palate to shades of pink.
22. '*Et dukkehjem*'. 1879. Directed by H.P. Holst. Performed by Betty Hennings as Nora. Det Kongelige Teater, Copenhagen, Denmark. December 21. *IbsenStage*, Event 75660. https://ibsenstage.hf.uio.no/pages/event/75660.
23. '*Et dukkehjem*'. 1990. Directed by Tormod Skagestad. Performed by Gro Ann Uthaug as Nora. Sogn og Fjordane Teater, Angedalsvegen 5, Førde,

Norway. *IbsenStage*, Event 75895. https://ibsenstage.hf.uio.no/pages/event/75895. '*Et dukkehjem*'. 1880. Directed by Johannes Brun. Performed by Johanne Juell. Christiania Theater, Bankplassen, Kristiania (Oslo), Norway. January 20. *IbsenStage*, Event 75479. https://ibsenstage.hf.uio.no/pages/event/75479. '*Et dukkehjem*'. 1957. Directed by Gerhard Knoop. Performed by Liv Strømsted as Nora. Nationaltheatret, Johanne Dybwads Plass 1, Oslo, Norway. August 15. *IbsenStage*, Event 75774. https://ibsenstage.hf.uio.no/pages/event/75774. '*Et dukkehjem*'. 1955. Directed by Gerda Ring. Performed by Ingeborg Brams as Nora. Det Kongelige Teater, August Bournonvilles Passage 8, Copenhagen, Denmark. November 19. *IbsenStage*, Event 76407. https://ibsenstage.hf.uio.no/pages/event/76407.

24. This analysis of facial emotions draws on Paul Ekman's book (2003).
25. The nine interviewees included the following actors who played Nora: Marit Synnøve Berg (2011), Vivi Sunde (2011), Marit Østbye (2011), Monna Tandberg (2011), Gisken Armand (2011), and Gro Ann Uthaug (2011), together with Edith Roger (director), Joachim Calmeyer (Dr Rank), and Espen Skjønberg (Helmer) (2011).
26. See the 'Ibsen Repertoire Database' (National Library of Norway 2015) for photographs from the following productions: *Et dukkehjem*, i Wesselsgate 15, Visjoner Teater, 20 May 2006; *Et dukkehjem*, Hålogaland Teater, 16 April 2008; *Et annet dukkehjem*, Hålogaland Teater, 17 April 2008; *Det vidunderlige—et enakters skuespill inspirert av 'Et dukkehjem'*, Interkulturelt Museum, 2 November 2008.
27. The festival has also presented works inspired by *Et dukkehjem*, like the sequel *Nora's Daughters* written by Swedish novelist Henning Mankell for the Mutumbela Gogo Theatre Ensemble in Mozambique.
28. As Bernadette Quinn (2010) observes, '[a]rts festivals have been in the ascendant since the late 1980s' when they began to be framed within the neoliberal agendas of culture-led regeneration and urban tourism.
29. The figures in Australia are a clear demonstration of this trend. Ostermeier's productions of *Nora*, *Hedda Gabler*, and *An Enemy of the People* all played major city arts festivals in Australia and the number of Ibsen productions presented by major state theatres showed a marked increase, but when a production of *A Wild Duck* presented by Belvoir Theatre in Sydney was invited to Oslo, it sparked six new productions of Ibsen's dramas the following year.
30. See Zaman and Amin (2006) for the 'Centennial Essays on Ibsen'. This 2006 event also included a student production of *Et dukkehjem*, directed by Tahmina Ahmed.

31. These four productions were a one-woman show, *Ibsen's Women*, by Norwegian performer Juni Dahr in 2008; a production by the Egyptian director Nora Amin entitled *Nora's Doors* in 2009; a film version of *Mabou Mines Dollhouse—From Henrik Ibsen's* A Doll's House *with snippets of* The Vikings of Helgeland in 2010; and an adaptation of the play by the Pakistani women's company Tehrik-e-Niswan, entitled *Gurrya ka Ghar*, in 2012.
32. *'Nuola (Wan'ou Zhi Jia)'*. 2010. Directed by Un-Magritt Nordseth. Performed by Liu Minzi, Dai Shaoting, Xie Xin, Jin Xing, Sun Zhuzhen, and Talisi as Nora. No. 22 Wangfujing Street, Dongcheng District, Beijing, China. October 22. *IbsenStage*, Event 77765. https://ibsenstage.hf.uio.no/pages/event/77765. *'Nora–A Contemporary Opera'*. 2014. Directed by Victoria H. Meirik. Grand Theatre, Tianjin, China. October 30. *IbsenStage*, Event 91522. https://ibsenstage.hf.uio.no/pages/event/91522.
33. For details of all the winners of International Ibsen Scholarships see Ibsen Awards (2015). *'Nora/Nurê'*. 2010. Directed by Jale Karabekir. Performed by İsmail Yildiz as Nora. Painted Bird Theatre, Van, Turkey. April 14. *IbsenStage*, Event 77572. https://ibsenstage.hf.uio.no/pages/event/77572. *'Nora's Doors'*. 2010. Directed by Nora Amin. Ibsenhuset, Lundegata 6, Skien, Norway. September 8. *IbsenStage*, Event 77751. https://ibsenstage.hf.uio.no/pages/event/77751. *'Nora's Cloth'*. 2014. Designed by Issraa El-Kogali. W3 Gallery, 185 High St, London, England. May 6. *IbsenStage*, Event 91521. https://ibsenstage.hf.uio.no/pages/event/91521. *'Hedda's Sisters'*. 2015. Directed by Dani Buglea. Teatrul Odeon, Bucharest, Romania. October 3. *IbsenStage*, Event 91520. https://ibsenstage.hf.uio.no/pages/event/91520. While the Ibsen Award Scholarships scheme has an annual budget of one million Norwegian kroner (approx. €115,000), the mega-prize is the biannual International Ibsen Award, which is worth 2.5 million Norwegian kroner (approx. €300,000). The prize is intended to 'honour an individual, institution or organisation that has brought a new artistic dimension to the world of drama or theatre' (International Ibsen Award 2015).
34. *'A Doll's House'*. 1990. Directed by Clare Stopford. Performed by Grethe Fox. Market Theatre, Johannesburg, South Africa. May 8. *IbsenStage*, Event 77726. https://ibsenstage.hf.uio.no/pages/event/77726. *'Independence Day'*. 2003. Directed by Sithokozile Mhlanga. Performed by Swallen Sibanda as Nora. Amakhosi Theatre, Bulawayo, Zimbabwe. October 26. *IbsenStage*, Event 76066. https://ibsenstage.hf.uio.no/pages/event/76066.
35. In a speech opening the 2012 International Ibsen Festival, Jonas Gahr Støre declared, 'the name "Ibsen" is a more familiar "brand"—if one can use such a term—than "Norway"' (Støre 2012).

36. In 2008, the Afghanistan seminar was cancelled after the death of the journalist Carsten Thomassen during the attack on the Kabul Serena Hotel, where a Norwegian delegation, led by Jonas Gahr Støre, was staying ('Director-General Condemns Killing of Norwegian Reporter Carsten Thomassen in Kabul Hotel' 2008).
37. This image of a country where all gender-related issues are solved—that gender balance and equality are accomplished facts—is critiqued within Norway as false and ideological in the simple sense that it serves to hide the many challenges still at hand. Progress has taken place, but there are still gender-based income differences, and problems associated with domestic violence and sexual abuse.
38. *'Breaking the Pot'*. 2006. Directed by Melissa Eveleigh. Performed by Mbumba Mbewe as Nora. Nanzikambe Theatre, French Cultural Centre, Blantyre, Malawi. April 17. *IbsenStage*, Event 75839. https://ibsenstage.hf.uio.no/pages/event/75839.
39. James McFarlane points to this aspect of Norwegian nation building in the nineteenth century, and quotes Bjørnson's words about his own early works: 'We had come to understand that the language of the sagas lived on in our peasants, and their way of life was close to that of the sagas. The life of our nation was to be built on our history; and now the peasants were to provide the foundations' (1993, 132).
40. This sum is calculated on the amount of government money allocated for Ibsen-related activities by Norwegian Embassies and the Ministry of Foreign Affairs; the grants to Ibsen Museums in Skien, Grimstad, and Oslo; the Centre for Ibsen Studies at the University of Oslo; public funding given to the production company Ibsen International; indirect support to the Ibsen Festival provided through infrastructure funding to Nationaltheatret; and the annual open-air performance of *Peer Gynt* with associated events in Gudbrandsdalen. It does not include regular productions of Ibsen plays outside these festival contexts. The currency conversion was calculated via http://www.oanda.com/currency/converter/ as at 13 August 2016.

PART II

Adaptation

The first adaptation of *Et dukkehjem* was written by Henrik Ibsen. In a letter to the editor of *Nationaltidende* written in Munich (1880a, 24–25), he explains why he adapted his own work:

> Immediately after *Nora* was published, I received from my translator and business manager for the North-German theatres, Mr. Wilhelm Lange in Berlin, a message that he had reason to fear that another translation or 'adaptation' of the play with a changed ending would be published, and that this would most likely be preferred by several North-German theatres.
>
> To prevent such a possibility I sent him a proposal for a change to be used in case of [emergency] in which Nora does not manage to leave the house but is forced by Helmer over to the children's bedroom door; here they exchange a couple of lines, Nora sinks down at the door and the curtain falls.
>
> I have myself described this change to my translator as a 'barbaric act of violence' against the play. Thus it is entirely against my wishes to use it; but I entertain the hope that it won't be employed by too many German theatres.[1]

Ibsen never enjoyed full copyright protection. Artists have been free to cut, substitute, condense, reorder, retitle, and add new material to *Et dukkehjem* from the beginning of its production history.[2] As a consequence, we include every performance described by producing artists as a version of *Et dukkehjem* within IbsenStage, however far it strays from Ibsen's text. In the first hundred years, changes to the text were handled by translators, actors, and directors, and only 59 artists in 1809 records of *Et dukkehjem* productions are credited for adaptation. In the 1978 records of productions since 1980, this number has risen to 328, signalling not only a change in theatrical practice, but also the growing demand for adaptations of canonical dramas in the international arts market.[3]

Adaptation has been taken up as a genre in film studies (Leitch 2009) in particular, with adaptations of classic writers like Shakespeare being perhaps the most popular in execution and in analysis. Understood frequently as a literary analytical tool, adaptation is less well articulated in performance, perhaps because theatre is already adaptive. Linda Hutcheon (2006, 2013) and Julie Sanders (2006) are the best-known commentators in the field, and both of them argue that adaptation is about transformation and change. Like many other scholars, they bridge the divide between the natural sciences and the humanities by appropriating evolutionary theory to argue that art is an adaptive human function developed through natural selection (Hutcheon 2006, 31; Sanders 2006, 160). Hutcheon's *A Theory of Adaptation* provides an approach to analysing adaptation, while Sanders's *Adaptation and Appropriation* tackles the politics of form. Hutcheon uses the model of the palimpsest, insisting that 'an adaptation is a derivation that is not derivative—a work that is second without being secondary. It is its own palimpsestic thing' (2006, 9). Sanders, on the other hand, explores adaptation 'as a form of collaboration across time and sometimes across culture or language' (2006, 47). They agree that adaptation changes the original, with Hutcheon suggesting that 'traveling stories adapt to local cultures, just as populations of organisms adapt to local environments' (2006, 177), while for Sanders, '[t]exts feed off each other and create other texts' (2006, 14).[4]

Hutcheon and Sanders make reference to Richard Dawkins's meme theory, the most prevalent application of Darwinian thought in the field of literary and dramatic adaptation, to suggest parallels between genetic and cultural reproduction (Dawkins [1976] 1989). Meme theory has achieved some traction in adaptation studies because it suggests that ideas or stories propagate themselves like selfish genes within the human imagination (Hutcheon 2006, 31; see also Sanders 2006). This theory has been used by Nina Witoszek to explain the global success of *Et dukkehjem*. In her study of the foundations of modern Nordic identity, she argues that a powerful meme lies at the heart of the play: 'the emancipatory ideal of modernity yielded a new meme authored by Henrik Ibsen: that of Nora, a disillusioned female leaving a bourgeois "doll house" in pursuit of self-realisation' (Witoszek 2011, 18). Yet if a selfish meme is a replicator 'in its own right', as is suggested by Susan Blackmore in her development of meme theory (1999, 24), where does this leave the agency and creative energies of artists? To follow Witoszek and adopt meme theory as the cross-disciplinary theoretical model for our study of *Et dukkehjem* would result in analysing the similarities within *Et dukkehjem* adaptations as naturally occurring phenomena. As it is a physical impossibility to replicate a live performance, it makes little sense to work from a theory that makes replication the default position. By following the gestalt shift in evolutionary thinking proposed by McShea and Brandon (2010), we view sameness as the result of constraint and increasing diversity as unforced. To further support this premise we have taken inspiration from a compelling rereading of Darwin's theoretical writings on sexual as opposed to natural selection by the philosopher Elizabeth Grosz (2011). Darwin devoted many hundreds of pages in *The Descent of Man* to documenting the extraordinary complexity with which the energy associated with sexual selection is deployed, diversified, and made manifest in the activities of living beings (1871). He suggested possible connections between the aesthetic production of song in birds and music in humans. Following Darwin, Grosz argues that artists engaging in cultural production are drawing on the same reservoirs of excess energy that are used in the aesthetic activities of other living creatures, because '[s]exual selection unveils the operations of aesthetics, not as a mode of reception, but as a mode of enhancement' (Grosz 2011, 132). The possibility that there is a reservoir of natural energy fuelling aesthetic production adds further weight to our argument that it is not creative innovation but interpretative repetition that requires explanation.

Despite our hesitations regarding meme theory, we agree with Sanders's broader premise that '[a]daptation studies are, then, not about making polarized value judgments, but about analyzing process, ideology, and methodology' (2006, 20). Our analysis of *Et dukkehjem* adaptations in Chapter 4 shifts from visualisations of touring maps and networks of productions to visualisations that compare dramaturgical structures, the manipulation of character, and narrative substitutions. The patterns they produce lead to explorations of the social and aesthetic forces that have influenced the adaptation process. One of the strongest patterns we uncover concerns the representation of female characters; to explore this pattern further, Chapter 5 zooms in on a single moment within Ibsen's play-script to find repetitions in multiple adaptations of Nora's tarantella dance. We take images of this performance moment from seventy-nine productions and arrange them in a tree diagram according to choreographic repetitions in the dance or overall conceptual approaches to the scene. The trunk and branches of this tree reflect different interpretative strategies; they are composed of images from different eras, geographical locations, political systems, and theatrical cultures. The analysis looks at each of these strategies to consider the ways in which distinct social, aesthetic, and ideological forces intersect to produce similar constraints over the representations of sexuality and gender.

Notes

1. In his letter to Heinrich Laube (1880c, 25–27), Ibsen included his German ending:

   NORA That we could make a real marriage out of our lives together. Farewell. (*begins to leave.*)
   HELMER Well then—go! (*seizes her arm.*) But first you shall see your children for the last time!
   NORA Let me go! I *will* not see them! I *cannot*!
   HELMER (*draws her towards the door, left*). You shall see them. (*Opens the door and says softly*) Look, there they sleep, so carefree and calm. Tomorrow, when they wake up and call for their mother, they will be—motherless.
   NORA (*trembling*). Motherless…!
   HELMER As you once were.
   NORA Motherless! (*struggles with herself, lets her travelling bag fall, and says*) Oh, this is a sin against myself; but I cannot forsake them. (*half sinks down by the door*)
   HELMER (*joyfully but softly*) Nora!
   [*The curtain falls.*]
   Both letters are translated by May-Brit Akerholt with amendments by Frode Helland.

2. The first international copyright agreement, the Berne Convention, was drawn up in 1886. Norway signed the agreement in 1896, but as Ibsen published the Dano-Norwegian texts of his plays in Copenhagen, he was not covered by the Convention until Denmark signed in 1903. Every country where his work was published and performed represented a new arena in which he had to establish his rights as a dramatist, maximise possible royalties, and ensure the quality of the translations of his plays. His strategies included citing bilateral trade agreements, publishing his own translations, signing an agreement with a major European theatre agency, working with

a publisher in London to secure British performance rights, joining the French Société des auteurs et compositeurs dramatiques, authorising translations of his work, and controlling simultaneous publications of his work to maximise royalty protection in different nation states.

3. A further discussion of this phenomenon appears in the last part of Chapter 3, which deals with the international 'Ibsen industry'.
4. Sanders expands the effects of adaptation, arguing 'how frequently adaptations and appropriations are impacted upon by movements in, and readings produced by, the theoretical and intellectual arena as much as by their so-called sources' (2006, 13). Hutcheon's revised edition, meanwhile, expands the concept in a different direction, focusing on new ways in which adaptation is being addressed. In this second edition, she writes with Siobhan O'Flynn to address a broader scope of objects of analysis, specifically incorporating intermediality and the even faster and more diverse ways in which multimedia have an effect on the adaptive process (Hutcheon and O'Flynn 2013). Both critics seek a greater depth of response to texts and 'intertexts' (Sanders 2006, 160).

CHAPTER 4

Adaptation at a Distance

A secret lies hidden in the past of a couple, in an unequal sexual relationship, living with little financial security. The subordinate partner has committed a crime involving the illegal acquisition of capital or goods, motivated by the desire to protect the dominant partner. A hostile intruder appears and tries to blackmail the guilty partner. Eventually the secret is revealed, but catastrophe is averted with the help of a friend. Despite the removal of the threat, the relationship between the couple is temporarily, or more permanently, damaged.

This scenario is a composite of narrative elements common to all the *Et dukkehjem* adaptations consulted for this study. These elements come from four scenes: the opening conversation between Torvald and Nora linking money with sexuality; Krogstad's first threat to expose Nora; the revelation of the hidden secret and removal of the blackmail threat; and the final confrontation between Nora and Torvald. The gendered indeterminacy of our skeletal scenario reflects the practice of transgender casting that has emerged in the past thirty years. While the scenario retains a strong connection between an intimate sexual relationship and money, it does not carry any of the supposedly universal themes cited by previous scholars, in particular the nineteenth-century discourses on subjectivity and the emancipation of women.

Apart from this common narrative that continues to be modified by new adaptations, the production history of *Et dukkehjem* is impressive for its diversity. Adaptations have been performed in over 3000 venues,

J. Holledge et al., *A Global Doll's House*, Palgrave Studies in Performance and Technology, DOI 10.1057/978-1-137-43899-7_4

everywhere from major national theatres, to open-air rural venues in sub-Saharan Africa, a car park in Los Angeles, a traditional Noh theatre, and a late nineteenth-century agricultural fair in New Zealand. The play has been transformed into musicals, dance works, and puppet shows; adapted into every possible electronic medium, including YouTube; produced by queer, avant-garde, and women's companies; and recreated by applied theatres of development, education, and social justice. Even the early performances of the play in Europe veer between genres of naturalism and symbolism. Ibsen's dialogue has been translated into thirty-seven languages; it has been rewritten countless times; and has disappeared from the silent films, dance versions, and photographic still-image re-creations.[1] Thousands of new scenes have been added to *Et dukkehjem* through the assimilation of the play into non-European cultures and the recent practices of free adaptation. One might imagine that the characters are consistent, but they have been renamed, resexed, cut, combined, or doubled, and their class, caste, ethnicity, gender assignment, and sexual preferences have been changed. In addition, the physical differences between individual actors mean that the audience's interpretation of characters will differ from production to production; and as adaptations use multiple geographical and temporal contexts, there are no common features in the scenography, or costume, sound, and lighting design. When the entire production history of the play is considered, *Et dukkehjem* has proved to be such a flexible sign system that its only common feature is a skeletal scenario of sex, money, blackmail, and relationship breakdown.

To create the distant visions that guide this chapter, we visualised dramaturgical structures to highlight repetitive patterns in the inner workings of a *sample* of adaptations. Initially we created visualisations of performances that incorporated plot sequencing, character interactions, narrative locations, and performance time. Subsequently, we simplified these to emphasise three structural elements: character interactions as social structures; character dominance with regard to dramatic action; and plot sequencing showing the relationship between the dialogue written by Ibsen, and the cuts, substitutions, and new material in adaptations. The patterns that we found were cross-checked against additional productions from the performance history of the play. When a pattern was repeated in the wider data set, we looked for its cause. Was it the result of an external social, political, or economic force, or was it internal to the creative process and reflective of generic conventions? Then we asked whether any of these constraining forces held clues regarding the global success of the play.

Although IbsenStage holds records on thousands of *Et dukkehjem* adaptations, the documentation on productions varies from the most basic information about the time, place, cast, and title of a performance to extensive electronic recordings, reviews, photographs, and artistic statements. Only the best-documented productions are suitable for a comparative analysis of the inner workings of the adaptation process. We chose eleven such productions as the sample to give the greatest possible geographical, temporal, and interpretative range: Britain 1889, the USA 1938 and 1987, India 1958, Germany 1981, Nigeria 2006, Japan 2006, Pakistan 2006, Malawi 2006, China 2010, and Chile 2012.[2] To distinguish between this sample and the additional thirty productions cited in this chapter, we refer to the former by country and date and the latter by company.

Comparing visualisations of dramaturgical structures has made us think in new ways about theatrical adaptation. As we move backwards and forwards in this chapter from the patterns we find in distant visions to the close-ups on details of specific performances, four key areas emerge: the importance of temporal structures; the relationship between genres and spatial relocations; the importance of empathy in the manipulation of character; and the cultural constraints on narrative relocation. Dramaturgical structures, with all their narrative detail stripped away, provide our first set of distant visions.

Pattern One: The Dramaturgical Structures of Plot, Time, Space, and Genre

Et dukkehjem consists of seventy plot events when the play is divided up according to changes in dramatic action, the introduction of new information, the exit and entrance of characters, and major emotional transformations. Plot events form the building blocks for our graphics, because it is at this level of structural detail, rather than acts and scenes, that patterns emerge between adaptations. As the analysis of the cuts, condensations, substitutions, elaborations, and additions to plot events is central to our comparative study of adaptations, Fig. 4.1 provides a list of the seventy events from Ibsen's play-script with titles that indicate their content. The abstract plot structures of nine out of our sample of adaptations are reproduced as Figs. 4.2, 4.3, and 4.4. These productions span one hundred and twenty-three years, come from five continents, and include theatre, radio, and dance adaptations. The structures are arranged by date from

ACT 1

1. The Xmas Tree Tip
2. The Evils of Borrowing
3. Money, Presents, Sex
4. Inherited Traits of Financial Incompetence
5. The Macaroon Interrogation
6. Introducing Rank and the Secret from Last Xmas
7. Introduction of Two Visitors
8. Nora tells Mrs Linde's Story
9. Nora's Good News
10. Nora tells the story of Torvald's Illness
11. Mrs Linde tells her Story
12. Nora's Great Secret
13. Nora's Past as a Worker
14. Krogstad's Arrival
15. Rank Introduced, Illness, and Moral Corruption
16. Nora Celebrates Money and Power with Macaroons
17. Nora Gets Mrs Linde a Job
18. Mother and Children at Play
19. The Intruder
20. Krogstad's Evidence
21. Krogstad asks Nora to use her Influence
22. Krogstad tells Nora's Story
23. Nora Reflects on Past Actions and Lessons
24. Helmer Chastises Nora for Lying
25. Nora Works on Helmer
26. Helmer's Lesson: Morality and Maternal Corruption
27. Nora consider the Lesson and Fears the Worst

ACT 2

28. Nora's Emotion Reprise
29. Anna's Story
30. Nora asks Mrs Linde to Sew Costume
31. Mrs Linde Investigates Relationship with Rank
32. Nora Gets an Idea
33. Survival Seduction
34. Nora's Plea for Krogstad is Rejected
35. Torvald's Heroic Delusions
36. Rank Enters Nora's Nightmare
37. Rank's Story of Illness and Death
38. Melancholic Intimacy
39. Silk Stockings
40. Re-establishing Boundaries
41. Naming the Relationship
42. Announcing an Unwelcome Visitor
43. Shared Secrets
44. Krogstad Reads Nora's Mind
45. A Letter Reaches its Destination
46. Nora Distraught, Mrs Linde Takes Control
47. Nora's First Attempt at Distraction
48. Tarantella Rehearsal
49. The Reprieve
50. Counting the Hours

ACT 3

51. Bitter Recriminations
52. Facing Grim Realities
53. Mrs Linde's Proposal
54. Removing the Blackmail Threat
55. Party Return, Performance Described
56. An End to Subterfuge
57. Helmer's Lesson on Craft Aesthetics
58. Helmer's Sexual Fantasies
59. Rank's Reason for Celebration
60. Masquerade of Death & Last Cigar
61. Open the Letter Box
62. Black Ice
63. Helmer Exposed
64. Helmer Saved, Forgiving, and Forgetting
65. Future Pleasures
66. Serious Business
67. Living Like a Doll
68. Education, Duty and Doubt
69. Love and Disillusionment
70. Ring Exchange and Closing Doors

Fig. 4.1 Ibsen's *Et dukkehjem* divided into a plot structure of seventy events

Fig. 4.2 Dramaturgical structures of adaptations—Britain 1889, USA 1938, India 1958. Close to Ibsen's play-script in light grey; cuts or substitutions in dark grey; new material in black

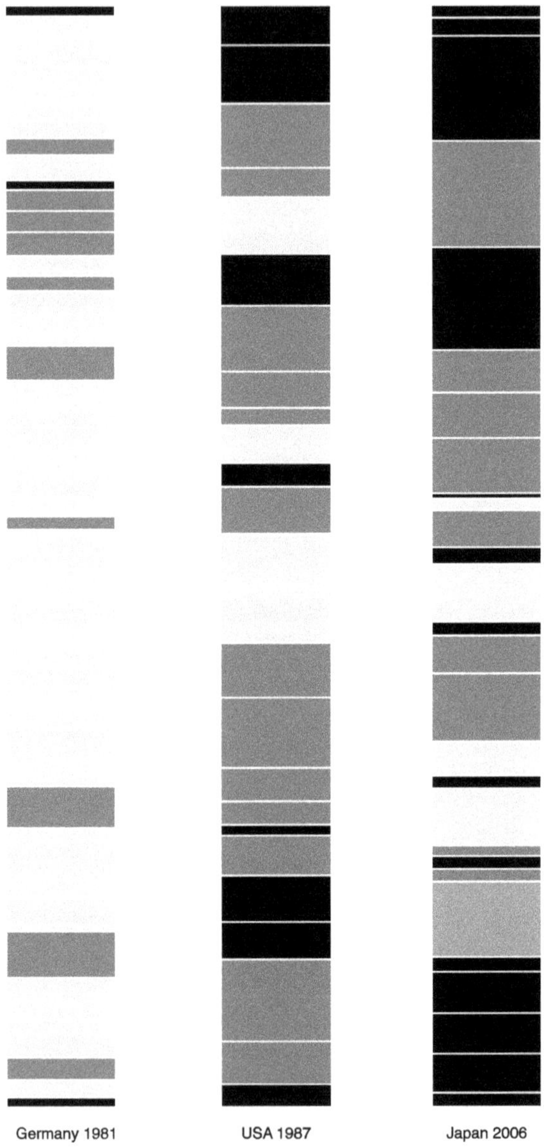

Fig. 4.3 Dramaturgical structures of adaptations—Germany 1981, USA 1987, Japan 2006. Close to Ibsen's play-script in light grey; cuts or substitutions in dark grey; new material in black

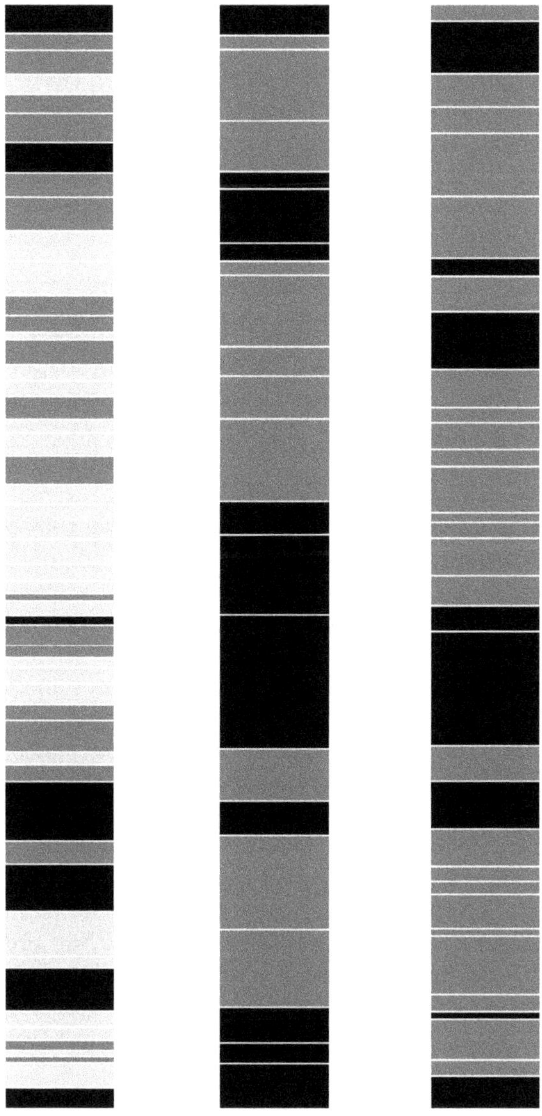

Fig. 4.4 Dramaturgical structures of adaptations—Malawi 2006, Pakistan 2006, China 2010. Close to Ibsen's play-script in light grey; cuts or substitutions in dark grey; new material in black

1889 to 2012. With the exception of the 1889 production, all the structures contain fewer than the seventy plot events of Ibsen's play-script; the maximum number is sixty-five and the minimum twenty-two. We use three basic categories to distinguish between plot events in the graphical layouts: events that are directly imported from *Et dukkehjem*; events that involve significant cuts or substitutions that shift the meaning of Ibsen's text; and new events containing material that is unique to the adaptation.

Temporal Structures

The most striking pattern across Figs. 4.2, 4.3, and 4.4 is the gradual increase over time of new material inserted into the adaptations. Equally significant, though less visible, is the fact that the plot event sequence never changes: all the adaptations follow the temporal organisation of Ibsen's narrative. We checked other productions to see whether this is a common feature and found that even when past events recounted by Ibsen's characters are dramatised as new plot events, they are added as a prologue. Conversely, when new material is added relating to events that take place after the ending of Ibsen's narrative, they are added as a sequel. This is the case even in film and radio adaptations where flashbacks and flashforwards are part of the dramaturgical language. The only production we have found that disturbs the temporal structure is an Italian production by Teatrino Clandestino from the late 1990s, which doubles a live and projected version of the same performance.[3] The play began with the stage action and projected version synchronised, as it progressed the two versions separated and the electronic image anticipated or fell behind the stage action; the linear structure remained intact even with this mismatching and doubling of the live and projected versions. A Brazilian company, Teatro de Narradores in São Paulo, attempted a more radical shift in the temporal structure by reversing the plot sequence, but after one performance they abandoned the experiment as theatrically unworkable.[4] Even when all psychological motivation has disappeared from the characterisations, as in the production by Theater Oberhausen in Germany, the plot sequence remains unaltered.[5]

In contrast to this unchanging linear structure of narrative time, the overall performance time of adaptations and the timing of individual plot events are extremely flexible. Ibsen's text has a performance time of approximately two and a half hours. The shortest adaptation in our sample is the radio version that lasts for forty-five minutes; the only evidence of further compressions come from the eight silent films and YouTube versions. The majority of the sample fall between sixty and ninety minutes; there are both historical and recent adaptations that equal the playing time of Ibsen's text, but none of them exceeds it. The cutting process significantly alters the internal rhythm of the text, particularly as the amount of performance time allocated to each event varies considerably. A common dramaturgical technique within the adaptations is the manipulation of playing time to maximise or minimise the importance of plot events. In the radio version recorded in front of a live audience in Los Angeles (USA 1938), the time allocated to events connected to the blackmail plot increases; in the dance version, the events that lend themselves to spectacle are given additional playing time (China 2010); and in the Noh adaptation, the events tied to character transformations slow to a meditative pace to increase their temporal weight (Japan 2006).

This contrast between an unchanging plot sequence on the one hand, and the highly variable playing time of separate plot events on the other, is particularly marked in adaptations of *Et dukkehjem* across cultures. The linear cause-and-effect sequencing is symptomatic of a European discourse of scientific rationality tied to the Enlightenment; its presence in *Et dukkehjem* reflects the European origins of the play. This does not mean that scientific rationality or linear thinking in terms of cause and effect is unique to a European discourse, nor does it mean that the European tradition is homogenous or unified in its Enlightenment discourse.[6] It just signifies that at a deep structural level the cultural origins of the drama remain untouched even when the narrative details of the plot are changed to fit new locations. Yet the linear structure can be challenged by other temporal structures used in theatre cultures through manipulations of the performance time of selected plot events. The dynamic between performance and narrative time, particularly in non-European adaptations, signals the relative strength of the cultural forces meeting within the production. In the Noh theatre performance the ritual time of transformation associated with Zen Buddhism overrides the linear cause-and-effect structure, making it seem a mere preamble to the serious business of transformation between states of existence. This suggests that a fruitful way of looking at adaptation across cultures might be to explore contestations within the temporal structures of performances.

Returning to the proportion and placing of new material within the dramaturgical structures, these elements also produce interesting patterns with wider implications for studies of theatrical adaptation. Productions that break away from an implied fidelity to Ibsen's text and freely integrate new material restrict it to approximately one-third of the overall playing time; this suggests that there is a rough limit to the amount of original material that can be absorbed into a production before its claim to be an adaptation of *Et dukkehjem* is contested. When it comes to the placing of this material, our sample of adaptations shows a repetitive pattern of new plot events at beginnings and endings of performances. Further investigations confirmed that this technique of framing adaptations with new material was occurring on three continents over a period of seventy-five years. The framing devices tend to be used as cultural bridges to link audiences to the imaginary world of *Et dukkehjem*. While each frame is unique, they are all strongly influenced by the materiality of the venue used for performances; this suggests that spatial relocation is a robust force within the adaptation process. Since this possibility has implications not only for *Et dukkehjem* but for all theatrical adaptations, we consider it at some length.

Spatial Constraints, Framing Devices, and Genres

The importance of theatre architecture in determining cultures of spectatorship through the spatial relationship between performers and their audiences is widely accepted, but the impact of physical relocations on dramaturgical structures is less clear. Our comparative analysis of plot structures suggests that it is performance spaces that are determining the new content at the beginnings and endings of adaptations. That performance spaces exert this influence is not surprising; treating theatres as inert containers reproduces the binary that the geographer Doreen Massey has been at pains to dispel. She has challenged the philosophical tradition that relegates space to a static background for the dynamic workings of time, and sees spatiality as a changeable and fluid dimension enabling the trajectories of multiple stories (2005, 39). Transposed to theatre, her views suggest an interactive dynamic between performance spaces and their time-based narratives.

The framing devices in adaptations of *Et dukkehjem* depend on performance spaces to determine their content. The Malawi 2006 adaptation, which played in twenty-two outdoor and indoor community venues, reinforced the collective ownership of these spaces by framing the story with a chorus of four men and four women representing the on-stage community. The performance recorded in front of a live audience in the Lux Radio Studio in Los Angeles (USA 1938) opened and closed with soap advertisements and actors' product endorsements; and fifty years later in the same city, an adaptation performed in a city car park began with all the characters in their cars. In Pakistan 2006, the touring company Tehrik-e-Niswan created a framing device that emphasised the temporary nature of their venues by presenting the performance as a rehearsal with the stage manager, stagehands, and actors interacting at the beginning and end of their day's work. Relocations to intimate theatres, where the scenography and lighting technology make it possible for individual spectators to imagine that they can read characters' minds, tend to produce framing devices that are psychological. In Germany 1981, the performance began with light on an isolated Nora tearing at Christmas presents and ended with Torvald weeping on the bed. More recently, the Chile 2012 performance was set in a *huis clos* black box and began with all the actors trapped, dressed identically as women, and spouting misogynistic insults; it ended with only Torvald, now dressed in male clothing, in the same enclosed space, with all the invisible doors firmly locked against him. In Japan 2006, the adaptation designed for a traditional Noh theatre framed the performance with a ritualised slow entry and exit of the entire company along the *hashigakari*, the long walkway that links the main entrance to the central playing area on the Noh stage.

All of these examples demonstrate the importance of performing spaces in determining framing devices, but is this spatial influence limited to the new plot events inserted at the beginnings and ends of adaptations? If the framing devices are influencing the playing of plot events within the body of the adaptations, particularly those events that are tied directly to Ibsen's play-script, then the frame is also signalling to the audience the generic conventions that will be used in the adaptation. This raises the question of how artists select genres for *Et dukkehjem* adaptations: are they choosing genres from a possible list of abstract conventions, or are they allowing the performance space to dictate their choice of genres? There are no hard-and-fast rules that can help us to answer this question, but following the line of argument suggested by the pattern of framing devices, we explore the latter possibility further by looking in depth at two productions from Asia and Africa where space and genre are inseparable.

Tokyo, Japan 2006

In Japan 2006, Mitsuya Mori created *Double Nora* with Umewaka Noh, a theatre with a lineage dating back six hundred years (Mori 2011). The spatial determinants of the stage were so integral to the dramaturgy of Noh theatre that this production perfectly illustrates the interrelationship between material space and generic conventions. *Double Nora* created a dialogue between traditional Noh theatre and the Japanese modern drama form *Shingeki*, which dates from the beginning of the twentieth century and is associated with the introduction of Ibsen to Japan. Nora was split into two, with the role shared by a female impersonator from the Umewaka Noh theatre and a 'modern female actor' (Mori 2011, 84). The core plot events from Ibsen's play-script absorbed approximately forty minutes of the seventy-minute playing time, and were performed by the *Shingeki* actors on the central square stage. The remaining thirty minutes of the adaptation were played on both the square and the *hashigakari*. The bridge not only signifies the major arrivals and departures of characters, it is also the location of their major transitions and transformations. Movements between states—whether emotional, corporeal, or supernatural—are far more significant than plot in Noh drama, and the *hashigakari* is a spatial signifier of transition.[7] This concentration on changing inner states is reflected in the Japanese performance tradition of interpreting *Et dukkehjem* as a transformation drama about the awakening of the new woman. The term awakening is ubiquitous in the early critical writings on the play, and the major debates after the first performances in the early twentieth century revolved around whether or not it was possible for a woman to achieve a real awakening in three days. *Double Nora* resolved this dilemma by replacing the naturalistic time-frame of Ibsen's drama with the ritual temporal structure of Noh. The awakening of the character was performed by the Noh Nora on the *hashigakari*, the liminal space of ritual transformation. The emotional and intellectual turmoil of the awakened character was symbolised by the Noh Nora's attempts to leave the stage along the walkway. Accompanied by an emotive musical score, she travelled up the *hashigakari* only to stop and retrace her steps, her feet seemed uncertain and she hesitated, until once again she moved along the *hashigakari*, only to falter and return. Finally, a new resolve appeared to calm her body and together with the modern Nora she walked with determination, very slowly, up the *hashigakari* and exited. The whole performance can be seen as merely a prologue to this enactment of a character transformation. This one action, which in Ibsen's text is completed in less than a minute, is developed into a seven-minute spatially rich sequence that is the aesthetic climax of the performance.

Blantyre, Malawi 2006

Breaking the Pot, the Malawi 2006 adaptation, was performed in community venues: schools, colleges, hostels, hotels, town assemblies, and entertainment and cultural centres. The boundaries between the spectators and the performers were deliberately blurred, with actors directly addressing the audience, the addition of a chorus on the stage, and characters entering and exiting through the middle of the audience. There was little distinction between private and public worlds in telling this story of marital breakdown. As the audience was always the custodian of the site of performance, the story was literally being enacted in the midst of their social world. The visual documentation of this production comes from an outdoor venue in which the stage was surrounded on three sides by eight rows of tiered bench seating. The playing space and the audience were protected from the sun by a thatched roof and the whole area was surrounded by rich tropical vegetation. The back of the stage had a very simple low, pink wall of painted flats draped with Christmas decorations of coloured tinsel and fairy lights. This background defined the imaginary location of the story, but there was no naturalistic illusion: the materiality of the community space dominated the spatial awareness of the audience throughout the performance. The eight members of the chorus represented the community witnessing the family drama and were a constant presence on the stage; they provided a musical score of harmonic song for the whole performance and created a corporeal link between the audience and the individual characters. At key points in the story, they took over the playing space to provide a choreographic text that highlighted the social and gender implications of the drama. The open and fluid performance space encouraged a presentational genre that lent itself to comedy and buffoonery, and in this performance the audience responded very warmly to the comic charm of the actor playing Jere/Torvald, even when the character joked about domestic violence. All the actors expressed their feelings openly to the spectators as if they were talking to friends and neighbours, and the constant presence of the chorus set up a triangular relationship that encouraged a collectivised (as opposed to individualised) response to the dramatic conflict. The chorus performed Nora's resolve to sacrifice herself; they brought to the surface the possibility of violent conflict in tableaux in which the four men threatened and restrained the four women; the women showed their strength by nurturing the men during Jere's expressions of despair; they performed the joyous reaction that Jere had to the second letter, which removes the threat of blackmail. In the final scene, they split into gendered groupings to bear witness to Nora's momentous decision to leave Jere and her children. The musical score of the chorus signified a communal response to the action and was inseparable from the community spaces used for the performances.

These performance spaces in Malawi and Japan shaped the generic conventions used in the *Et dukkehjem* adaptations. As genres are rules governing representational practices, they act as powerful constraints over creative innovation. It follows that if material spaces influence genres, then the physical relocation of *Et dukkehjem* to new venues will influence the dramaturgical structures of adaptations. The logic of this argument does not stop with adaptations: it can also be applied to the analysis of the very first performance of *Et dukkehjem* at the Royal Theatre in Copenhagen in 1879, which we briefly examine now.[8] The play is so firmly associated with the beginnings of naturalism in Scandinavian theatre that it is easy to assume that the first performance was the prototype for this genre. Yet there is often a time lag between dramaturgical innovations foreshadowed by playwrights and the development of the acting techniques necessary to give their innovations the fullest expression. The notion of any play having an original and definitive performance is erroneous: a premiere may be the first attempt at its staging, but it is not the definitive benchmark against which other interpretations or adaptations can be judged. It may take a considerable time before a genre foreshadowed in a written text is capable of being realised on the stage. This raises interesting questions about the genres attached to the European theatre spaces that premiered Ibsen's plays.

Copenhagen, Denmark 1879

Historians have described the premiere of *Et dukkehjem* in 1879 at the Royal Theatre in Copenhagen as the 'true turning point' in the introduction of naturalism to Scandinavian theatres, but they still recognise that this first performance was a 'stylistic hybrid' (Marker and Marker 1996, 164–67). It is difficult to imagine this hybrid, as the Royal Theatre specialised in the standard fare of the mid-nineteenth-century European repertoire: melodramas, '*la pièce bien faite*', and light comedies. The actors only had eleven rehearsals for *Et dukkehjem*, including the dress rehearsal, which suggests that they were using the dominant acting techniques of the day. Ibsen was highly critical of these techniques: they involved stock characters, the placing of actors on the fore-stage facing the audience, and declamation. The critics attacked the first performance of the play for its implausible ending, but perhaps it was the architecture of the theatre and the generic codes of acting tied to its spatial configuration that made it impossible for the final scene to work. The transition from the second to the third act requires an acting technique of double consciousness; in a letter to Hans Schrøder in relation to another of his female characters, Ibsen referred to this technique as 'seemingly easy but overlayered conversations' (Ibsen 1887). This doubling involves splitting what is said from what is thought. In Ibsen's works this is often connected with contradictory memories of characters' shared experiences. As the production stayed in the repertoire for twenty-eight years, Betty Hennings, who played Nora, may have acquired the technique she needed to play this double consciousness, but the techniques of creating a subjective interiority for a character were still in their infancy in 1879. The Théâtre Libre in Paris pioneered naturalism as a theatrical genre nearly ten years later. Crucially, André Antoine's experiments were conducted in a relatively small venue in which the relationship between the stage and the auditorium, together with the use of electric light, produced a compelling intimacy. These skills were transferable to larger theatres, but auditoriums like the Royal Theatre with its 1600 seats were soon considered too large for the modern drama. In Copenhagen, a new playhouse was built leaving the old stage for opera and ballet, a decision that supported the contention that the scale of the Royal Theatre was ill-suited to playing *Et dukkehjem*. If this is the case, it suggests that more consideration needs to be given to the materiality of performance spaces, not just in the adaptation process but also in the performance analysis of the first productions of Ibsen's plays.

Abstract visualisations of dramaturgical structures have led us from a discussion of temporal and spatial relocation in adaptation to an examination of the relationship between theatrical genres and material spaces, and the reception of the first performance of *Et dukkehjem*. Our analysis of a second set of patterns, based on abstractions of character interaction and function, repeats this methodology of using distant visions to direct our explorations through the history of *Et dukkehjem*.

Pattern Two: Character Interactions, Manipulations, and the Importance of Empathy

Character Interactions

A central feature of adaptations in literature is the retelling of a familiar narrative from the point of view of a secondary character; an obvious example is Jean Rhys's *Wide Sargasso Sea*, which retells the story of

Charlotte Brontë's *Jane Eyre* from the point of view of the mad wife in the attic. However, in dramatic adaptations, whether on stage or screen, there are many ways of influencing the audience's perceptions of characters that do not necessarily involve complete rewritings of the dialogue. Our examination of character begins with a distant look at patterns of social relationships in adaptations of *Et dukkehjem*. Precedents for this approach exist at the Stanford Arts Lab, where Franco Moretti uses network analysis for the comparative study of canonical plots. He is interested in these structures as abstractions of the social relationships in different cultures. He notes that 'comparative morphology is such a fascinating field: studying how forms vary, you discover how symbolic power varies from place to place' (2000, 66). Our visualisations of plot differ from Moretti's: whereas he depicts each scene as a network of characters, our approach depicts the movement of characters through the sequence of interactions.[9] This is because our interest is in changes to the dramaturgical structure of a single text as it adapts to different cultures. These changes are subtle, but it is possible to see a continuum of cultural forms of social organisation reflected within *Et dukkehjem*: at one extreme there is a privileging of individual experience and at the other an emphasis on collectivised social engagement.

As Ibsen's play-script is dominated by duologues, the patterns created by character interactions are very simple: it is the maid, an otherwise minor character, who links interactions together by introducing visitors, communicating new information, or delivering letters. When the interactions with the maid and the other representatives of the servant class are lost from an adaptation, the pattern loses many of its connections; as more characters are added from the world beyond the domestic realm, the connections increase. In depicting the movement of characters between interactions in each of the sample productions, the Noh theatre adaptation with its ritual dramaturgical structure yields the simplest and most symmetrical network (left of Fig. 4.5), while Pakistan 2006, which emphasised the importance of social class, yields the most convoluted and connected network (bottom right of Fig. 4.5). The German 1981 production, which was a study of Nora's psychology, yields a network that shifts from a web of social connections to a simple line depicting Nora's progression: here there are no servants or children, and characters appear and disappear like figments from Nora's disturbed imagination (centre of Fig. 4.5). At the other end of the continuum are the densely connected networks created by the community chorus in Malawi 2006 and the multiple Noras and Krogstads in the dance version in China 2010 (top right

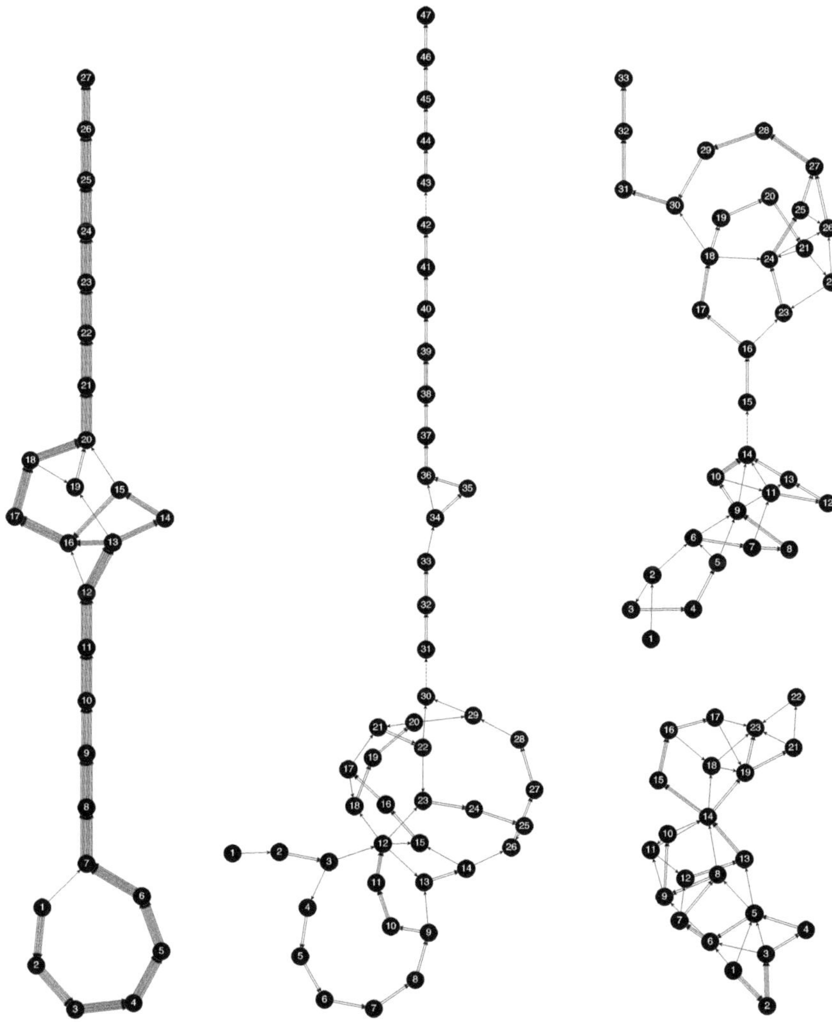

Fig. 4.5 Networks showing how characters progress through adaptations of the *Et dukkehjem* plot in Japan 2006 (*left*), Germany 1981 (*centre*), China 2010 (*top right*), and Pakistan 2006 (*bottom right*); plot events are numbered in sequence

of Fig. 4.5). The variety of patterns revealed by analysing the network of character interactions in the sample of adaptations demonstrates the flexibility with which the *Et dukkehjem* narrative can be integrated into different social structures: it can be contracted into an intensely private world, expanded into a community drama, or incorporated within the form of ritual drama.

In Ibsen's play-script there are five central and six minor characters who have also proved to be remarkably flexible. Changing the names of characters is a standard technique of artists who indigenise or domesticate *Et dukkehjem* for non-Norwegian audiences. In the past one hundred and thirty-five years, the five central characters have been significantly altered: Nora became a chorus of women in both China 2010 and in *Putuler Itikatha* in Bangladesh[10]; she was doubled in Japan 2006; Dr Rank disappeared in the Iranian film *Sara*[11]; and Krogstad and Rank were combined into a single character with access to the home as the children's tutor in Pakistan; while in the same production Mrs Linde appeared as a woman from a battered wives' shelter and as the representative of the working class/caste she became a major protagonist.[12] Surprisingly, it is Torvald and not Nora who is the most stable character across the adaptations, but in *Een Poppenhuis*, the Toneelgroep ADODVS production, he swapped roles with Nora and was transformed into a house husband, while she became a successful career wife.[13] The children disappear from the stage, though they may be given life through sound effects or inanimate objects signifying their presence; in recent years they are often present throughout the play. Anne-Marie, Nora's old nurse, is frequently cut from adaptations, particularly when the role of the maid is expanded into a composite domestic servant responsible for everything in the house, including the children. Both of these female characters disappear in productions that dispense with the servant class, as in Germany 1981; or their roles are adapted to reflect the social organisation and gender of domestic servants in other cultures, as in India 1958. The porter has the most nebulous existence of all the characters, although it could be argued that he transforms into a stagehand in productions like Pakistan 2006 that emphasise the theatrical framing of the drama. There are also new characters being added to the cast list who usually provide additional layers of social context: choruses representing the wider community are popular, while all the film versions and some stage versions create a spectacle out of the Stenborg party with additional masked dancers.[14]

Character Manipulations

As Ibsen's characters are so changeable, we compared their relative dominance in the sample of adaptations. We defined character dominance not in terms of social status or power, but by the function of the character as an instigator of dramatic action. Sometimes this function is the responsibility of one character, sometimes it is shared between two or more characters, and sometimes it shifts backwards and forwards in some form of contestation. Analysing changes in character dominance is an interpretative exercise: our evaluations are based on a character's ability to change or shape the direction of the narrative. There are clearly dominant characters in 80% of the plot events in Ibsen's text; in the remaining 20%, dominance is shared between all the characters on the stage. In our sample, the adaptations have a tendency to lose this clarity in assigning dominance, particularly when an editing process collapses several events together. The only adaptations where this was not the case were from theatre cultures where Ibsen's characters were transformed into archetypes with clearly defined primary or secondary dramatic functions, as in Japan 2006. Of the plot events in Ibsen's play-script where there is a clearly dominant character, Nora drives approximately half, Torvald is responsible for just under a quarter, and the remaining three characters share the rest. The most interesting pattern from our comparative study of character dominance is the degree to which Nora's role as a protagonist diminishes, which suggests that an erosion of the importance of this central character is a typical feature in the process of adapting *Et dukkehjem*. In our sample, the proportion of plot events in which Nora dominates drops from a half to as little as a twentieth. Figure 4.6 compares the dominance of Nora in three of the sample productions, reflecting the performance time of each plot event in the horizontal bars. Britain 1889 (left of Fig. 4.6) closely resembles the structure of Ibsen's play-script and replicates Nora's dominance within the seventy plot events. The most dramatic loss of dominance in the character of Nora is visible in the pattern from USA 1987 (right of Fig. 4.6). In adaptations where the character of Nora is supported by a chorus, loss of dominance is compensated for by the introduction of the additional performers, as in China 2010 (centre of Fig. 4.6).

As the originality of Ibsen's vision in the writing of the play is so often attributed to the revolutionary status of Nora as a female protagonist within the European theatre repertoire, it is surprising to find a tendency for the character's importance within the dramatic action to diminish.

Fig. 4.6 Relative dominance of Nora in relation to other characters in Britain 1889, China 2010, and USA 1987. Nora in black; chorus in dark grey; other characters in light grey

Our interest was further alerted when we found that the only other central character dropping in dominance was Mrs Linde; a pattern emerged that both female characters were losing agency with regard to shaping the dramatic action. In contrast, the scenes in which the male characters were dominant were less liable to be cut, hence the increase in their relative importance. The big winner in the reorganisation of dominance was Torvald, and the next was Krogstad.

Our analysis of character dominance was based on adaptations produced by artists from a broad spectrum of cultural and ideological positioning, including a major women's theatre group and a theatre for social justice. Was there a common problem faced by these adaptations in reproducing Ibsen's expression of female agency? This prompted us to look for the specific elements in the plot events dominated by Nora and Mrs Linde in Ibsen's play-script that were disappearing. The problematic areas centred on the depiction of heterosexual power relations, specifically where the female characters manipulated or controlled the actions of the male characters; the agency that was disappearing involved the female manipulation of male desire. Ibsen's Nora may have limited access to a wider social world, but within the confines of her domestic environment she can and does exert influence through her sexuality. She indulges Torvald in his sexual fantasies of nymphs and peasant girls, and plays erotic games with the family friend Dr Rank. We found that Nora's agency was being diminished by multiple small cuts in the plot events connected with these encounters. Although a very different life-world is embodied in the character of Mrs Linde, her agency is equally tied to the influence she wields through her sexuality. She marries her first husband to provide financial security for her mother and siblings. Finding herself a widow and free of her earlier family responsibilities, she initiates the relationship with Krogstad, the man she rejected in her youth. This reversal of orthodox gender roles in a proposal of marriage is reinforced by Mrs Linde's refusal to give up her position at the bank, even though it was previously occupied by Krogstad and represents his best hope of future employment. In the interests of supposed verisimilitude, her proposal to Krogstad and decision to retain her employment were removed from the story when transposed to India 1958 and Pakistan 2006. In the condensed adaptations her subplot was treated as superfluous: she disappeared in Japan 2006 and was reduced to a voiceover in the live performance recorded for radio in Los Angeles 1938.

Looking beyond our sample of adaptations confirmed our suspicions that agency through sexual manipulation was being cut cross-culturally. Where there is a strong binary in theatre cultures controlling the depictions of a virtuous passive female sexuality and a dangerous active female sexuality, female villains exhibit this behaviour as a signifier of moral corruption. If Nora is to function as a sympathetic figure, she must be distanced from this manner of sexual agency. In theatre cultures where it is considered derogatory or demeaning to represent a woman as manipulative and scheming, there is an equal disincentive to show Nora and Mrs Linde exerting control over men through their sexuality. Even in adaptations that focus on the mechanics of sexual power in heterosexual relationships, Nora's flirtatious world of sexual foreplay is replaced by Torvald's sexual use or abuse of her body, which can be traced visually through the presence on stage of the marital bed: it first appeared in the 1951 Mae Zetterling production in London and travelled as far afield as Cape Town and Tel Aviv.[15] Depicting women on stage using their sexuality to manipulate men appears to have negative connotations in a wide variety of theatre cultures. When all these cultural prohibitions converge, Nora and Mrs Linde lose agency everywhere from Australia to Zambia.[16]

Did a similar problem exist with regard to the representation of female sexual pleasure? We found that it was only sexual manipulation that was falling under a global blanket of censorship, and aside from theatres subject to religious and moral censorship, the female characters could express an active sexuality. In Los Angeles 1987, Nora took a lover to save her sexually unsatisfying marriage, and in *Independence Day!*, the Amakhosi Theatre production from Bulawayo, a sexually frustrated Sara/Nora put an aphrodisiac into Ndlovini/Torvald's food, and led him into an erotic dance simulating intercourse accompanied by loud music and flashing disco lights.[17] While there are no equivalently raunchy substitutions for Mrs Linde's marriage proposal, there are numerous versions of the reunion of Mrs Linde and Krogstad that emphasise mutual sexual attraction.

As the cross-cultural rationale for removing sexual manipulation from Nora and Mrs Linde appears to be a fear of alienating audiences, we wondered whether the decrease in character agency might be compensated for by an increase in audience empathy. This seemed plausible, as the sexually manipulative agency has reappeared recently in postdramatic adaptations where empathy is minimised: it was expressed as a parody of learnt gestures when Nora transformed into a wind-up bourgeois doll in the La Boite Theatre Company production from Brisbane[18]; and overwhelmed the characterisation of Mrs Linde as the cartoon predatory lesbian in the *grand guignol* adaptation by Theater Oberhausen.[19] As the presence or absence of empathy appears to correlate with the presence or absence of this problematic female agency, we decided to probe deeper into the workings of empathy within *Et dukkehjem* adaptations.

The Importance of Empathy

Empathy is such a nebulous quality in performance and is so dependent on the interaction of actors and audiences that it is difficult to translate it into a distant vision. Not only is empathy tied to the emotional expressions used by an actor in the embodiment of character, it is also culturally determined by the systems of emotional contagion used within different theatre cultures. Despite the obvious difficulties of tackling a comparative study of these complex dynamics, we approached the working of empathy by concentrating on the emotional states and situations most likely to elicit sympathies from audiences cross-culturally: sorrow, pain, grief, and being subjected to unjustified criticism or aggression.

We began with empathy structures that privileged the female characters. In the case of Nora, there was a clear indication that loss of agency was being compensated for with an increase in empathy. Where gender discrimination against women is highlighted as the cause of social inequality, adaptations tend to encourage audiences to empathise with Nora as a victim of circumstance trapped within a social structure that she neither understands nor controls. She commits a crime through ignorance, making herself vulnerable to blackmail, but she responds to adversity in a manner worthy of sympathy. When alone on the stage, Nora reveals her inner turmoil to the audience using an emotional range intended to trigger audience empathy; this includes sorrow, pain, and resolve in the face of despair. As empathy tends to increase for characters depicted as victims of injustice, there is a concomitant increase in the negative behaviour of the male characters. This pattern is illustrated within our sample by the productions from Pakistan 2006 and Malawi 2006: they made major changes to the forgery plot to make Nora's innocence plausible to their contemporary audiences, while exaggerating the antipathetic qualities in Torvald through male narcissism in Pakistan 2006 and hints of domestic violence in Malawi 2006. In *Independence Day!*, the Amakhosi Theatre Bulawayo production of 2003, the domestic violence became explicit.[20] In these adaptations gender discrimination against women is the major cause of social inequality, and any loss of agency in Nora and Mrs Linde is compensated for by an increase in empathy. However, this is not always the case.

The patterns of repetition between adaptations suggest that empathy is organised according to representations of symbolic power. While the operations of social power based on gender, sexuality, class, race, and age all figure in the social world of Ibsen's play, there is a tendency for artists to choose one of these structures as the dominant social framework and to use empathy as a means of highlighting the injustices associated with this instance of symbolic power. It is the characters who are most oppressed by this social framework, and not necessarily Nora and Mrs Linde, who are offered up to the audience for empathetic connection. Instead of portraying gender discrimination as a system that oppresses women, many of the adaptations of *Et dukkehjem* depict gender as a mechanism that oppresses men and women equally. This is typical of productions from cultural contexts experiencing major challenges to the dominant norms regarding gendered behaviour. Its popularity reached a height during the second wave of the women's rights movement in the 1970s in the screen adaptations by male directors in Europe.[21] In these productions, the differences in symbolic power accessible to men and women in nineteenth-century Europe were replaced by the depiction of equality in oppression, where women and men are both victims of rigid gender roles. In these adaptations, empathy was elicited for Torvald, who became as much of a manipulated doll within the domestic world as Nora. He joined Nora as a victim of circumstance trapped within a social structure that he neither understood nor controlled. In the Nordic television versions he was cast as significantly older than Nora and assumed a role of parental indulgence with his naïve and childlike wife. While there may not be an increase in the antipathetic qualities in the female characters, the emotional binary of the final scene depicts the departing wife as strong and fearless and the abandoned husband as vulnerable and destroyed. In this respect the ending of the German 1981 adaptation is archetypical: a half-naked Torvald 'bathed in a searing white light, is left weeping on the bed' (Marker and Marker 1999, 99).

When an adaptation introduces transgender characters and homosexual relations, empathy is assigned according to a hierarchical structure of oppression. Heterosexual men dominate the structure and are placed at the top of the system; heterosexual women are lower down the power scale and function as allies of the sexually oppressed, who occupy the base of the structure. Torvald becomes the controlling patriarch and Nora the sympathetic helper of the 'othered' sexualities represented by secondary characters, as was the case in the Los Angeles 1987 production. In this adaptation, Dr Dick/Dr Rank was dying of AIDS and was the most empathetic of the characters. Playing the family friend as a sympathetic gay, bisexual, or transgender character is not uncommon in the twenty-first century; a notable cross-dressed version of the Dr Rank character was created in Chile in 2012.[22]

Antipathy for both Nora and Torvald replaces empathy in the adaptations that depict class relations as the dominant form of social oppression. In these productions, Krogstad and the servants assume a new importance as identification figures for the audience. Nora's behaviour becomes increasingly obnoxious: she begins to abuse not only the general servants but also her devoted erstwhile nanny.[23] Meanwhile, Krogstad is transformed into a single father struggling to support his children; his desperate efforts to protect them force him into the role of blackmailer. In the film adaptation by Joseph Losey, Krogstad's devotion to his children was contrasted with Nora's self-obsession. An exception to this polarisation of empathy by means of class affiliation can be found in Pakistan 2006, in which women transcended class boundaries. Mrs Linde was transformed into the heroic working-class woman who re-educated a sympathetic middle-class Nora along Marxist-feminist lines.

There are isolated adaptations of *Et dukkehjem* that use ethnic differences as a mechanism for building a character's empathetic link to an audience. The intercultural adaptation by the National Experimental Theatre in Beijing set the play in the 1930s: Torvald was Chinese, and Nora was Norwegian.[24] Here the audience was invited to build empathetic relationships with both characters as they attempted to overcome the cultural conflicts that were eroding the basis of their marriage. Another cross-cultural marriage was at the centre of a recent radio version broadcast by the BBC and adapted by Tanika Gupta. The play was relocated to Calcutta in 1879, to where Tom/Torvald had been posted as a colonial administrator and had married Nira/Nora, a Bengali woman. The power relation between the husband and wife was a mirror image of the colonial relation between the two countries: Tom had few redeeming features and all the empathy was with Nira.[25] Ethnicity was used in a different way in the Schaubühne *Nora*: here the nanny was a marginalised foreign worker, she was ignored by her employers, protected the children from the violence that erupted in the bourgeois household, and at the end of the play took the children with her as she left the house.[26]

A new empathetic structure that focuses on the children in *Et dukkehjem* has emerged in twenty-first-century adaptations, implying that previously unacknowledged power relations between generations are becoming a popular subject for social critique. It may also indicate a theatrical interest in exploring social anxieties and fears that are associated with feelings of abandonment.[27] In the past, the interactions with the children were used in adaptations to convey information to the audience about the adult characters: Nora could be seen to be a good or bad mother, the nurse as a good or bad surrogate mother. The vulnerability of the children has been increased by the introduction of a newborn baby onto the stage in the 2012 Young Vic production in London[28]; and the possibility of an empathetic connection between the children and the audience has resulted in new plot events featuring parent–child interactions. In yet another child-focused production from Belvoir Theatre in Sydney, Nora ended the play trying to explain her actions to her uncomprehending daughter.[29] At Nationaltheatret in Oslo, all the adult actors doubled as the children in the Helmer nursery, the world of the children being the framing device for the entire play.[30] The most unnerving adaptation that places the audience in an empathetic relationship with a child is the recent production by Toneelgroep Amsterdam.[31] Directed by Thibaud Delpeut, who trained as a clinical psychologist, this Nora was trapped in an unspecified childhood trauma. All the characters seemed to be images of her lost parents and her identity was blurred with that of her daughter, who was old enough to silently observe the psychological violence invading the home. In the final scene, as Nora escaped from this chilling environment, her daughter ran after her and their bodies merged in the door frame; as Nora disappeared behind the closing door, her daughter turned back into the room to be trapped in the gaze of her unrepentant father. History was about to repeat itself and there was no escape for the daughter, or for the audience.

The relationship between agency and empathy in the characters of Nora and Mrs Linde triggered this investigation, but the variety of empathetic structures that we have encountered is unexpected. The ease with which *all* of the five main characters, a composite maid/nanny, and the children have assumed empathetic centrality may have some bearing on the global success of the play. Notably, this has been achieved without necessarily altering the characters' involvement in the plot, or providing additional back stories and complex psychological motivations. The inequalities expressed within sexual, familial, friendship, and economic relations within *Et dukkehjem* have been adapted to critique an extraordinary range of culturally diverse social structures. In every case, there has been a character created by Ibsen that is suitable for empathetic identification.

Narrative Substitutions

We have touched indirectly on narrative adaptation by considering manipulations of character and the placing of new material in dramaturgical structures (Figs. 4.2, 4.3, and 4.4), but we have not yet examined patterns of narrative substitution. In the production history of *Et dukkehjem* there are two ubiquitous substitutions: in the first, Nora stays or hesitates in the door; in the second, Nora leaves with her children. Both of these substitutions are significant for the global success of the play, but the forces behind them are so different that we will consider them separately.[32]

Hesitations

Ten years after Ibsen was asked to leave Nora in her home for the ending of the first German production, he wrote to his French translator, Moritz Prozor: 'I can almost say that the whole play is written exactly for the sake of the final scene. [...] With the changed ending, the play did not stay long in the repertoire. Unchanged [on the contrary], it is still being played' (Ibsen 1891). While time has shown that Ibsen was correct in assuming that the original ending would survive, he was wrong to imagine that all changed endings would disappear from *Et dukkehjem*. There is a basic acceptance across five continents that a woman deciding to leave her husband is a plausible dramatic story, even though there are instances (notably Malawi) where there are concerns that audiences will find it difficult to understand her decision when her husband is neither an adulterer nor explicitly violent; but the finality with which Nora exits is open to a wide spectrum of interpretations. Many of the Noras leave the door faintly ajar. This strategy was used in the critically acclaimed Egyptian production that opened the first National Theatre Festival in Cairo in 2006. The director, Gamal Yakout, felt that this final image allowed for Nora's possible failure, Torvald's possible change, or another unforeseen outcome.[33] While the major Egyptian theatre critic, Nehad Selaiha, suggests that the ending is true to the spirit of Mediterranean culture 'where women invariably forgive, or overlook, the silly foibles of men and never take quite seriously what they say' (Selaiha 2006), this ambiguity is not restricted to southern Europe. It is something of a tradition within the German production history of the play to create ambiguous endings. In 1922, the silent film starring Olga Chekhova was shot with two possible endings, both of which were screened: in the first Nora left, in the second she stayed.[34] Rainer Werner Fassbinder was similarly equivocal in his 1974 television version, which ended with Nora standing at an open door.[35]

In recent years, creating new and shocking endings has become almost *de rigueur* in Germany, but definitive departures of Nora are still rare. The most notable recent re-creation by Thomas Ostermeier has Nora shooting Torvald: as the bullet hit him, he fell dead into the giant fish tank that had dominated the stage.[36] Less violent endings involve Nora returning home through the window after a dramatic exit[37]; or engaging in a theatrical boxing fight with Torvald that is juxtaposed with an image of the homeless living on the streets outside the doll home[38]; or Nora exiting to the balcony where she chain smokes[39]; or standing under falling stars with a ghoulish chorus of Mrs Linde, Krogstad, and Torvald chanting her name.[40] If there is any similarity between these substitutions, it is depictions of bourgeois women as pathologically unstable, emotionally labile, or downright mad. The artists behind these productions are part of an ongoing tradition that demands aesthetic originality in the staging of the ending of the play. The symbolic capital that accrues to those who succeed in this task is considerable, and the competition between artists to demonstrate inventiveness increases the value of *Et dukkehjem* as a 'stake in the game' (Bourdieu 1996, 111).

Nora Leaves with Her Children

Outside Europe, particularly in post-colonial theatres where Western dramatic narratives are appropriated, changes to the ending have been motivated less by aesthetic considerations and more by the cultural specifics of the place of performance. Here we find that women tend to exit with their children, either to defy the local social and legal position of women with regard to divorce law and child custody, or to affirm the social status of women as mothers. The theory of moral degeneracy that Ibsen uses to justify Nora's decision to leave her children is a by-product of mid-nineteenth-century European thinking about society and evolution; since its disappearance is a perfect illustration of the severing of the ideological content of a play in the process of adaptation, we take a moment to consider the motivation that Ibsen has given to Nora.

There is nothing inevitable or innate about good mothering in Ibsen's worldview: it is important work and requires skill and education.[41] To explain Nora's decision to give up this role, he weaves a discourse on the effects of moral contagion into the fabric of the play. In an early draft, Ibsen has Dr Hank (later Rank) explaining to Nora and Mrs Linde that Krogstad is one of those '[ruined] specimens of the race' because he resembles those 'persons who take advantage of the weakness of their superiors to obtain advances or loans that they can never repay' (Archer 1917, 112). This echoes the transgression at the heart of Nora's secret: she learns that her 'great thing', which she sees as ethically faultless, is interpreted by the wider society as a signifier of moral corruption. Torvald creates a further link between degeneracy and the corruption of children when he tells Nora that Krogstad has 'been poisoning his own children for years past by a life of lies and hypocrisy—that is why I call him morally ruined' (Archer 1906, 60). Nora absorbs this lesson and a moment later refuses to see her children. Confirmation that degeneration is a reality comes in the guise of Dr Rank's announcement that his terminal illness has been caused by his father's physical and moral corruption. Nora's belief that she is an unfit mother is unshakable: 'No, I won't go to the children. I know they are in better hands than mine. As I now am, I can be nothing to them' (1906, 153). It is too late for Torvald to argue that biology is the only qualification necessary for mothering. While Nora refuses to accept that her past actions were unethical, the moral degeneracy argument undermines her confidence as a mother: by remaining ignorant and uneducated, she has placed her children at risk. In the final twist of self-revelation, she understands that she has a duty to know herself and to 'try and become' a 'human being' (1906, 147). It is only this last stage in the complex thought process crafted by Ibsen that is retained in the majority of adaptations of the play. The anachronistic evolutionary theories about degeneration increasingly evaporate from adaptations the further away in time and space they are from nineteenth-century Europe.[42] What is of interest here is how easily the whole discourse on degeneration disappears, to be replaced by culturally diverse social constructions of motherhood, particularly in recent adaptations from low- or middle-income countries, where the tendency is for Nora to take her children with her. The rationales for these rewritings either refer to motherhood as central to a woman's social status, or insist that Nora must take the children in defiance of local laws that treat children as a father's property, as is illustrated by the following substitutions from Iran, Nigeria, and Zambia (Holledge and Tompkins 2000, 39; Asiedu 2011, 173).

Tehran, Iran 1993

Dariush Mehrjui's film *Sara* (1993) was made in Iran at a time when public theatres were banned; film production was (and still is) controlled by pre- and post-production censorship.[43] The final shot was of Sara/Nora in a taxi with her daughter looking back at the receding figure of Hessam/Torvald wrapped only in a bed sheet, standing in the road looking lost. Mehrjui worked through the framework of 1990s Islamic family law to create his adaptation of *Et dukkehjem*. Under Article 1170, a mother could be given custody of her daughter until the age of seven, and of her son until the age of two; if she remarried she lost all rights over her children (Mir-Hosseini 1993, 67). In Mehrjui's film, Hessam/Torvald tried to separate Sara from her daughter; she defied her husband and insisted on taking her three-year-old with her when she left her doll's house. In the context of Iran at that time, it was more confrontational for a Nora to claim custody of her children than leave them in the home of her estranged husband.[44]

Awaka, Nigeria 2002

Tracie Chimo Utoh-Ezeajugh's adaptation *Nneora* ended with Nneora/Nora preparing to leave her marital home with her children.[45] In her critique of this adaptation, Awo Mana Asiedu suggests that Utoh-Ezeajugh deliberately separates out the role of wife from the role of mother, 'signaling quite a significant difference in African feminism as opposed to Western feminism' (2011, 178). Being a mother in Nigerian society gives a woman status, but there is a catch: she must produce sons. The fate of a woman who gives birth to daughters was at the core of this adaptation. Nneora had four daughters and was pregnant with twins. Reacting to the possibility that the twins may be girls, Ikenna/Torvald exclaimed: 'What do you mean? Don't tell me you are going to give birth to girls again, oh no!' (Utoh-Ezeajugh 2005, 102). It was only in the last moments of the play that he discovered she was carrying twin boys and this opened up the possibility of reconciliation between husband and wife. Nneora declared her intention to leave and went into another room to pack her things.

Ikenna was left alone on the stage to deliver the final lines of the play, which were filled with his self-criticism and remorse.

Lusaka, Zambia 2006

Cheela Chilala writes a more definitive departure for Nora in his Zambian version of the play, entitled *Forbidden Ground*.[46] Unlike *Nneora*, which took place in an urban environment, this version adapted the story to village life, where Nora's debt involved borrowing livestock rather than money. Yet the importance of motherhood as the core of female identity was crucial once again to the rewriting of the ending. When Nora told Hema/Torvald that she was leaving him, he asked her to stay for the sake of the children. She replied, 'I will come back for them tomorrow morning. I will never abandon my children.'

The motivations for these Noras to take their children are culturally specific, but they all affirm that the bond between mother and child is unbreakable. Yet the most controversial aspect of Ibsen's narrative is that this natural bond can be severed by the power of rational argument. We have not found any adaptations that use narrative substitutions to shock audiences into rethinking assumptions about motherhood. This is not the case with substitutions to the marriage relationship: when Bulu/Nora wiped the vermillion sindur from her hair as she gave back her ring to Tapan/Helmer in Calcutta 1958, there was an audible gasp in the audience (Roy 2003, 145): a Bengali woman only removes the sindur if her husband is dead. In *Nora/Nûre*, a recent Kurdish adaptation, Saliho/Torvald accused Nûre of having 'trespassed into male society'; he took her to the town centre and killed her in front of the mosque.[47] These adaptations shock audiences into reconsidering power relationships within marriage; they challenge normative thinking. Although there is no equivalent challenge in adaptations where Nora takes her children, the fact that the play can critique the lack of legal rights of mothers in one culture while representing their social power in others points once again to the flexibility with which *Et dukkehjem* can represent multiple social structures.

Conclusion

This chapter began by describing the background of increasing diversity in *Et dukkehjem* before examining adaptations for repetitive patterns in dramaturgical structures, character manipulations, and narrative substitutions.

These patterns are symptomatic of forces internal to the creative process, some of which are specific to *Et dukkehjem*, while others are more generally applicable to theatrical adaptation. We review these forces and consider whether any of them are relevant to the global success of the play.

The common narrative core of *Et dukkehjem* adaptations relies on archetypical dramatic tropes: intimate relationships, sex, money, and secrets. Ibsen appropriated these tropes from nineteenth-century theatre and modified them to fit his dramaturgical needs, but it is the tropes rather than the modifications that have persisted in the narrative core of *Et dukkehjem* adaptations. As there are other nineteenth-century dramas containing similar tropes that have not survived into the twenty-first century, the cultural forces that maintain these archetypes in popular narratives are not responsible for *Et dukkehjem's* global success.

Our analyses of repetitive patterns in dramaturgical structures have pointed to a number of interesting factors: limitations governing the amount of new material that can be absorbed into adaptations; the use of framing devices; and, most importantly, temporal and spatial constraints. The linear cause-and-effect structure, which reflects a European perspective of temporal progress, persists within *Et dukkehjem* adaptations. This treatment of narrative time is countered by temporal structures from other cultures that are expressed through the manipulation of performance time. Time can be a site of contestation within the creative process if opposing cultural forces occupy the parallel temporal structures of imaginary narrative time and the playing time allocated to separate plot events. There is no equivalent cultural tension in the spatial dimension, as physical relocation can shape the variety of performance techniques that artists use in the adaptation process. For this reason, the materiality of the performance space can override the European theatrical conventions embedded in the play. These forces of temporal and spatial constraint may have some bearing on theatrical adaptations of European canonical dramas and therefore warrant further investigation, but they are too generalised in their impact to be relevant to our investigation into the *Et dukkehjem* phenomenon.

Turning to character, we found patterns of manipulation that pointed to the influence of external social forces in the adaptation process. Ibsen created a social world in *Et dukkehjem* that is highly culturally adaptive. Examining the patterns produced by the interactions of his characters drew our attention to the dramaturgical function of the servant class: when adaptations focus on the inner psychology of the central characters and the servant class is lost from the play, the social context attenuates, as visualised in our network analyses of plots; at the other extreme, this social context expands when the inner life of characters is replaced in adaptations by community involvement in the lives of the couple at the centre of the narrative. The network analysis shows the flexibility with which *Et dukkehjem* can be adapted to reflect radically different social structures. A similar finding was apparent in our study of the manipulation of character through empathy. Ibsen's characters are constructed with such complex backgrounds that they can fit into multiple empathetic structures and critique a variety of social inequalities. All the characters, except for the porter and the maid (when not merged into a single character with the nurse, Anne Marie), have been used as empathetic figures in productions intent on highlighting different forms of social discrimination. The ease with which *Et dukkehjem* can be used by artists to reflect social structures and to critique power relations is arguably a contributing factor in the ongoing success of the play.

Theatrical constraints on the representation of female characters produced the final patterns examined in this chapter. The most surprising was the loss of female agency; we traced this pattern to culturally diverse forces censoring positive female characters' use of a manipulative sexuality. This agency was removed rather than substituted in many adaptations. The second representational constraint that we uncovered was in the depiction of motherhood, specifically the severing by a mother of an anaclitic bond with her children. While this form of female agency was also cut in multiple adaptations, there were numerous substitutions in the representations of cultures of motherhood. It would be absurd to suggest that the cross-cultural prevalence of theatrical censorship over representations of female agency has contributed to the global success of *Et dukkehjem*, but there may be an indirect link. It is possible that the strength of the provocations within the play regarding the representation of female characters may have contributed to the continuing artistic interest in Ibsen's play-script. There is a metatheatrical sequence in *Et dukkehjem*, not of a play within the play, but of a rehearsal within the play, where Ibsen throws down the gauntlet to artists and challenges them to critique the theatrical representation of the female performing body. In Chapter 5 we use images from seventy-nine productions to find patterns of repetition in the staging of this metatheatrical moment. Our intention is to examine how artists have responded to Ibsen's challenge and to pursue the possibility that problems surrounding the representation of the female characters have some bearing on the global success of the play.

Notes

1. Jules Wright, the director of the Wapping Project in London, together with her photographer collaborator, Thomas Zanon-Larcher, created a new genre with *Et dukkehjem* in their installation version using contemporary fashion images that 'raises questions about their representation as contemporary "dolls" and affirms as an aside a fresh, filmic way to tell fashion stories' ('Ibsen's Nora Is Haute Couture in London' 2006).
2. '*A Doll's House*'. 1889. Directed by Charles Charrington. Performed by Janet Achurch as Nora. Novelty Theatre, Great Queen's Street, London, England. June 7. *IbsenStage*, Event 75649. https://ibsenstage.hf.uio.no/pages/event/75649. '*Joan Crawford and Basil Rathbone Perform* A Doll's House'. 1938. Performed by Joan Crawford as Nora. Lux Radio Theatre, Los Angeles. June 6. *IbsenStage*, Event 91399. https://ibsenstage.hf.uio.no/pages/event/91399. Available via YouTube. '*Putul Khela*'. 1958. Directed by Sambhu Mitra. Bohurupee, Calcutta, India. January 10. *IbsenStage*, Event 76759. https://ibsenstage.hf.uio.no/pages/event/76759. '*Nora*'. 1981. Directed by Ingmar Bergman. Performed by Rita Russek as Nora. Königliches Residenz-Theater, Munich, Germany. April 30. *IbsenStage*, Event 76728. https://ibsenstage.hf.uio.no/pages/event/76728. '*The Former Miss Barstow with Every Tom, Dick and Harry in a doll's house*'. 1987. Directed by Richard Newton. Performed by Nancye Ferguson. 315 South Hewitt Street, Los Angeles, California, USA. September 19. *IbsenStage*, Event 85351. https://ibsenstage.hf.uio.no/pages/event/85351. Also serialised on YouTube, see '*The Former Miss Barstow*' (1987). '*Nneora*'. 2002. Directed by Ihentuge Chisimdi Udoka. Performed by Amechi Somto, Nzegwu Ngozi, Nwora Chimma, and Ihedioha Chigoziri as Nora. University Auditorium, Nnamdi Azikiwe University, Awaka, Nigeria. September 11. *IbsenStage*, Event 91583. https://ibsenstage.hf.uio.no/pages/event/91583. '*Double Nora*'. 2005. Directed by Mitsuya Mori. Umewaka Nohgaku Gakuin Kaikan Theater, Tokyo, Japan. August 9. *IbsenStage*, Event 75988. https://ibsenstage.hf.uio.no/pages/event/75988. '*Breaking the Pot*'. 2006. Directed by Melissa Eveleigh. Performed by Mbumba Mbewe as Nora. Nanzikambe Theatre, French Cultural Centre, Blantyre, Malawi. April 17. *IbsenStage*, Event 75839. https://ibsenstage.hf.uio.no/pages/event/75839. '*Gurrya ka Ghar*'. 2006. Directed by Anwer Jafri. Tehrik-e-Niswan, Alhamra Hall No. 2, The Mall, Lahore, Pakistan. April 23. *IbsenStage*, Event 77324. https://ibsenstage.hf.uio.no/pages/event/77324. '*Nuola* (*Wan'ou Zhi Jia*)'. 2010. Directed by Un-Magritt Nordseth. Performed by Liu Minzi, Dai Shaoting, Xie Xin, Jin Xing, Sun Zhuzhen, and Talisi as Nora. No. 22 Wangfujing Street, Dongcheng District, Beijing, China. October 22.

IbsenStage, Event 77765. https://ibsenstage.hf.uio.no/pages/event/77765. '*Persiguiendo a Nora Helmer*'. 2012. Directed by Alexandra von Hummel. Performed by Tamara Acosta. Teatro La María, Centro Cultural Gabriela Mistral, Sala N1, Santiago, Chile. June 15. *IbsenStage*, Event 85748. https://ibsenstage.hf.uio.no/pages/event/85748.

3. '*Si prega di non discutere di casa di bambola*'. 1999. Directed by Pietro Babina. Performed by Fiorenza Menni as Nora. Teatrino Clandestino, Interzona, Via Santa Teresa, 6, Verona, Italy. October 7. *IbsenStage*, Event 76690. https://ibsenstage.hf.uio.no/pages/event/76690. Available via Vimeo, see '*Si prega di non discutere di casa di bambola*' (2015).
4. The experiment was attempted in front of a live audience, but in production reverted to the conventional temporal structure (Fernando Peixoto de Azevdeo and Maiello 2012). '*Nossa casa de boneca*'. 2005. Directed by José Fernando Peixoto de Azevedo. Performed by Teth Maiello as Nora. Teatro de Narradores, Teatro Fábrica, Rua Consolação, 1623–Consolação, São Paulo, Brazil. October 22. *IbsenStage*, Event 77617. https://ibsenstage.hf.uio.no/pages/event/77617.
5. '*Nora oder Ein Puppenhaus*'. 2010. Directed by Herbert Fritsch. Performed by Manja Kuhl. Theater Oberhausen, Will-Quadflieg-Platz 1, Oberhausen, Germany. October 29. *IbsenStage*, Event 77580. https://ibsenstage.hf.uio.no/pages/event/77580.
6. This temporal logic is central to the plot structure of Ibsen's plays. For further discussion on this point see Sen (2005), Chakrabarty (2000), Toulmin (1990), and Harding (2008).
7. Zeami Motokiyo, whose fifteenth-century writings established the aesthetic principles of Noh, said that it was by finding the inner truth of an object or consciousness that the performer touches 'some great primal force that flows through life and death' (Ueda 1961, 77). Zen Buddhism influenced his thinking, and the practice of detached contemplation of animate and inanimate matter has had a significant impact on Japanese performance aesthetics.
8. '*Et dukkehjem*'. 1879. Directed by H.P. Holst. Performed by Betty Hennings as Nora. Det Kongelige Teater, Copenhagen, Denmark. December 21. *IbsenStage*, Event 75660. https://ibsenstage.hf.uio.no/pages/event/75660.
9. Our network analysis of plot in adaptations of *Et dukkehjem* is similar to the visualisation of storylines in Tanahasi and Kwan-Liu (2012); Roberts-Smith et al. (2013); and Hoyt et al. (2014).
10. '*Putuler Itikatha*'. 2001. Directed by Kamaluddin Nilu. Performed by Sheuly Akhter, Shipra Das, Tahmina Sharif, and Sabina Sultana as Nora. Shawkat Osman Memorial Auditorium Public Library, Dhaka, Bangladesh.

April 27. *IbsenStage*, Event 76947. https://ibsenstage.hf.uio.no/pages/event/76947.

11. '*Sara*'. 1993. Directed by Dariush Mehrjui. Performed by Niki Karimi as Sara. H. Seifi and D. Mehrjui. Farabi Cinema Foundation, Tehran. Video recording. *IbsenStage*, Event 75342. https://ibsenstage.hf.uio.no/pages/event/75342.
12. '*A Doll's House*'. 2006. Directed by Gamal Yakout. Performed by Eman Emam. Cultural Palaces' Sidi Gaber Creativity Centre, Alexandria. June 24. *IbsenStage*, Event 91394. https://ibsenstage.hf.uio.no/pages/event/91394.
13. '*Een Poppenhuis*'. 2009. Directed by Manon van Gelder. Performed by Marten van der Meijden as Torvald. Toneelgroep ADODVS, Drang Studio, Schelpkade 45 te Den Haag. February 12. *IbsenStage*, Event 90958. https://ibsenstage.hf.uio.no/pages/event/90958.
14. The expansion of the tarantella scene into spectacular ballrooms is discussed further in the next chapter.
15. Zetterling's first name is also spelt 'Mai'. '*A Doll's House*'. 1953. Directed by Peter Ashmore. Performed by Mae Zetterling. Tennent Productions, Lyric Theatre, Hammersmith, London, UK. September 8. *IbsenStage*, Event 76448. https://ibsenstage.hf.uio.no/pages/event/76448. '*A Doll's House*'. 1990. Directed by Clare Stopford. Performed by Grethe Fox. Market Theatre, Johannesburg, South Africa. May 8. *IbsenStage*, Event 77726. https://ibsenstage.hf.uio.no/pages/event/77726. '*Nora*'. 2000. Directed by Ilan Ronen. Performed by Anat Waxman as Nora. Te'atron ha-Kameri shel Tel-Aviv, Da Vinci, Hahashmona'im 93, Israel. January 5. *IbsenStage*, Event 76635. https://ibsenstage.hf.uio.no/pages/event/76635.
16. '*Nora*'. 2014. Directed by Anne-Louise Sarks. Belvoir Street Theatre, Surry Hills, Sydney, Australia. August 9. *IbsenStage*, Event 91397. https://ibsenstage.hf.uio.no/pages/event/91397. '*Forbidden Ground*'. 2010. Directed by Benne Erastor Banda. Performed by Gift Muneka as Nora. Lusaka Playhouse, Cnr Church and Nasser Rds, Lusaka, Zambia. October 8. *IbsenStage*, Event 77141. https://ibsenstage.hf.uio.no/pages/event/77141.
17. '*Independence Day*'. 2003. Directed by Sithokozile Mhlanga. Performed by Swallen Sibanda as Nora. Amakhosi Theatre, Bulawayo, Zimbabwe. October 26. *IbsenStage*, Event 76066. https://ibsenstage.hf.uio.no/pages/event/76066.
18. '*A Doll's House*'. 2014. Directed by Steven Mitchell Wright. Performed by Helen Christinson as Nora. La Boite Theatre Company, Roundhouse Theatre, Kelvin Grove, Queensland, Australia. September 6. *AusStage*, Event 107978. www.ausstage.edu.au/pages/event/107978.

19. '*Nora oder Ein Puppenhaus*'. 2010. Directed by Herbert Fritsch. Performed by Manja Kuhl. Theater Oberhausen, Will-Quadflieg-Platz 1, Oberhausen, Germany. October 29. *IbsenStage*, Event 77580. https://ibsenstage.hf.uio.no/pages/event/77580.
20. '*Independence Day*'. 2003. Directed by Sithokozile Mhlanga. Performed by Swallen Sibanda as Nora. Amakhosi Theatre, Bulawayo, Zimbabwe. October 26. *IbsenStage*, Event 76066. https://ibsenstage.hf.uio.no/pages/event/76066.
21. '*A Doll's House*'. 1973. Directed by Patrick Garland. Performed by Claire Bloom as Nora. Elkins Productions, Freeward Films, England. Film. *IbsenStage*, Event 75341. https://ibsenstage.hf.uio.no/pages/event/75341. Available at National Library of Norway. 2015. Accessed July 31. ibsen.nb.no/id/6230.0. '*A Doll's House*'. 1973. Directed by Joseph Losey. Performed by Jane Fonda as Nora. World Film Services, Les Films la Boétie, UK, France. Film. *IbsenStage*, Event 75340. https://ibsenstage.hf.uio.no/pages/event/75340. Available at National Library of Norway. 2015. Accessed July 31. ibsen.nb.no/id/6206.0.
22. '*Persiguiendo a Nora Helmer*'. 2012. Directed by Alexandra von Hummel. Performed by Tamara Acosta. Teatro La María, Centro Cultural Gabriela Mistral, Sala N1, Santiago, Chile. June 15. *IbsenStage*, Event 85747. https://ibsenstage.hf.uio.no/pages/event/85747.
23. '*A Doll's House*'. 2012. Directed by Carrie Cracknell. Performed by Hattie Morahan as Nora. Young Vic, 66 The Cut, London, UK. June 29. *IbsenStage*, Event 85776. https://ibsenstage.hf.uio.no/pages/event/85776.
24. '*A Doll's House*'. 1998. Directed by Wu Xiaojiang. Performed by Agnete G. Haaland as Nora. China National Experimental Theatre, Beijing, China. April 1. *IbsenStage*, Event 75393. https://ibsenstage.hf.uio.no/pages/event/75393.
25. '*A Doll's House*'. 2012. Directed by Nadia Molinari. BBC Radio 3, BBC Broadcasting House, London W1A 1AA, UK. Radio Play. October 7. *IbsenStage*, Event 91398. https://ibsenstage.hf.uio.no/pages/event/91398.
26. '*Nora*'. 2002. Directed by Thomas Ostermeier. Performed by Anne Tismer as Nora. Schaubühne am Lehniner Platz, Kurfürstendamm 153, Berlin, Germany. November 26. *IbsenStage*, Event 76838. https://ibsenstage.hf.uio.no/pages/event/76838.
27. Social anxiety about abandonment may also explain the recent interest in sequels that focus on the experiences of the motherless children: *Nora's Daughters* written by Henning Mankell (2006) and *Nora's barn* by Jesper Halle, developed at Ibsen Teater (Halle 2005). (*Nora's barn* premiered in early January 2005 at a school in Telemark and it has since been performed in China in 2006 and by the Danish company Teamteatret in 2013.)

However, there is a long history of sequels using this conceit, including Emile Fabre's 1907 drama *La Maison d'Argile* (*The House of Clay*) and *Encore Cinq Minutes* (*Five Minutes More*) by Françoise Loranger ([1967] 2011).

28. '*A Doll's House*'. 2012. Directed by Carrie Cracknell. Performed by Hattie Morahan as Nora. Young Vic, 66 The Cut, London, UK. June 29. *IbsenStage*, Event 85776. https://ibsenstage.hf.uio.no/pages/event/85776.
29. '*Nora*'. 2014. Directed by Anne-Louise Sarks. Belvoir Street Theatre, Surry Hills, Sydney, Australia. August 9. *IbsenStage*, Event 91397. https://ibsenstage.hf.uio.no/pages/event/91397.
30. '*Et dukkehjem*'. 2010. Directed by Laurent Chétouane. Performed by Ågot Sendstad as Nora. Nationaltheatret, Nationaltheatret Amfiscenen, Johanne Dybwads Plass 1, Oslo, Norway. August 27. *IbsenStage*, Event 77716. https://ibsenstage.hf.uio.no/pages/event/77716.
31. '*Nora*'. 2012. Directed by Thibaud Delpeut. Performed by Halina Reijn as Nora. Toneelgroep Amsterdam, Stadsschouwburg Amsterdam, Leidseplein 26, Amsterdam, Netherlands. November 6. *IbsenStage*, Event 85785. https://ibsenstage.hf.uio.no/pages/event/85785.
32. For readers unfamiliar with the series of actions that mark the final moments of the play, they can be summarised as follows: Nora puts on her hat and shawl and says she will not see the children before she goes; she insists on a ring exchange that symbolically annuls the marriage; she puts down the house keys and refuses to accept any future help from Torvald. A future marriage of equality is held up as a distant possibility before Nora's exit through the hall door; Torvald expresses a moment of hope, followed by the reverberations of a heavy door closing.
33. Unpublished statement provided to authors. For a further discussion of this production, see Holledge (2011).
34. '*Nora*'. 1922. Directed by Berthold Viertel. Performed by Olga Chekhova as Nora. Projektions-AG Union, Berlin, Germany. Silent Film. *IbsenStage*, Event 76130. https://ibsenstage.hf.uio.no/pages/event/76130.
35. '*Nora Helmer*'. 1974. Directed by Rainer Werner Fassbinder. Performed by Margit Carstensen as Nora. Telefilm Saar/Saarländischer Rundfunk. Video recording. February 3. *IbsenStage*, Event 76104. https://ibsenstage.hf.uio.no/pages/event/76104.
36. '*Nora*'. 2002. Directed by Thomas Ostermeier. Performed by Anne Tismer as Nora. Schaubühne am Lehniner Platz, Kurfürstendamm 153, Berlin, Germany. November 26. *IbsenStage*, Event 76838. https://ibsenstage.hf.uio.no/pages/event/76838. See also the televised version, *Nora* (2003).

37. '*Nora oder Ein Puppenheim*'. 1972. Directed by Hans Neuenfels. Performed by Elisabeth Trissenaar as Nora. Staatstheater Stuttgart, Oberer Schloßgarten 6, Stuttgart, Germany. January 8. *IbsenStage*, Event 76675. https://ibsenstage.hf.uio.no/pages/event/76675.
38. '*Ein Puppenheim* (*Nora*)'. 1990. Directed by Leander Haußmann. Performed by Steffi Kühnert as Nora. Deutsches Nationaltheater, Theaterplatz 2, Weimar, Germany. June 22. *IbsenStage*, Event 76673. https://ibsenstage.hf.uio.no/pages/event/76673.
39. '*Nora*'. 2002. Directed by Stephan Kimmig. Performed by Susanne Wolff. Thalia-Theater, Hamburg, Germany. September 14. *IbsenStage*, Event 76628. https://ibsenstage.hf.uio.no/pages/event/76628. For an article on contemporary German endings, see Kalb (2004).
40. '*Nora oder ein Puppenhaus*'. 2010. Directed by Herbert Fritsch. Performed by Manja Kuhl. Theater Oberhausen, Will-Quadflieg-Platz 1, Oberhausen, Germany. October 29. *IbsenStage*, Event 77580. https://ibsenstage.hf.uio.no/pages/event/77580.
41. Ibsen summarised his own views on motherhood in his speech to the Norwegian League for Women's Rights in Kristiania, on 26 May 1898. He placed the hope of cultural regeneration with mothers, which would suggest that he also considered cultural degeneration a possible consequence of denying women education:

    It is for the mothers, by strenuous and sustained labor, to awaken a conscious feeling of culture and discipline. This feeling must be awakened before it will be possible to lift the people to a higher plane. It is the women who shall solve the human problem. As mothers they shall solve it. And only in that capacity can they solve it. Here lies a great task for women. (Ibsen [1898] 1910, 65–66)

42. For an in-depth discussion of the relevance of nineteenth-century evolutionary thought in Ibsen's dramaturgy, see Shepherd-Barr (2015).
43. '*Sara*'. 1993. Directed by Dariush Mehrjui. Performed by Niki Karimi as Sara. H. Seifi and D. Mehrjui. Farabi Cinema Foundation, Tehran, Iran. Film. *IbsenStage*, Event 75342. https://ibsenstage.hf.uio.no/pages/event/75342.
44. The early 1990s were a time of political uncertainty following Ayatollah Khomeini's death in 1989. Shirin Ebadi, the Nobel Peace Prize winner, wrote of the morality police during this period: 'they harassed people because they felt like it […]. [B]efore you knew it, you were three days into an interrogation, being accused of anything from adultery to treason' (Ebadi and Moaveni 2006, 99). As a human rights lawyer, Ebadi succeeded in improving the legal status of women and children by arguing over interpretations of the Qur'an: 'Islam, like any religion, is subject to interpretation. It can be interpreted to oppress women and it can be

interpreted to liberate them […]. If I'm forced to ferret through musty books of Islamic jurisprudence and rely on sources that stress the egalitarian ethics of Islam, then so be it' (2006, 122). For further discussion on this production, see Holledge (2011) and Helland (2015).

45. '*Nneora*'. 2002. Directed by Ihentuge Chisimdi Udoka. Performed by Amechi Somto, Nzegwu Ngozi, Nwora Chimma, and Ihedioha Chigoziri as Nora. University Auditorium, Nnamdi Azikiwe University, Awaka, Nigeria. September 11. *IbsenStage*, Event 91583. https://ibsenstage.hf.uio.no/pages/event/91583. See also Utoh-Ezeajugh (2005) for the published script.
46. '*Forbidden Ground*'. 2010. Directed by Benne Erastor Banda. Performed by Gift Muneka as Nora. Lusaka Playhouse, Cnr Church and Nasser Rds, Lusaka, Zambia. October 8. *IbsenStage*, Event 77141. https://ibsenstage.hf.uio.no/pages/event/77141.
47. '*Nora/Nurê*'. 2010. Directed by Jale Karabekir. Performed by İsmail Yildiz as Nora. Painted Bird Theatre, Van, Van, Turkey. April 14. *IbsenStage*, Event 77572. https://ibsenstage.hf.uio.no/pages/event/77572. See also Ibsen Awards (2014).

CHAPTER 5

Ibsen's Challenge: The Tarantella Rehearsal

Our distant visions have uncovered two major forces shaping the global transmission of *Et dukkehjem*: the late nineteenth-century European women's movements, and the ongoing involvement of Norwegian institutions guaranteeing the position of the play in the canon of world drama. Deciphering repetitive patterns in the adaptation process has proved more difficult than analysing cultural transmission because the general forces have to be distinguished from those specific to *Et dukkehjem*, but, as Chapter 4 demonstrated, there are strong representational constraints producing repetitive patterns in the depiction of the female characters. Character manipulations in multiple adaptations of *Et dukkehjem* suggest that these constraints have a long history and are still present in diverse theatre cultures; the desire to break through them may be a factor in attracting artists to adapt the play. In this chapter, we pursue our analysis of this force by conducting a comparative study of multiple versions of the dramatic climax of Ibsen's second act: the tarantella rehearsal.[1]

At a plot level, Ibsen uses the rehearsal of the tarantella as an obstacle created by Nora to prevent Torvald from opening the mailbox that contains the letter from Krogstad. At a metaphorical level, the letter is as deadly as the venom of the tarantula spider, which can only be expelled from the body by a frenetic dance. The narrative justification for the scene is that Nora is to perform the tarantella at the Stenborgs' party in the costume of a Neapolitan fisher girl and that she must rehearse her dance.

J. Holledge et al., *A Global Doll's House*, Palgrave Studies in Performance and Technology, DOI 10.1057/978-1-137-43899-7_5

Torvald wants Nora to perform the tarantella because he takes pleasure in the public display of her performing body; this exhibitionist scenario is a trigger for his sexual fantasy of abducting a peasant virgin. That this game has had a long history within their relationship is clear from the costume Nora wears to act out this fantasy foreplay of the *droit de seigneur*; that the costume is torn implies that he tears the clothes off her body.

The scene has a metatheatrical structure in which four of the major characters play a role: Nora is the performer, Torvald the director, Rank the rehearsal pianist, and Mrs Linde the star's dresser. Even the stage space is implicated in this metatheatrical structure, since Mrs Linde listens to the off-stage sound of the tarantella performance while she sits in the drawing room as if she were backstage in a theatre. When the star (Nora) returns to her dressing room, as in so many backstage dramas, she is accompanied by an ardent admirer (Torvald) who provides us with an account of her triumphant performance. Yet the rehearsal of the dance that precedes this scene is a disaster: Torvald's choreography for Nora conforms to the representational norms of aestheticised femininity, but these norms are broken when Torvald realises that she is dancing 'as if it were a matter of life and death' (Archer 1906, 106) and her movements become wilder and more exaggerated, her hair falling onto her shoulders. Torvald loses directorial control and Mrs Linde and Rank see a transgressive female body that shocks them.

Nora's rehearsal of the tarantella dance is triangulated within three gazes: a husband who stops his wife dancing; a doctor who explains the incident by referring to a medical discourse linking pregnancy to mental instability; and an empathetic friend who witnesses her dancing. Mrs Linde is so appalled by the scene that she engineers the final confrontation between husband and wife. When Nora begins to dance, the audience is invited to look at Nora through the eyes of the male characters on the stage. This can be a comfortable position for both male and female spectators because it is one of control, but when Nora begins to dance as though her life depends on it, the audience is forced to relinquish this powerful viewing position. To interpret and understand her dancing body, they must empathise with Nora's subjective experience, give up the voyeuristic pleasure of gazing at her body, and replace it with a kinaesthetic empathy with this same body's subjective pain. Confronted with this metatheatrical conceit, interpreters of the scene, whatever their cultural context, are faced with the same problems: what is Nora doing when she complies with the accepted aesthetic conventions of the dance, and what does she do when she breaks them?

Our comparative study of tarantella rehearsals is based on seventy-nine images selected from 150 productions of *Et dukkehjem*; these images have been sourced from illustrations, photographs, and film and video recordings. When considering dramaturgical structures in Chapter 4, we found that new material in *Et dukkehjem* adaptations contributed up to one-third of the total playing time of a performance, but this assessment took no account of innovations in the embodiment of character. It is rare to find a performance of *Et dukkehjem* from the last fifty years that pays heed to any of the physical directions for characterisation that are embedded in Ibsen's play-script. These adaptations are so diverse that throughout this chapter when we mention the 'tarantella rehearsal' or the 'tarantella dance' we are referring to all the variants and substitutions on Ibsen's text, whatever the music or dance steps used within a particular performance. As the body language and stage movement in theatrical adaptations are so open to interpretation, finding recurring physical patterns between adaptations is intriguing. They are like the imprints of social, aesthetic, political, cultural, and religious constraints over the representation of the performing body. Although we have sourced and sorted these images ourselves, the possibilities for this kind of analysis will increase when visual searching (as opposed to text-based searching) across performing arts digital archives becomes a reality. This technology would have assisted us in sourcing images according to repetitions in the choreographic patterns of the dance, but our analysis is not restricted to physical patterns and also embraces repetitions in conceptual strategies and in dramaturgical approaches to substituting or censoring the scene.

We have arranged the tarantella images into a tree structure that records the relationships between images. Similarities between performances and the dates of productions determine the ordering of the images in the trunk, branches, or sub-branches. Where images are layered with multiple interpretative elements, the dominant feature dictates the placement. Figure 5.1 displays a version of this tree as a simplified text-based graphic, with each image identified by place and year of the performance together with the number of the corresponding IbsenStage record.

The trunk of the visual tree (the strongest and most recurring pattern) is the iconic image of Nora with the tambourine raised above her head performing an Italian folk dance. The five branches that depart from this interpretation can be broadly described as *the branch of cuts and substitutions* in which the scene is cut back, replaced, or disappears; *the voyeuristic branch* where the possibilities for spectacle in the early part of Nora's dance are indulged or critiqued; *the branch of transgressions* where Nora breaks through respectable

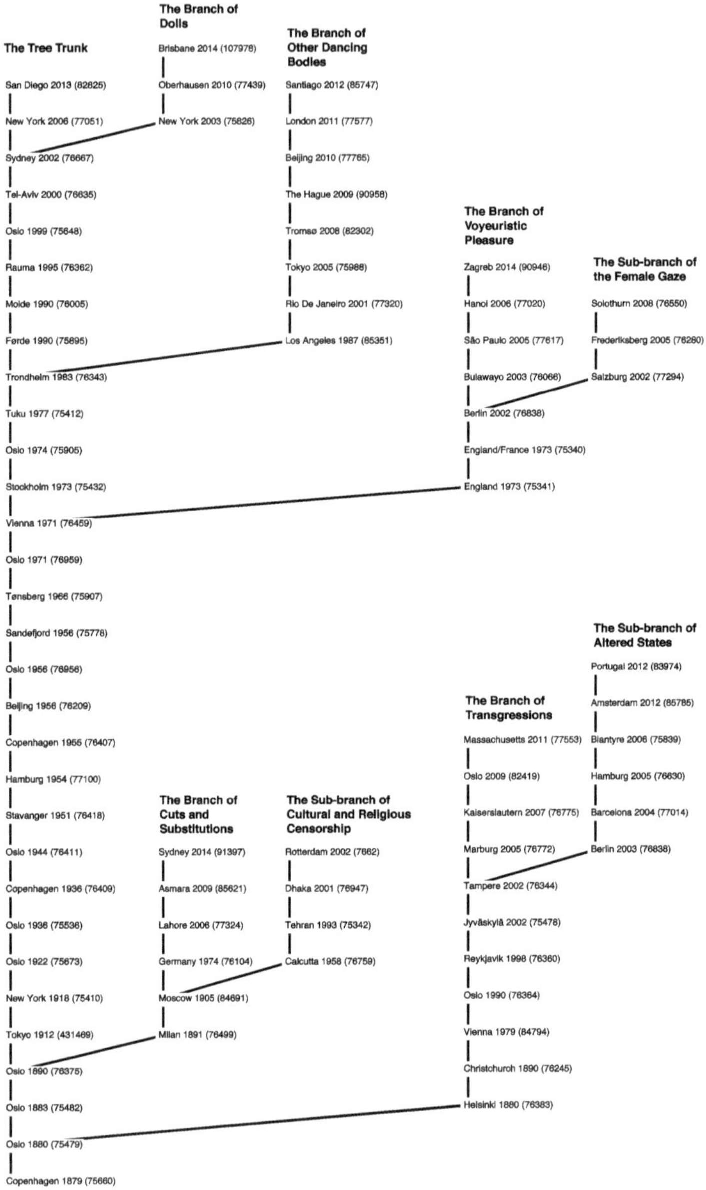

Fig. 5.1 Visual schema for the tarantella tree indicating the placement of images by location, year of production, and event identifier in IbsenStage

conventions of drawing-room entertainment to embody some form of social negation; *the branch of other dancing bodies* in which assumptions about the normality of heterosexual desire and the social organisation of gender are interrogated; and finally *the branch of dolls* that critiques theatrical representation itself. Unexpected connections across space and time appear in the tree; images from adaptations created in Chile, China, and Denmark sit together in a single branch. A variety of cultural, aesthetic, and ideological forces have shaped these branches, but they combine to produce clear interpretative strategies for embodying the tarantella rehearsal.

Before we can proceed with the analyses of these interpretative strategies, we need to pause and consider the basic premise behind this study: that Ibsen wrote the tarantella scene primarily in the *language of the body*. The importance of the body in Ibsen's dramaturgy has received very little scholarly attention. John Northam's monograph on the symbolic meaning of the stage objects and costumes that 'supplement' Ibsen's 'verbal characterisations' is still the major work on this aspect of Ibsen's dramaturgy (1953, 32). We argue that the tarantella is an integral part of a carefully devised physical score crafted by Ibsen with the same degree of meticulous detail as his dialogue. This assertion contradicts William Archer's judgement that the tarantella 'was a theatrical effect, of an obvious, unmistakable kind' (1906, xi). In his opinion, it was only in the middle of the third act that Ibsen outgrew 'the theatrical orthodox of his earlier years' (Archer 1906, xi). Archer's view was echoed by Elizabeth Robins (the first actress to play Hedda Gabler in London): she dismissed the tarantella rehearsal as an *entr'acte*, a *divertissement*, and 'Ibsen's one concession to the effect-hunting he had come to deliver us from' (1932a, 13). To dispel this perception, which persists today in the lack of scholarly interest in Ibsen's dramaturgy of movement and gesture, we touch on his theatrical training in the Bergen theatre, and contextualise the tarantella rehearsal within his physical score for *Et dukkehjem*.

Et dukkehjem's Physical Score

The sophistication of Ibsen's use of the performing body in his dramaturgy can be traced back to his theatrical apprenticeship at the first national theatre in Norway, founded in Bergen in 1850. He joined the theatre as the resident playwright in 1851 and stayed with the company for five seasons. During this time the company presented 122 plays, including five by Ibsen. Although Ibsen was employed as a playwright, his day-to-day responsibilities expanded far beyond this job description. He shared the role of 'scene instructor' or director with an older and more experienced theatre practitioner. This unusual arrangement, which was constantly renegotiated by the board of the theatre, gave his senior colleague the task of instructing the actors in the interpretation and delivery of their lines, leaving Ibsen with responsibility for the sets, costumes, lighting and sound designs, production management, and, crucially for his development as a playwright, the movements and gestures of the actors. For nearly six years, Ibsen's artistic influence was expressed through the *mise-en-scène* and the physicality of actors' characterisations.[2] His experiments with the physical and visual languages of theatre were anything but orthodox and had a lasting influence on his dramaturgy. In the year before the premiere of *Et dukkehjem*, he wrote to the Christiania Theatre about plans for the production of *Samfundets Støtter* (*Pillars of the Society*): 'I hope proper attention will be paid to groupings and positions. Actors being marched up in the foreground must be avoided, the individual positions changing as often as is natural; overall, each scene and each picture ought to, [as far as possible,] be a reflection of reality' (Ibsen 1878a). Rather than leave these matters to chance, he incorporates a physical score into *Et dukkehjem* that ensured that the Helmer household was 'a reflection of reality'. All the physical movements embedded in the dialogue and stage directions are justified by characters' intentions with a degree of detail unusual in a play written almost ten years before the Théâtre Libre was pioneering naturalism on the stage in Paris, and nearly twenty years before Stanislavski founded the Moscow Art Theatre. In the tarantella scene, it is Nora's overwhelming fear of Torvald reading Krogstad's letter that causes her to take drastic action to stop him reaching the letter box: desperation fuels the excessive energy of the dance. This dramaturgical logic that ties together action and thought is exemplified by the tarantella; it may be the most extreme physical expression within the play, but it is far from theatrical 'effect-hunting'.

Eric Østerud (1997) argues that Nora's compliant and erotic dancing body is a key to the theme of social masquerade that runs through the play: it is highlighted by the preparations for the costume party at the home of the neighbouring Stenborgs, developed in the post-party scene with Rank's farewell, and resolved with the final stripping away of the fancy-dress costumes.[3] The most significant mask-like gesture that Ibsen creates for Nora occurs before the intimate scene with Dr Rank: '*Nora draws her hands over her face, pulls herself together, goes to the door and opens it. RANK stands outside hanging up his fur coat*' (Archer 1906, 79). The passing of one's hands over one's face signifies the donning of a facial mask that hides an emotional interiority; for Nora it marks the return of her light and playful gestures from the beginning of the play, before the blackmail threat overwhelms her. The ease with which Ibsen's Nora resumes the demeanour of the charming little bird or squirrel, and the speed with which she drops it again as soon as Rank declares his true feelings, reveals the artifice of her innocent, childlike femininity. This movement of drawing the hands over the face signifies her awareness that the image she presents to family and friends is a social mask. The gesture is a subtle manifestation of the masquerade theme, which becomes explicit when the mask cracks during the tarantella rehearsal and Nora's body transgresses the boundaries of the acceptable in drawing-room performances.

The tarantella may be the most obvious thematic use of a physical action within the narrative, but there are other examples. A subliminal warning of future catastrophe is physicalised in Nora's 'hide and seek' game with the children. The stage direction reads: '*Nora hides under the table*; *the children come rushing in*, [*look*] *for her*, *but cannot find her*' (Archer 1906, 41). This image of the children running through the house searching for their absent mother is a game that is destined to become their reality. The complexity and subtlety of Ibsen's physical score are evident in the final scene when Nora asks Helmer: 'Does it not strike you that this is the first time we two, you and I, man and wife, [are talking] together seriously?' (Archer 1906, 142). This moment is visually reinforced by the tableau of Nora and Helmer sitting opposite each other at the table. The strength of this image is magnified retrospectively because Ibsen has engineered all their previous scenes to avoid the couple being seated together. This theatrical sleight of hand reinforces Nora's contention that rational discussion has been absent from their marriage. It is a considerable dramaturgical feat to write a domestic drama involving a married couple, set in their living room, and keep them standing through all their major scenes until late into the third act. Given that the whole artifice of Ibsen's physical score is that it functions at a subliminal level, the audience is likely to believe Nora's statement because it is being visually reinforced by the novelty of seeing the seated husband and wife.

The metatheatrical element within the tarantella rehearsal sets it apart from these other more subliminal aspects of Ibsen's physical score, but this dramaturgical layer was a late addition to the play. In an earlier draft there is no rehearsal, just a private performance. Nora distracts Torvald from Krogstad's letter by singing Anitra's song from Ibsen's *Peer Gynt*. This is a song of adoration, describing how Peer is revealed as the Prophet, spreading light as he rides on his white horse across the North African desert. As Nora sings, Torvald turns to Dr Rank and says: 'But we must have cigarettes with it; real Turkish ones.' The men sit and smoke, echoing the figure of

Peer listening to Anitra while reclining on cushions in his Arab chieftain's tent, drinking coffee and smoking a long pipe. When Mrs Linde enters, Helmer says: 'A picture of family life. What do you say to it?' Dr Rank adds, 'Turkish, but [beautiful] is it not?' Mrs Linde agrees to play the piano, and Nora dances, draped in her multiple veil-like shawls. Torvald surveys her body, comments on 'the fine curve of the neck', Dr Rank replies 'A wife is a good thing', and Torvald concludes 'A wife like her' (Archer 1917, 148).[4] All the references to Turkish cigarettes and Turkish families have disappeared from the final version of *Et dukkehjem*, to be replaced by Torvald's erotic fantasy of abducting a virgin peasant girl from southern Europe who dances the tarantella. In this fantasy there is an echo of Anitra, the sex slave from North Africa, and, as Franco Perrelli has pointed out, the Neapolitan tarantella contains both Spanish and Arabian influences (2001, 120).

The shift from the orientalist fantasy of the early draft to the Neapolitan tarantella in the finished script is accompanied by a move from the representation of a domestic performance to the metatheatrical conceit of a rehearsal. The earlier draft highlights the orientalist fantasies underpinning the unacceptable face of gendered power relations in the bourgeois households of northern Europe, but it could still be perceived in performance as a musical interlude. The voyeurism of Dr Rank and Torvald is explicit, but Nora remains trapped in their gaze as a desirable dancing girl. It is only when Ibsen transforms the performance into a rehearsal that her escape route becomes possible. We now explore how artists have used this route and the obstacles placed in their way.

The Tarantella Tree Trunk

The images in the trunk of our visual tree come from the dominant aesthetic tradition of *Et dukkehjem*: this tradition emerged in the Nordic region in the late nineteenth century, was exported internationally by Norwegian institutions during the twentieth century, and still influences adaptations today. Twenty-two of the Nordic images form the trunk in Fig. 5.1, but since this tradition has travelled globally, a further nine images are scattered across North America, Australasia, Europe, and Asia. In Chapter 3 we traced the emergence and cultural transmission of this performance tradition from 1879 to its decline within Norway in the 1990s, but the trunk demonstrates that interpretations based on this tradition have appeared sporadically, both locally and globally, to the present day. The four images from the trunk reproduced in Fig. 5.2 show the

Fig. 5.2 (**a**) Betty Hennings, Det Kongelige Teater, Copenhagen, 1879 (Source: The Royal Library, Copenhagen). (**b**) Tore Segelcke, 1936 (Source: photographer Ernest Rude, photo archive of National Theatre, National Library, Oslo). (**c**) Ji Shuping, China, 1956 (Source: Gerda Ring's Album, Theatre Collection, National Library, Oslo; photographer unknown). (**d**) Miranda Otto, Sydney, 2002 (Source: photographer Heidrun Löhr, Sydney Theatre Company)

similarities between the first performance by Betty Hennings in 1879; the Norwegian Nationaltheatret's first international tour with Tore Segelcke that premiered in 1936; the Ji Shuping 1956 Beijing production that was connected to the Nordic *Et dukkehjem* artistic network through Gerda Ring; and a 2002 production from the Sydney Theatre Company starring Miranda Otto.[5] The Australian image is a clear demonstration of the pervasive influence of this tradition. The last image included in the trunk comes from a 2013 student production in San Diego.

The dominant performance tradition has constrained interpretative innovation in the staging of the tarantella rehearsal for more than a hundred years. In a superficial way it is faithful to Ibsen's play-script, since his Nora does rehearse the dance with a tambourine, but the more controversial elements in the tarantella scene are underdeveloped, possibly because the tradition was exported to secure a place in the world canon for a national icon. As the forces that lie behind this tradition were explored at some length in Chapter 3, we focus here on the branches that *diverge* from the trunk to create a variety of counter-traditions. The first branch has even less interest in developing the controversial elements of the scene than the adaptations that form the trunk. Here, aesthetic objections to the scene mingle with censorship over the representations of the female body as an object of voyeuristic pleasure.

The Branch of Cuts and Substitutions

The nine images representing this branch in Fig. 5.1 span a hundred years and come from Europe, South Asia, and the Middle East. While the artistic rationales behind these interpretations differ, they converge on the supposed links between exhibitionist female bodies and prostitution.

The branch emerges from the tree trunk early in the *Et dukkehjem* history with aesthetic censorship. William Archer believed that '[u]ndoubtedly the great attraction of the part of Nora to the average actress was the tarantella scene' (1906, xi), but many of the first European Noras were not average actresses. They were struggling to carve out space as serious artists and to distance themselves from nineteenth-century prejudices that assumed that all of their kind were sexually promiscuous. Vera Komissarzhevskaya reduced the tarantella to 'a series of expressive poses during which the feet simply tapped out a nervous rhythm' (Braun 1991, 25), while Eleanora Duse performed a few cursory steps and rejected the image of a Neapolitan fisher girl in favour of a masquerade costume of a *commedia dell'arte* character,

Arlecchino, the male servant who entertains and tricks his master.[6] Born into a Venetian theatrical family, Duse had a direct link to this theatrical tradition through her grandfather.[7] Perhaps she was too familiar with the lived reality of peasant women in Naples to find the drawing-room version of the tarantella compelling. Duse and Komissarzhevskaya cut the tarantella to a physical quotation because it was antipathetic to their professional identities to portray a 'dancing girl'. This elision or avoidance of the tarantella continues throughout the production history of *Et dukkehjem* whenever the physical display of Nora is at odds with the aesthetics of a production; an obvious example is the 1974 television version by Rainer Werner Fassbinder, entitled *Nora Helmer*.[8] This doll home was created out of cut-glass mirrors, glass etched with lace patterns, white wrought iron, chandeliers, gauze curtains, and chiffon and satin costumes. The characters were isolated from each other by multiple transparent surfaces that signified the layers of lies, secrets, and illusions at the centre of this bourgeois marriage. In this highly aestheticised world, a peasant dancing girl from Capri had no place.

The Sub-Branch of Cultural and Religious Censorship

The branch of substitutions divides in the middle of the twentieth century when cultural taboos banning the female dancing body start appearing in post-colonial productions of *Et dukkehjem*. We mark this break with the famous Bengali production where Ganesha, the Hindu Elephant God, replaces Christian iconography in the Helmer household. In 1958, Sambhu Mitra and his company, Bohurupee, adapted the play from the William Archer translations, but omitted the tarantella.[9] As the play was domesticated into the Bengali cultural context, Mitra considered it inappropriate for a middle-class woman to perform a dance to entertain a social gathering of friends and neighbours and decided to replace the dance with a recitation. The poem he used was entitled 'Jhulan' (Swaying), published in 1893 by the Nobel laureate Rabindranath Tagore in his volume *Sonar Tari*. As this first verse demonstrates, the text reflects an existential crisis in the speaker that Mitra used to verbally express the physical angst embodied in the tarantella metaphor:

> I play today with my Self
> A game of death
> In the dead of night.

In deep dense monsoon
The darkening sky.
See how the rain falls weepingly on all sides.
In intense playfulness
My raft floats on the currents of life;
I have spurned the comforts of my dream world
And stepped out in this dark dark night. (Gupta 2015)[10]

After the first verse, Bula/Nora stops speaking, the stage directions stating that she is confused and frightened. Tapan/Torvald tries to calm her and she continues reciting, he joins in softly keeping the rhythm by clapping his hand, but he loses the words while she becomes more and more disconnected, speaking fragments of the poem, revolving around the room as if 'under her own spell' (Mukhopadhyay 2014).[11] The structure of a rehearsal spiralling out of control is retained, but the words of the great Bengali poet of Indian independence replace the potential angst of Nora's dancing body. The inner conflict of the character is signified through the words, though it is implied that her body exhibits confusion and distress as she tries to remember the poem.

Substituting the female dancing body with a more respectable cultural entertainment has had a long history; our last image of this kind comes from the 2009 Eritrean production where Nora, played by Birikti Woldeselassie, sang the aria 'O Caro Babbino Mio' from Giacomo Puccini's one-act comic opera, *Gianni Schicchi*.[12] However, most of the post-1990 images in this sub-branch are the result of religious taboos and come from productions in cultures radicalised by the resurgence of Islamic values in public life; here the depiction of a positive female character breaking through the religious constraints of modesty and piety has become unthinkable. Ibsen's early draft of the tarantella scene implied a connection between a decadent sexuality and Islam through Anitra, the slave girl, singing her song of adoration to Peer Gynt, in his guise as the Prophet. It is ironic to find that the exhibition of Nora's dancing body has now become a signifier in the Islamic world of Western decadence.

In *Sara*, the 1993 film version directed by Dariush Mehrjui, the whole scene was cut.[13] There could be no tarantella in this Iranian film because the exhibition of the female performing body is censored.[14] The scene was substituted with a party to celebrate Torvald/Hessam's promotion, and it was the men who danced. There was no lack of spectatorial pleasure in the camera's relationship with Sara/Nora played by Niki Karimi, and the other characters were kept at a visual distance. A close-up of Sara showed her gently swaying to the music as a tear fell from her eye. Was she crying for the pain to come, or did her body sway in grief for the lost joy of the dance? The technique of substituting the tarantella with a social dance is a common strategy in productions subject to religious prohibitions over the display of a female dancing body. When Nora does dance in Islamic cultures, the tarantella morphs into a social dance in which she is partnered either by Torvald or Dr Rank. In Gerrit Timmers's Arabic production for the Moroccan immigrant community of Rotterdam in 2002, Nora rehearsed a traditional Berber dance with both male characters.[15] Social dances have also been used to defuse the potential exhibitionist presence of the female dancing body in productions created in Egypt in 2006 and Bangladesh in 2001.[16]

Although cutting or minimising the tarantella is typical of recent adaptations created in or for Islamic cultures, it would be wrong to suggest that these adaptations are necessarily conforming to religious prohibitions. To stress this point, an image from the Pakistan women's movement company, Tehrik-e-Niswan, is included in this branch, but it reflects aesthetic rather than religious censorship. This 2006 Urdu adaptation might well have cut the dance to avoid confrontation with fundamentalist elements within Pakistan, but given the personal history of the artistic director, Sheema Kermani, this is unlikely. She was the only major exponent of classical Indian dance in Pakistan in the latter years of the military dictatorship of General Muhammad Zia-ul-Haq. The draconian Islamic laws imposed by his regime banned all public dancing by women, yet Kermani evaded censorship by performing within the framework of 'cultural evenings' (Kermani 2009). In the Tehrik-e-Niswan adaptation, *Gurrya ka Ghar*, the metatheatrical conceit of the tarantella scene became the frame for the whole production and there was no place for a rehearsal within a rehearsal. The aesthetics of the adaptation merged two kinds of realism: the psychological realism of Henrik Ibsen, and the dialectical realism of Bertolt Brecht (Jafri 2009).[17]

As the organising principle behind the *branch of substitution* is the absence of the tarantella, it throws together images created by artists imposing their own aesthetic constraints on *Et dukkehjem* with those of artists intent on negotiating external forms of censorship. The background to religious censorship is easy to explain, as the representation of the female body on the public stage has been an ongoing problem for Judeo-Christian and Islamic cultures. Theatre has fallen foul of religious dictates in numerous societies. In Islamic cultures the theological debate revolves around whether representation challenges the authority of God by usurping the act of creation.[18] Medieval Christianity and Judaism banned theatre on the grounds of the prohibition against cross-dressing in the Book of Deuteronomy (22:5) in the Old Testament of the Bible. All of these religions of the book have a history of censoring the public display of the female body. The forces of cultural and religious censorship and the forces of aesthetic practice could not be further apart, the only connection being a shared distance from popular entertainments where associations between exhibitionist female bodies and promiscuity are at their strongest. That this association still lurks within many of the adaptations where Nora dances is reflected in the number of images we have gathered of her dressed in red for the masquerade party. In many European cultures strong associations exist between red dresses and prostitution, not to mention danger and murder; and it has become a theatrical cliché to bathe the stage in red light to signify a brothel. Colour symbolism is culturally specific and colour photography of theatre productions is comparatively recent, but there is strong evidence that red has become globally the most popular colour for Nora's masquerade costume. At the very least, this suggests that in theatre cultures influenced by European theatrical conventions, Nora's performance at the Stenborg party has associations with a sexuality that is both dangerous and for sale.

The Branch of Voyeuristic Pleasure

Ibsen's tarantella contains a voyeuristic pleasure where sight is close to touch. *Et dukkehjem* is a remarkably tactile text: Ibsen uses touch as a way of defining the relationships between characters and Torvald is always touching Nora's body. He puts his arm around her, holds her in his arms, and kisses her forehead; he takes her by the ear and chin, and seizes her hands; he holds her back, drags her, and leads her gently. With the exception of his preoccupation with shuffling and sorting papers, every movement given by Ibsen to Torvald is fixated on his wife's body—some are overtly sexual, others parental. By encouraging Nora to perform the tarantella, Torvald stimulates his own desire by allowing his friend and neighbours to look but not touch: Nora's body is his property. The audience is also implicated in this voyeuristic conceit. Images that indulge or critique the voyeuristic pleasure of watching Nora dancing fill the next branch of our tree. Fig. 5.3b typifies this pattern, with both audience and actors indulging in the pleasure of watching Nora dancing in her red dress; this adaptation by the Croatian National Theatre was framed as a ballroom spectacle.[19] The ten images that

Fig. 5.3 (**a**) Teth Maiello (Nora), Teatro de Narradores, São Paulo 2005 (Source: Teatro de Narradores). (**b**) Daria Lorenci (Nora), Croatian National Theatre, 2014 (Source: Croatian National Theatre)

represent this interpretative approach in Fig. 5.1 cross the divide between film and theatre: the first images come from feature films that encouraged the voyeuristic pleasure of the audience; the middle images are from theatre productions that used film icons to reference this pleasure; and in the final images the male gaze became the theatrical spectacle.

In the hands of the film directors who adapted the play in the 1970s, the voyeuristic pleasure of consuming Nora found its most uncritical expression. The two best-known English-language films, directed by Patrick Garland and Joseph Losey, were both released in 1973.[20] Typical of film adaptations of plays set in domestic environments, both versions moved the action beyond the confines of the home to create cinematic extravaganzas out of the masquerade party with large casts of costumed characters, music, and dance. As the parties are major spectacles in these films, the tarantella rehearsals lost their dramaturgical importance and became a mere foretaste of the visual pleasures to come.

In Patrick Garland's film starring Claire Bloom, re-released in 2003, the climactic moment of the tarantella rehearsal disappeared together with the final dialogue and the scene segued into the Stenborgs' party. In what remained of the tarantella rehearsal, Torvald was depicted as a caring husband and sensitive aesthete who is deeply worried about Nora's mental state. As he sat at the piano, he implored Dr Rank to 'do as much as you can to control her'. A lock of Nora's hair fell, but nothing shocking happened to signify her inner angst, and Mrs Linde never appeared. The performance at the party emerged seamlessly out of the rehearsal and a series of close-ups on Anthony Hopkins as Torvald invited the audience to empathise with his expressions of paternalistic pride in his wife's efforts. It was the displaced male gaze of the camera that fixated on the spectacle of Claire Bloom as she danced the tarantella. The camera lingered on her white stockings and the laced boots of the peasant costume, referencing not only the earlier 'silk stocking' scene, but also the risqué glimpses of actresses' legs that were ubiquitous in the popular entertainments of the late nineteenth century.

In the Joseph Losey film, the party began with an extended sequence showing the guests dancing, intercut with Mrs Linde's visit to Krogstad's lodgings. Nora's performance was delayed while she returned home to fetch the forgotten tambourine and visit the nursery to look at her sleeping children. A parallel sequence showed Krogstad, the poverty-stricken single parent, putting his children to bed. When Nora returned to the party, the tarantella (as performed by Jane Fonda) was the dance of an innocent but seductive girl. Once again, it was the camera, abstracted from any character's point of view, that zoomed in until it almost touched her swirling body and long, flowing hair.

These two films, commonly referred to as the Claire Bloom or Jane Fonda versions, are interpretations authored by directors reflecting on the challenges faced by men during the second wave of the women's movement in Europe and America. Garland featured Torvald as the mild-mannered and empathetic husband, who was more of a misguided aesthete than a male chauvinist; while Losey dismissed his Torvald as an irrelevant bore, treated his film star Nora as a spoilt bourgeois, and privileged the emotional and psychological angst of Krogstad, played by Edward Fox, the single parent who was the victim of a moralising, hypocritical world. As Fonda had won an Oscar in 1971 for her performance as Bree Daniels, the prostitute in *Klute*, and had been labelled a political activist through her opposition to the Vietnam War, Losey's decision to cast her as Nora was already overdetermined.[21]

The voyeuristic power of cinema is echoed in the next set of images from stage adaptations that use film icons for Nora's masquerade. There are two linked productions, one in Germany that uses the image of Angelina Jolie as *Lara Croft: Tomb Raider* (2001), and the other from Brazil that uses images of Marilyn Monroe from *Let's Make Love* (1960) and *The Seven Year Itch* (1955). The images of Jolie and Monroe were superimposed on German and Brazilian Noras as signifiers of Torvald's sexual fantasies, but it is arguable whether the critique implicit in the use of these icons subverts or legitimates voyeuristic pleasure. In the Schaubühne production of 2002, Anne Tismer lay almost unconscious, wet and bleeding, at the end of the tarantella rehearsal; this physical state anticipated her masquerade costume, which referenced Jolie's Lara Croft warrior covered in cuts, bleeding, bruising, and smeared with gel.[22] Ostermeier's explanation for this costume is challenging: 'we thought to incorporate into our production a sense of the way women seek to express themselves based on influences they get from looking at magazines and watching commercials and videos and also animated films' (2005). This tarantella rehearsal was visually stunning, but arguably it is Jolie as an undefeated warrior, not as a battered and bleeding victim, who holds the lure for female expression.

José Fernando Peixoto de Azevedo, the director of Teatro De Narradores in Brazil, acknowledges that he was influenced by Ostermeier's production in his creation of *Nossa casa de boneca*.[23] Seeing *Nora* at the Schaubühne inspired him to translate Ibsen's play into the Brazilian present (Fig. 5.3a). In this 2005 production, Nora morphed into Marilyn Monroe for the entire play and the tarantella scene was transformed into a rehearsal of 'My Heart Belongs to Daddy', the Cole Porter song that Monroe performed as a dance number in a cabaret rehearsal in the 1960 film *Let's Make Love*. The superimposition of Monroe's cabaret on Ibsen's tarantella rehearsal fits well: Monroe, having introduced herself as Lolita, rehearsed her number watched by two men, a billionaire sugar daddy and his nervous assistant. In the Brazilian production, Teth Maiello, who played Nora, described her performance of the song as initially nervous, with a slowly increasing tension leading to an excruciating agony that is only brought to a halt by Dr Rank's intervention (Azevedo and Maiello 2012). The off-stage performance at the masquerade party was signified by favela funk, popular dance music associated with working-class culture, but appropriated by the Rio middle classes. The lyrics of the music were deliberately aggressive and overtly sexist. On the return from the party, Maiello was costumed as Monroe in the iconic white dress from the 1955 film *The Seven Year Itch*, made famous by the sequence where her skirt billowed upwards from the draft of the subway grating; it was only during the rehearsal that she wore red. Superimposing the Monroe image onto the Brazilian Nora made Torvald's pleasure in objectifying Nora's body explicit and the use of the song paralleled the context of the private rehearsal, but there was yet another level of meaning to be derived from the introduction of Marilyn into the Brazilian doll home. Azevedo described the production more in terms of class than sexual politics: the Helmers represented a Brazilian middle class enamoured with the consumerist culture of the USA (Azevedo and Maiello 2012).

If Lara Croft and Marilyn Monroe are sex goddesses of the twentieth and twenty-first centuries, the character of Georges Bizet's *Carmen* predates them as the sex symbol of the nineteenth century. In the 2006 Vietnamese production directed by Le Hung, Nora assumed an image reminiscent of Carmen rather than a Capri peasant girl.[24] Carmen rivals Nora as the most-adapted female character in the Western dramatic canon, appearing in Bizet's opera only four years before Nora's debut in Copenhagen. However, the transgression that fascinates in this character is somewhat different for Susan McClary: 'That Carmen has long stood as a moral lesson about the dangers of female sexuality is evident from much of what has been written about it from the very first Parisian reviews up to the present' (1992, 125). In this cross-ethnic production, Vietnamese actors played Caucasian characters and the Carmen image referenced the French colonial culture imposed on Vietnam after its absorption into French Indochina in 1887, a colonial entity that was eventually dissolved in 1954 (Helland 2015, 81). Nevertheless, while Carmen may be a cultural import from France, the character transgressed boundaries of French identity, as she was variously identified as Jewish, Romany, Spanish, and Basque. None of this was overt in the performance by Lê Khanh as Nora, which references Carmen through the image of a red Spanish flamenco dress.[25] Monroe, Jolie, and Carmen all satisfy Ibsen's requirement that Nora begins her dance by reproducing an alluring image of femininity, designed by Torvald to gratify the sexual tastes of his friends and himself. Yet these icons are so fixed in a global cultural imaginary that it is difficult to manipulate them to express Nora's crisis as she tries to break through their representational hold.

The Sub-Branch of the Female Gaze

Separating from this branch are images from recent productions that suggest a new approach to critiquing the voyeuristic potential of the tarantella rehearsal. In an image from the Betty Nansen Theatre in Denmark, Torvald and Dr Rank became the objects of the audience's gaze. Nora, played by Marie Louise Wille, was on display, but the female director, Katrine Wiedermann, staged the dance so that the audience watched the male characters watching the dancing Nora.[26] An early production directed by Katharina Rupp in Salzburg used similar staging to highlight the voyeurism of male characters.[27] Both of these productions presented images of men trapped in fantasies of consumption of a woman's body. This pattern was repeated in the last image in this sub-branch, which comes from Solothurn and once again was the work of Katharina Rupp, suggesting that this interpretative pattern has a female gaze.[28]

Although the images in this branch and sub-branch all shared an interest in the female performing body as spectacle, they fall into interesting cultural patterns. The first images came from film adaptations untouched by the film theories of the 1970s that critiqued the voyeuristic cinematic.[29] Still, these theoretical writings informed both the use by male directors of Monroe and Jolie, and the counter-strategy by female directors. Separating these images are the different levels of critique structured into the productions, but uniting them is a concentration on the voyeuristic pleasure that has been repressed for aesthetic, religious, or cultural reasons in the branch of substitutions. They all addressed the first part of Ibsen's challenge to represent the cultural norms of an aestheticised femininity and most of them also critiqued its social construction, but they were less engaged with the second part of Ibsen's challenge, which involves the depiction of a transgressive female body.

The Branch of Transgressions

The branch of transgressions emerges within months of the premiere of *Et dukkehjem*. It represents an interpretative concentration on the dance's frenetic aspects, which were minimised in the dominant performance tradition. Ida Aalberg came close to 'the edge of madness' in her portrayal of Nora in 1880, and 'in the wild tarantella scene she expressed dramatic strength with great, touching power' (Koski 2006, 527). According to Pirkko Koski, excessive tarantellas were typical of Finnish Noras and this approach is still current today in the 'animalistic tarantella' performed by Minttu Mustakallio in the Suomen Kansallisteatteri production of 2002 (2006, 528).[30] Janet Achurch was also renowned for her wild tarantella, which was condemned by George Bernard Shaw: 'The tarantella began at a pitch which it should only have touched for the 1/10000000th (one ten millionth) of a second at the end' (Shaw 1892). Yet in New Zealand, according to the *Auckland Evening Star*, it was precisely the same theatrical moment that reviewers considered the theatrical highpoint of the performance: 'The wild scream of laughter with which she ends up and collapses is a thousand times more full of terror of realistic suffering than were the most awful scene of other plays in which we have seen Miss Achurch' (Review of Janet Achurch in *A Doll's House* 1891, 5). Physically excessive tarantellas became increasingly popular in the twentieth century with Noras dancing on chairs, tables, even on a piano. Their gestures were expansive, growing in intensity, and increasingly frenetic, but these Noras were still contained by the choreographic structures of their dance. There is one strain of transgressive bodies that breaks this containment to form a sub-branch consisting of animalistic images and depictions of madness, hysteria, and trance. All of these altered states share a quality of dehumanised irrationality placing the female body beyond the realms of the social; the images come from a wide variety of cultures.

The Sub-Branch of Altered States

In the popular imagination there are clear animalistic associations with the tarantella folk dance, since it was believed to be a cure for the venomous bite of the tarantula spider. In his famous study of tarantism in the 1950s, Ernesto de Martino identified the mythical and ritual origins of the dance as a cultural phenomenon, rather than a folk cure for a deadly poison (de Martino [1961] 2002). Women were the major tarantella participants from as early as the seventeenth century. Historically, the dance consists of frenetic ecstatic movements, leading to trance, which sometimes include features that are explicitly orgasmic. An ecstatic dance, referencing the healing rituals of tarantism and using trance possession, is a highpoint of the 2006 adaptation from Malawi (*Breaking the Pot*) where the tarantella was substituted with the *vimbuza*, a women's healing dance from northern Malawi, eastern Zambia, and southern Tanzania.[31] Declared by UNESCO intangible cultural heritage, this ritual is traditionally associated with the exorcism of spiritual and physical illness, primarily mental disturbances and epilepsy (UNESCO 2005). It belongs to the matriarchal Tumbuka people, who lost land and power to the patriarchal Ngoni people during European colonisation in the mid-nineteenth century. The psychological impact of this double colonisation on the Tumbuka was so devastating that the *vimbusa* became used as a healing ritual for the whole community. The Malawian production used the *vimbusa* because it highlights the gender conflict of the play by referencing Ngoni and Tumbuka colonial history. Melissa Eveleigh, the director of the production, explains the concept behind the tarantella:

> They are rehearsing for the dance the next night, and Torvald begins with the drum beat from a Ngoni ritual which involves women kneeling in front of men. Nora wants to do her own dance, the *vimbusa*. He is doing a slow drum beat, but she is not following. She just gets faster and faster using a different rhythm and the chorus, who provide the cultural context for the dance, support her with their drums. The *vimbusa* is competing with the Ngoni drum beat. In five minutes, Nora goes through the dance that would usually take a whole night: very fast drumming, very fast turning, very fast shoulders, a trance state and collapse[s] on the ground. Her wig has fallen off. The meaning of the dance is very clear to the audience. (Eveleigh 2009)

Finding a trance ritual as specific as the *vimbusa* is rare in this sub-branch, which is largely composed of non-specific images of altered states. Recent German adaptations tend to substitute the Italian folk dance with ecstatic elements combined with features of expressionistic modern dance. Compositionally, these performances are built out of the repetition of everyday movements that merge theatre and dance and are reflective of the Pina Bausch legacy. In 2002, Susanne Wolff performed Nora for the Thalia Theatre in Hamburg in a domestic setting without intimacy, its coldness evoking an asylum or a warehouse. Her tarantella was fixed to a single spot consisting of full body movements referencing street dance, martial arts, gym aerobics, and a foetal slump, a combination that became progressively more frenetic and uncoordinated.[32] In the 2012 production by tg STAN, the Belgian actors' company, Wine Dierickx improvised her five-minute dance to the repetitive lyric of 'power' from the song of the same name by Kanye West.[33] She had conscious control over the dance until her limbs started to twitch to the counter-rhythms of the musical jazz score, as if they had a life of their own. Dierickx fell, crawled in time with the music, rolled over, and arched her back, her shoulders on the ground, with her feet propelling her across the floor (Fig. 5.4b). She jumped up and immersed herself again in an ecstatic dance. Mrs Linde gently took hold of her, and calmed her body into stillness. There is no overt reference to animality in Dierickx's performance, but an animal-skin rug and stuffed pig, dog, and kangaroo surrounded her. This animal theme, while not directly referencing the tarantula spider, was everywhere in the Teatre Nacional de Catalunya production directed by Rafel Duran and performed in Barcelona in 2004. Laura Conejero's sexually provocative dance took her audience on a journey from a drawing room, to a popular dance hall, a sleazy bar, and, finally, a circus, before she collapsed on the ground.[34] The image of Nora as a domesticated performing animal reaching the climax of her dance on all fours was reinforced by the animal imagery that filled this production: a reindeer with candelabra antlers stood in front of the Christmas tree; Dr Rank wore a polar-bear suit to the masked ball and left it on the ground like a hunting trophy; and Torvald returned drunk from the party dressed as a ring master, with a Moorish fez and a whip in his hand. All these excessive tarantellas from Europe and Africa combined into a single dance in Halina Reijn's performance as Nora at Toneelgroep Amsterdam.[35] In her black leotard, she stood like a nervous child in a dance class reluctant to start, pulled down her leotard in an awkward gesture, straightened her back, and assumed a pose to begin. The dance rapidly disintegrated into a series of disconnected movements: the thumb-sucking child, the cat with outstretched paws that snarls and roars, the hysterical screaming mouth, the limbs convulsed by fits, and the constant movement between aggression and submission.

However hard artists try to create transgressive bodies using altered states, they end up with a representation of the feminine that has committed symbolic suicide by being placed outside the social in a dissociated realm of pure corporeality. Trance, animality, madness, and hysteria are all bodily states that involve social negation. In Ibsen's tarantella, Nora still notices and talks with her childhood friend at the transgressive climax of her dance, but she is silenced by adaptations that place her in an altered state of consciousness. There are common physical elements in many of the excessive tarantellas: the arms and legs twitch or spasm as if in an epileptic

Fig. 5.4 (**a**) Arachne in Gustave Doré's illustration for Dante's *Purgatorio* of the Divine Comedy series (Source: Wikipedia). (**b**) Wine Dierickx (Nora), tg STAN, Portugal, 2012 (Source: Ann Selhorst)

fit, and in recent European productions Noras writhe with sexually explicit gestures. It is remarkable to compare these movements with the photographs taken in 1878 at the Salpêtrière Hospital in Paris as documentation of patients with hysteria. One of the classic poses is the hysterical arch, an intense muscular contraction of the whole body resulting in immobility and paralysis of the limbs; this hysterical arch in motion rather than paralysis is a popular trope in the performance of Nora's dance in the twenty-first century. This arch mirrors the images of spider women, the most famous of which is the Arachné in Gustave Doré's illustration for Dante's *Purgatorio* in his Divine Comedy series, which was published in 1868 and ran to 200 editions (Fig. 5.4a; Dante Alighieri and Doré 1868).[36] That these images from the nineteenth century should be attached retrospectively to a canonical play written within the same decade is a possibility, but no other visual element in these adaptations would suggest this interpretative strategy. A more depressing explanation is that the fear of imaginary spider women and the physical symptoms used to diagnose a nineteenth-century medical invention have had a deep impact on theatrical representations of transgressive female bodies. To find images that exceed these representational conventions, we need to look at the next branch of the tarantella tree, which introduces other dancing bodies into the scene.

The Branch of Other Dancing Bodies

The ballroom spectacles and social dances that we have already encountered in the tarantella tree have reinforced gender divisions while minimising the disruptive potential of the female dancing body. In this *branch of other dancing bodies*, Ibsen's challenge to transgress accepted aesthetic conventions governing the representation of the female dancing body is expanded to contest entire representational systems governing the depiction of masculinity and femininity. There are other dancing bodies everywhere: homosexual bodies, cross-dressed bodies, female impersonators, drag queens, and male-to-female transsexual and transgendered bodies. There are no consistent meanings attached to these other dancing bodies, but they all critique interpersonal power relations, while challenging assumptions about sex, sexuality, gender, the family, desire, and theatrical representations of masculinity and femininity. In northern Europe, cross-dressing and gender reversals have provided the basis for adaptations; in East Asia, the long history of female impersonation in traditional theatre has been used in adaptations of *Et dukkehjem* to critique representations of gendered behaviour; in Latin cultures, the dance traditions change the role of Torvald in the scene; whereas in North America, a deliberate queering of the male body appears as early as the mid-1980s. It is necessary to situate these images within the wider context of their adaptations, because these bodies do not just appear to dance the tarantella.

In the Netherlands production by Toneelgroep ADODVS, *Een Poppenhuis* directed by Manon van Gelder, women played the male characters of Torvald, Dr Rank, and Krogstad, and men played Nora and Mrs Linde.[37] This doll home was inhabited by a successful career woman and her house husband, the couple were still called Nora and Torvald, but Ibsen's names were reversed.

Torvald, the house husband, was physically soft and Nora, the career woman, was physically dynamic. The dance sequence that substitutes for the tarantella involved all the characters. It began with the female Dr Hank/Rank dancing alone to an up-tempo song. She took the hand of the seated house husband and pulled him to his feet. They danced together using a traditional ballroom hold. Nora interrupted them to partner Torvald. As ballroom dancing requires women to follow the movements initiated by men, it was transgressive for Nora to insist on leading Torvald from her 'feminine position'. The dance almost dissolved into a fight when Torvald tried to throw Nora into a back bend, she broke away leaving him to resume dancing with Dr Hank, and they were joined by the male Hansen/Mrs Linde. Nora turned the music off. As the body language of Torvald gradually transformed over the course of the evening into a theatrical representation of assertive masculinity, the choreography of the tarantella held the implication that Torvald should claim his status as the dominant partner in the marriage.

Hålogaland Teater in Tromsø used a similar conceit of gender reversal to tell the story of a successful career woman and her house husband. This Norwegian company created two versions of the same production, with Nora and Torvald swapping roles on alternate nights to become Norvald and Tora.[38] In *Et annet dukkehjem*, the cross-gendered version, a new gaze was introduced into the tarantella dance as Rank was played as a homosexual character. His familiarity with the male Nora gave their relationship a sexual ambivalence; both characters were cross-dressed for the masquerade party, the bald Rank in a black evening dress with drop diamante earrings, the bearded Norvald in a black corset with a red *décolleté* neckline. In the production photographs of the two versions, when Nora danced Torvald directed, but when Norvald danced Rank's voyeuristic gaze was privileged (Fig. 5.5).

Cross-dressed women replaced these cross-dressed men in Sophie Reynolds's adaptation by the British company Theatre Delicatessen in 2011.[39] In this all-women version directed by Frances Loy, the audience were handed flowers or fake moustaches on arrival at the theatre and were made aware that they were entering a male-dominated world. The performance began with all the cast in corsets or silk shorts on a catwalk, 'striking attitudes that flicker between the suggestive and the maternal, accompanied by that now-laughably sexist sixties Bacharach song "Hey, Little Girl!"—"For wives should always be lovers, too/Run to his arms, the moment he comes home to you"' (Taylor 2011). The reviews were effusive in their praise for the actors playing the male characters, particularly that of the critic Raylene Robertson: 'The visual transformation

Fig. 5.5 Tobias Santelmann (Norvald) and Nils Johnson (Dr Rank), Hålogaland Teater, Tromsø, 2008 (Source: Hålogaland Teater)

from the women dressed in corsets, to these powerful male characters was astounding! Each actor captured their characters amazingly.' She was particularly impressed by 'Dr Rank gazing longingly at Nora', yet Robertson does not suggest that the production aimed to introduce a transgressive lesbian gaze into the tarantella rehearsal (Robertson 2011).

In East Asia, where the traditions of female impersonation in theatre and opera forms are so strong, cross-dressing takes on different meanings. In *Double Nora*, the Japanese production discussed in Chapter 4, the tarantella dance was performed by the Noh Nora. The physical and vocal mannerisms used by the female impersonators are encoded within the Noh tradition. In Japan there is an art to embodying gender, and historically the female impersonator on the stage and the traditional geisha who entertained her private clients shared their skills to perfect an aesthetic practice of performing femininity. By contrasting the ways in which gender is signified on the Noh and *Shingeki* stages, *Double Nora* drew attention to the artificiality of these representational systems. In China, an equivalent codification of gender was developed in the all-male forms of traditional opera that influences the early performances of Ibsen; the first production of *A Doll Home* was presented by an all-male cast in Shanghai in 1912 (He 2016). This cultural context produced the first performance of the tarantella by a transsexual Nora, the celebrated Chinese dancer Jin Xing. This dance version of Ibsen's play began as an experimental contemporary dance work in Norway choreographed by Un-Magritt Nordseth. It was later adapted to suit the performance style of Jin Xing and her company. Jin Xing has undergone sex reassignment surgery, but as she explains, 'for the Opera performance if you put a character, cross dressing for man play woman, woman play man—this is OK because people take as entertainment, but when you bring this up as a social issue, that's tough' (qtd in Branigan 2012).[40] The tarantella as performed by Jin Xing mixed the fluidity, flexibility, and grace associated with conventional representations of femininity in classical Western dance with the language of a manipulated puppet that could be traced to the 1870 French ballet *Coppélia*. As this was a dance adaptation, the tarantella rehearsal became a prelude to the spectacular scene of the Stenborg party. Jin Xing's Nora was mirrored throughout by the identically dressed chorus who acted as her *corps de ballet*. The confusion created by her performance with regard to audiences' reception of corporeal authenticity, biological determinism, and gender representation cannot be definitively resolved because it is so tied to the idiolects of individual spectators. On a semiotic level, this tarantella was based on a conservative interpretation of femininity and does little to challenge representational conventions of gender difference, but there is no doubt that Jin Xing has added a new perspective to the performance history of the tarantella rehearsal.

In Latin America, where European, Indigenous, and African traditions combine to create rich popular dance cultures, Torvalds have had a tendency to take over the tarantella. As early as 2001, the production in Rio de Janeiro directed by Aderbal Freire-Filho had Torvald providing a virtuoso display of the dance steps that Nora should perfect, but this was a technical demonstration devoid of any seductive or erotic content.[41] This was not the case with the remarkable tarantella rehearsal from the Teatro La Memoria production directed by Alfredo Castro in 2011.[42] Nora began the dance by marking the steps in a staccato sequence of half-realised movements; Torvald lost his temper, shouted at her, and took over the dance. He was played by a paunchy, balding, middle-aged actor costumed in an old-fashioned cardigan, tie, and grey trousers, but he beautifully embodied the full fluidity of movement that he required of his Nora with sensuous hip movements, and arms caressing his imaginary breasts. He sat down on the sofa to spread his legs and move his pelvis up and down in time with the music, all the while adopting a seductive gaze to his intended audience. There was nothing comical in this performance, it was a classic female dance from a film representation of a strip club, and it made the point that this set of movements was both designed and consumed by men. The image of a dancing Torvald was developed even further a year later in a second Chilean adaptation by Teatro La María entitled *Persiguiendo a Nora Helmer* (*Searching for Nora Helmer*).[43] Once again, Nora reproduced the dance steps in an alienated and mechanical fashion and Torvald demonstrated a more complex counter-rhythm for her to follow. He did not embody any female eroticism in the choreography, but he was dancing in a skirt and high-heeled shoes. To disentangle this image, it needs to be contextualised within the cross-dressing theme in the production. The director, Alexandra von Hummel, explains:

> We worked in 'transvestating' men, I'm not sure if transvestite is the correct concept [… and] dress men with women's clothes, managing to reveal the differences under one equal platform, a common floor. In fact, I think that a man looks so much more virile when he is dressed as a woman. It is like if the real masculine space appeared—although this is cultural as well, there are many spaces that are culturally masculine—but this appears very clearly. (von Hummel 2013)[44]

In the prologue the whole company was dressed identically in high heels, short skirts, and smart little business jackets. Nora was recognisable, but the other actors playing these look-a-like women reflected in their improvised dialogue the misogyny that von Hummel believes is deep within the Chilean patriarchal culture. As the actors slowly began to switch to the dialogue based on Ibsen's text, the men lost their wigs, jackets, false breasts, and handbags. Complex images emerged through these transformations that defined the male characters: Krogstad, at his most desperate, embodied an extraordinary image of symbolic castration as he sat on a stool in his high heels applying lipstick, with his short skirt exposing his naked, flaccid genitals. Dr Rank, leaning on his crutch, with his naturally long hair pulled back from his bearded face, in a short skirt and high heels, with red Christmas-tree tinsel around his neck, emerged as the most empathetic character on the stage. By the final act Torvald had resumed his conventional male clothing, the strong drum beat from the party music was heard off stage, and he danced alone for over a minute, a drunken sexual dance full of pelvic thrusts; this was his own tarantella. Nora watched his dancing body and suddenly moved towards him, seizing him in a passionate embrace, thus reversing the physical directions implied in Ibsen's text.

Historically, transvestism on the Chilean stage signified opposition to the brutal version of masculinity promoted by the Pinochet regime, but when Richard Newton created a trans-world for his adaptation of *A Doll's House* in Los Angeles, it carried a very different meaning.[45] In his tarantella scene the bodies were straight and gay, transsexual, transgender, and transvestite. As Newton explains, 'The Tarantella is one of four places where I stop the play for a musical or dance number. I have always loved the golden era of Hollywood musicals and Bollywood. The opportunity to insert a musical number into the action is a delight' (Newton 2012, 5). The production started life as a fringe show in the Los Angeles Festival in 1987. It was presented in a car park and the tarantella musical number was performed around five door frames, with Nora dressed as a fairy-tale princess and all the other characters, including Krogstad, in long black skirts, red sequin eye masks, and white hoodies. In this adaptation, Nora has saved her sexually unsatisfactory marriage by taking a lover. Her husband has taken over the running of a local hospital, and as part of an AIDS awareness campaign decides that both he and Nora will undertake voluntary testing. Nora believes that she is HIV positive. Nora's childhood friend Harry (Mrs Linde) has become Harriet; Tom's childhood acquaintance (Krogstad), after winning the famous Miss Barstow beauty queen competition, has changed her sex to male and appears cross-dressed in a beauty pageant outfit. 'Oddly, balance is maintained', suggests Newton; 'whereas Harry and Miss Barstow were unable to be together when they were younger, Harriet and The Former Miss Barstow are on their way to making a life together' (2012, 2). In the musical number that substituted for the tarantella rehearsal, both Harriet/Mrs Linde and The Former Miss Barstow/Krogstad stood in doorways playing tambourines. Tom/Torvald also stood in a doorway staring angrily, watching Nora as she danced with Dr Dick/Dr Rank. Eventually he interrupted the dance, picked Nora up in his arms, and exited. While Newton's desire to create a Bollywood number out of the scene may appear merely iconoclastic, the adaptation was his response to the trauma of the AIDS plague in the mid-1980s:

> I wanted to do something not so much about living or dying with AIDS, but about the community's and society's judgements and morality regarding sex, sexually transmitted diseases, sexual orientation and identity. Ibsen's *A Doll's House* popped up from the back of my mind. The new wrinkles and quirks in the characters are there to update the play to the relationships of family, friends and community in the mid-eighties. Of course it helps if you lived in West Hollywood or the Castro in San Francisco. (Newton 2009)

In 1987, Newton's introduction of a trans-world into *Et dukkehjem* was iconoclastic; thirty years later this adaptation is just one of the images in the *branch of other dancing bodies* that undermines heteronormativity. The transgressive meanings in these images are being carried by cross-dressed and transgendered Torvalds, Ranks, Krogstads, and Mrs Lindes, together with male performing bodies playing Nora. However, they are not being carried by the female performing bodies playing Nora; even Jin Xing, who has transgressed these boundaries in her life, danced the tarantella without crossing them on the stage. In this branch of the tree it is the male performing bodies that are destabilising representational constraints.

The Branch of Dolls

The doll metaphor is a popular trope in adaptations of *Et dukkehjem*, and puppet strings, miniature furniture, and doll's houses are frequently used in set designs. The images in this final branch take the metaphor further by turning characters into doll automatons that replicate clichéd gestures signifying masculinity and femininity. The shift in the audience's relationship with Nora from objectified body to empathetic subject that is implied in

Ibsen's tarantella becomes irrelevant here, because there are no subjective interiorities to characters in a theatre that has rejected psychological realism: Nora's only manifestation is as an artificial object, a representational conceit. The Theater Oberhausen tarantella rehearsal was literally a two-dimensional world (Fig. 5.6). Nora was a child sex doll trapped in the arms of three ghoulish men and an evil lesbian. The female characters fell easily into archetypical clichés, but the ghoul surface sat like the make-up on the individuated male characters. To find a doll Nora who severs her representational chains, we turn to the first image in this branch, which comes from the Mabou Mines adaptation.[46] Here the tarantella was a wild dance with strobe lighting that included all the characters and the stagehands, but again this adaptation was not concerned with exploring the interiority of the doll Nora, and it was the transformation from doll automaton to new female performing body in the final moments of this performance that was transgressive. Since this image of Nora suggested that by returning to the origins of the female nude in Western art new representational possibilities for the female body might be envisaged, we take a moment to consider her construction.

Actors who are less than four-feet-six-inches tall played all the male characters in Lee Breuer's *Dollhouse*. From the moment they entered the stage, the absurdity of a power relation based on the notion of male strength and female frailty was exposed. The false consciousness of the female characters was visualised metaphorically by the efforts of female actors, who were of average height, to fit into the miniature furniture that had been scaled to the bodies of the small men. As Nora recognised her strength in the final scene, she grew ever taller until she was standing level with the theatre boxes far above Torvald. Her new body was born, a naked body capable of a different register of being and desire. The actor Maude Mitchell described the process that resulted in this new body for Nora:

> Initially I just removed the wig—but quickly I felt that it wasn't enough, that the 'prison' of the corset needed to go too, so I would fight my way out of the corset and bodice after removing the wig—underneath I wore an organza chemise. Lee and I agreed that removing the corset but still wearing the chemise didn't seem quite right—so I would take off the wig and then the bodice and corset—when I did that inevitably half the time my skirt would fall off so after a while it just got incorporated as it seemed odd standing there partly clothed. It felt better jettisoning all the 'doll trappings.'

Fig. 5.6 From left Nora Buzalka (Mrs Linde), Torsten Bauer (Torvald), Henry Meyer (Dr Rank), and Jürgen Sarkiss (Krogstad) holding Manja Kuhl (Nora), Theater Oberhausen, 2010 (Source: Theater Oberhausen)

> I'm not sure when we changed the order of the disrobing—I think it just seemed to us that the undressing didn't 'stop' at taking off the wig and we were interested in playing with a moment of total objectification and then flipping it. 'Venus on the half-shell deconstructed.'
>
> That moment for me has always been the least 'naked' in the piece, I feel very pure, and clean and free—it makes perfect sense to me that if Nora wants to seek her full humanity she has to rid herself of everything and begin anew. (Mitchell 2009)

The 'flipping' as described by Mitchell answered the metatheatrical challenge embedded in Ibsen's tarantella rehearsal. Her naked body signified a new beginning for Nora, and a new representational beginning for the female body as nude.

Conclusion

Our comparative study of dramaturgical structures uncovered a force of representational constraint in the depiction of *Et dukkehjem*'s female characters; in this chapter we have continued to explore this force by creating patterns from the images of one theatrical moment in multiple adaptations. Although the tarantella rehearsal in Ibsen's play-script has a playing time of a little over five minutes, it can have a major impact on an audience's understanding of the narrative. If Nora slips into madness at the end of the tarantella, how can we give credence to her rational arguments in the final scene? If she is dressed as Marilyn Monroe, how do we see beneath the surface of this icon? If the tarantella dance is cut to preserve Nora's modesty and her body loses all its flirtatious and seductive qualities, how do we view the power relationship in the Helmer household? If the tarantella rehearsal scene becomes an exploration of challenges to heteronormativity represented by male performing bodies playing Torvald, Rank, and Krogstad, what interest do we have in Nora's crisis? All these questions have been provoked by the interpretative strategies visualised in the tarantella tree, but our major interest has not been to critique the efficacy of these artistic approaches; rather, it has been to uncover the forces limiting creative diversity within *Et dukkehjem*.

The patterns created in the branches and sub-branches of the tree are produced by a wide variety of cultural, aesthetic, and ideological forces that have impacts on theatrical and cinematic representation. They suggest that in many cultures breaking conventions governing the representation of the female body is extremely complex and hazardous. The dominant performance tradition reflected in the tree trunk sought to increase the aesthetic value of *Et dukkehjem* and as a consequence reinforced socially acceptable and aesthetically desirable depictions of the female performing body. The long history of substitutions to the scene seems to be connected to intractable beliefs that the female dancing body is somehow tied to prostitution. These associations have had a long history in Judeo-Christian and Islamic cultures, but they are more widespread than 'the peoples of the book'. That the female body is offered as a spectacle for consumption in many cultures was confirmed by the interpretative strategies that manipulated the voyeurism of spectators to reaffirm, make conscious, or critique their visual pleasure. While the patterns from the branches of substitution and voyeurism reflect the prohibitions and pleasures tied to representations of the female dancing body, the branches of transgression and other dancing bodies exposed the hegemonic strengths of these conventions. What we found surprising was the repetition with which the transgressive body of Nora was depicted using altered states of consciousness involving some form of symbolic suicide through madness, ecstasy, and trance. Equally significant were the lack of transgressive Noras depicted by female performers in the *branch of other dancing bodies*. It was only in the final *branch of dolls* that we encountered an image critiquing the history of the female body in Western art.

Artists tackling the tarantella rehearsal are faced with a self-reflexive challenge: to reproduce and then break free of the conventions they use to represent the aesthetically desirable female performing body in their cultures. The difficulties that artists have had in answering this challenge point to the strengths of the representational conventions governing global depictions of women. Can this tell us anything about the success of *Et dukkehjem*? Only that Ibsen's challenge is a theatrical puzzle still waiting to be solved.

Notes

1. The critical literature on the tarantella rehearsal is ubiquitous. The dance has been variously characterised as a metaphor of life, death, masquerade, and carnival. It has been linked to Dionysian rites, the *entr'acte* of melodrama, and aesthetic modernism. Other accounts suggest that Ibsen saw a tourist performance in Italy; Ibsen knew an expert on the tarantella and tarantism; Betty Hennings danced the tarantella in Bournonville's ballet; Lady Hamilton made the dance popular at her evening soirees; and so on. See Østerud (1997, 2004, 2005) and Wicklund (2003). For a survey of the critical literature on the scene, see Colella (2007).

2. His responsibilities included maintaining detailed production books for the remounting of successful performances and his records for fifty-three productions include plans for the configurations of stage space, movement of characters, and the arrangement of tableaux. See Gjervan (2010).
3. Joan Riviere defined masquerade as an artificial femininity used to ward off reprisals for the appropriation of male power: 'Womanliness therefore could be assumed and worn as a mask, both to hide the possession of masculinity and to avert the reprisals expected if she was found to possess it' (1929, 308). When Nora dances the tarantella, she is delaying discovery of a secret that has allowed her to experience the thrill of being 'almost' like a man; her dance is thus a classic use of masquerade.
4. Ibsen's earlier draft is available within Archer (1917).
5. '*Et dukkehjem*'. 1879. Directed by H.P. Holst. Performed by Betty Hennings as Nora. Det Kongelige Teater, Copenhagen, Denmark. December 21. *IbsenStage*, Event 75660. https://ibsenstage.hf.uio.no/pages/event/75660. '*Et dukkehjem*'. 1936. Directed by Halfdan Christensen. Performed by Tore Segelcke as Nora. Nationaltheatret, Johanne Dybwads Plass 1, Oslo, Norway. October 13. *IbsenStage*, Event 75536. https://ibsenstage.hf.uio.no/pages/event/75536. 'Ji Shuping'. *IbsenStage*, Contributor 436834. https://ibsenstage.hf.uio.no/pages/contributor/436834. '*Nora*'. 1956. Directed Wu Xue. Performed by Ji Shuping as Nora. Beijing Dongdan Theatre, Beijing, China. July 28. *IbsenStage*, Event 76209. https://ibsenstage.hf.uio.no/pages/event/76209. '*A Doll's House*'. 2002. Directed by Robyn Nevin. Performed by Miranda Otto as Nora. The Wharf 1 Theatre, Pier 4/5, Hickson Road, Walsh Bay, Sydney, Australia. March 6. *IbsenStage*, Event 76667. https://ibsenstage.hf.uio.no/pages/event/76667.
6. 'Vera F. Komissarzhevskaya'. *IbsenStage*, Contributor 449852. https://ibsenstage.hf.uio.no/pages/contributor/449852. 'Eleonora Duse'. *IbsenStage*, Contributor 428954. https://ibsenstage.hf.uio.no/pages/contributor/428954.
7. He had created a *commedia* character known as Giacometto, and although Duse never saw him perform, his red velvet waistcoat was one of her most cherished possessions.
8. '*Nora Helmer*'. 1974. Directed by Rainer Werner Fassbinder. Performed by Margit Carstensen as Nora. Telefilm Saar/Saarländischer Rundfunk. February 3. Video recording. *IbsenStage*, Event 76104. https://ibsenstage.hf.uio.no/pages/event/76104.
9. '*Putul Khela*'. 1958. Directed by Sambhu Mitra. Performed by Tripti Mitra as Nora. Bohurupee, Calcutta, India. January 10. *IbsenStage*, Event 76759. https://ibsenstage.hf.uio.no/pages/event/76759. This production holds a major place in the post-colonial history of the play; it was kept in the company repertoire for twenty years. Tripti Mitra, Sambhu's wife, played Nora in the original production and created a new version in Hindi in 1981; their daughter, Saoli Mitra, also performed Nora in her own production in 2002.

10. Tagore wrote about this poem in 1934, noting that 'in pain and peril, rebellion and revolution, human beings wish to realise themselves with an intensity of emotion, shaking off the torpor of the unmanifested' (2001, 301). The poem was translated by Tapati Gupta for this publication.
11. Saranya Mukhopadhyay's unpublished translation of *Putul Khela* by Sambhu Mitra was commissioned for this publication.
12. From *Gianni Schicchi*, the last part of *Il trittico* (Puccini 1918). '*A Doll's House*'. 2009. Directed by Msgun Zerai. Performed by Birikti Woldeselassie as Nora. Cinema Asmara, Asmara, Eritrea. December 5. *IbsenStage*, Event 85621. https://ibsenstage.hf.uio.no/pages/event/85621.
13. '*Sara*'. 1993. Directed by Dariush Mehrjui. Performed by Niki Karimi as Sara. H. Seifi and D. Mehrjui. Farabi Cinema Foundation, Tehran, Iran. Film. *IbsenStage*, Event 75342. https://ibsenstage.hf.uio.no/pages/event/75342.
14. At the time the film was made, theatre as an art form was virtually banned in Iran. Ironically, Mehrjui is credited with persuading Ayatollah Khomeini that cinema should not share the same fate. He argued that film was important to the cultural development of the Islamic Republic. The mullahs accepted this view and devised a pre- and post-production censorship system that could control national cinema.
15. '*Nora*'. 2002. Directed by Gerrit Timmers. Performed by Saadia Ladib. Onafhankelijk Toneel Rotterdam, at Theater Kikker, Ganzenmarkt 14, Utrecht, Netherlands. April 17. *IbsenStage*, Event 76049. https://ibsenstage.hf.uio.no/pages/event/76049.
16. '*A Doll's House*'. 2006. Directed by Gamal Yakout. Performed by Eman Emam. Cultural Palaces' Sidi Gaber Creativity Centre, Alexandria, Egypt. June 24. *IbsenStage*, Event 91394. https://ibsenstage.hf.uio.no/pages/event/91394; '*Putuler Itikatha*'. 2001. Directed by Kamaluddin Nilu. Performed by Sheuly Akhter, Shipra Das, Tahmina Sharif, and Sabina Sultana as Nora. Shawkat Osman Memorial Auditorium Public Library, Dhaka, Bangladesh. April 27. *IbsenStage*, Event 76947. https://ibsenstage.hf.uio.no/pages/event/76947.
17. '*Gurrya ka Ghar*'. 2006. Directed by Anwer Jafri. Tehrik-e-Niswan, Alhamra Hall No. 2, The Mall, Lahore, Pakistan. April 23. *IbsenStage*, Event 77324. https://ibsenstage.hf.uio.no/pages/event/77324. Anwer Jafri, the adaptor and director, explains his decision to use this metatheatrical device as a reflection of the company's aesthetic: 'our approach to theatre is always minimal and we wanted to create a realistic play without constructing a set' (Jafri 2009).
18. We are indebted to Dr Mona Khedr for explaining that 'no direct ban on representation can be detected in the Qur'an, the first and principal source of Islamic legislation, except in the cases where its practice relates to idolatry and polytheism' (Khedr 2012). In her doctoral thesis on Islamic

identity in contemporary theatre, she draws on Muhammad Mandur's argument that performing a character in a play is merely an act of imitation that does not challenge God's absolute power of creation, and that theatre involves inventiveness and creativity, human attributes that are encouraged within the Qur'an (qtd in Khedr 2010).

19. '*Nora*'. 2014. Directed by Saša Božić. Performed by Daria Lorenci as Nora. Hrvatsko Narodno Kazalište U Zagrebu (Croatian National Theatre in Zagreb), Trg Maršala Tita 15, Zagreb, Croatia. May 9. *IbsenStage*, Event 90946. https://ibsenstage.hf.uio.no/pages/event/90946.
20. '*A Doll's House*'. 1973. Directed by Patrick Garland. Performed by Claire Bloom as Nora. Elkins Productions, Freeward Films, UK. Film. *IbsenStage*, Event 75341. https://ibsenstage.hf.uio.no/pages/event/75341. Available at National Library of Norway. 2015. Accessed July 31. ibsen.nb.no/id/6230.0. '*A Doll's House*'. 1973. Directed by Joseph Losey. Performed by Jane Fonda as Nora. World Film Services, Les Films la Boétie. Film. *IbsenStage*, Event 75340. https://ibsenstage.hf.uio.no/pages/event/75340. Available at National Library of Norway. 2015. Accessed July 31. ibsen.nb.no/id/6206.0. See also 'Claire Bloom'. *IbsenStage*, Contributor 426940. https://ibsenstage.hf.uio.no/pages/contributor/426940.
21. But the adaptation left her powerless to express the complexities of the character of Nora or the mixed emotions that lead to the tarantella rehearsal. Fonda was explicit in her criticism of the production: 'All the men involved decided that what Ibsen said about women didn't apply anymore. […] I found I had to become Nora with Losey […] bat my eyelashes, and make it seem as though it was his idea. Every day I realized how valid the play was, as Ibsen's whole thesis was being acted out' (qtd in Schanke 1988, 263).
22. '*Nora*'. 2002. Directed by Thomas Ostermeier. Performed by Anne Tismer as Nora. Schaubühne am Lehniner Platz, Kurfürstendamm 153, Berlin, Germany. November 26. *IbsenStage*, Event 76838. https://ibsenstage.hf.uio.no/pages/event/76838.
23. 'Teth Maiello'. *IbsenStage*, Contributor 438315. https://ibsenstage.hf.uio.no/pages/contributor/438315. '*Nossa casa de boneca*'. 2005. Directed by José Fernando Peixoto de Azevedo. Performed by Teth Maiello as Nora. Teatro de Narradores, Teatro Fábrica, Rua Consolação, 1623–Consolação, São Paulo, Brazil. October 22. *IbsenStage*, Event 77617. https://ibsenstage.hf.uio.no/pages/event/77617.
24. '*Nhà Búp Bê*'. 2006. Directed by Le Hung. Performed by Lê Khanh as Nora. Nhà Hát Tuổi Trẻ, Hanoi, Vietnam. November 1. *IbsenStage*, Event 77020. https://ibsenstage.hf.uio.no/pages/event/77020.
25. 'Lê Khanh'. *IbsenStage*, Contributor 430621. https://ibsenstage.hf.uio.no/pages/contributor/430621.

26. 'Marie Louise Wille'. *IbsenStage*, Contributor 434952. https://ibsenstage.hf.uio.no/pages/contributor/434952. '*Nora*'. 2005. Directed by Katrine Wiedermann. Performed by Marie Louise Wille as Nora. Betty Nansen Teatret, Frederiksberg, Denmark. September 24. *IbsenStage*, Event 76280. https://ibsenstage.hf.uio.no/pages/event/76280.
27. '*Nora. Ein Puppenheim*'. 2002. Directed by Katharina Rupp. Performed by Julia Urban as Nora. Salzburger Landestheater, Kammerspiele, Salzburg, Austria. November 17. *IbsenStage*, Event 77294. https://ibsenstage.hf.uio.no/pages/event/77294.
28. '*Nora*'. 2008. Directed by Katharina Rupp. Performed by Margit Maria Bauer as Nora. Stadttheater Solothurn, Theatergasse 18, Solothurn, Switzerland. January 17. *IbsenStage*, Event 76550. https://ibsenstage.hf.uio.no/pages/event/76550.
29. These debates were triggered by Laura Mulvey's article of generational significance (1975); for this and other major articles on feminism and film theory, see Penley (1998).
30. '*Nukkekoti*'. 2002. Directed by Katarina Lahti. Performed by Minttu Mustakallio as Nora. Suomen Kansallisteatteri, 1 Läntinen Teatterikuja, Helsinki, Finland. March 13. *IbsenStage*, Event 76963. https://ibsenstage.hf.uio.no/pages/event/76963.
31. '*Breaking the Pot*'. 2006. Directed by Melissa Eveleigh. Performed by Mbumba Mbewe as Nora. Nanzikambe Theatre, French Cultural Centre, Blantyre, Malawi. April 17. *IbsenStage*, Event 75839. https://ibsenstage.hf.uio.no/pages/event/75839.
32. 'Susanne Wolff'. *IbsenStage*, Contributor 434293. https://ibsenstage.hf.uio.no/pages/contributor/434293. '*Nora*'. 2002. Directed by Stephan Kimmig. Performed by Susanne Wolff as Nora. Thalia-Theater, Hamburg, Germany. September 14. *IbsenStage*, Event 76628. https://ibsenstage.hf.uio.no/pages/event/76628.
33. 'Wine Dierickx'. *IbsenStage*, Contributor 456806. https://ibsenstage.hf.uio.no/pages/contributor/456806. '*Nora*'. 2012. Directed by Jolente De Keersmaeker, Wine Dierickx, Tiago Rodrigues, and Frank Vercruyssen. Performed by Wine Dierickx as Nora. Tg STAN, Teatro Maria Matos, Lisbon, Portugal. July 6. *IbsenStage*, Event 83974. https://ibsenstage.hf.uio.no/pages/event/83974. The ethos of this company is to strip away unnecessary theatrical illusions and concentrate on the characters' interrelationships. The production has the feel of a rehearsal room, with the off-stage actors sitting watching the on-stage action. The production has toured to Greece, Japan, the Netherlands, Norway, Poland, and Portugal.
34. 'Laura Conejero'. *IbsenStage*, Contributor 428649. https://ibsenstage.hf.uio.no/pages/contributor/428640. '*Casa de nines*'. 2004. Directed by Rafel Duran. Performed by Laura Conejero as Nora. Teatre Nacional De

Catalunya, Barcelona, Spain. February 12. *IbsenStage*, Event 77014. https://ibsenstage.hf.uio.no/pages/event/77014.

35. 'Halina Reijn'. *IbsenStage*, Contributor 466121. https://ibsenstage.hf.uio.no/pages/contributor/466121. '*Nora*'. 2012. Directed by Thibaud Delpeut. Performed by Halina Reijn as Nora. Toneelgroep Amsterdam, Stadsschouwburg Amsterdam, Leidseplein 26, Amsterdam, Netherlands. November 6. *IbsenStage*, Event 85785. https://ibsenstage.hf.uio.no/pages/event/85785.
36. This extreme emotional state is captured in a famous sculpture by Louise Bourgeois; it is also reflected in images of women's bodies with legs of spiders that are part of the tarantism tradition.
37. '*Een Poppenhuis*'. 2009. Directed by Manon van Gelder. Performed by Marten van der Meijden as Torvald/Nora. Toneelgroep Adodvs, Drang Studio, Schelpkade 45 te Den Haag, Netherlands. February 12. *IbsenStage*, Event 90958. https://ibsenstage.hf.uio.no/pages/event/90958.
38. '*Et dukkehjem*'. 2008. Directed by Tyra Tønnessen. Performed by Marte Germaine Christensen as Nora. Hålogaland Teater, Teaterplassen 1, Tromsø, Norway. April 16. *IbsenStage*, Event 76285. https://ibsenstage.hf.uio.no/pages/event/76285; '*Et annet dukkehjem*'. 2008. Directed by Tyra Tønnessen. Performed by Tobias Santelmann as Norvald. Hålogaland Teater, Teaterplassen 1, Tromsø, Norway. April 17. *IbsenStage*, Event 82302. https://ibsenstage.hf.uio.no/pages/event/82302.
39. '*A Doll's House*'. 2011. Directed by Frances Loy. Performed by Polly Eachus as Nora. Theatre Delicatessen, 35 Marylebone High Street, London, UK. January 5. *IbsenStage*, Event 77577. https://ibsenstage.hf.uio.no/pages/event/77577.
40. '*Nuola (Wan'ou Zhi Jia)*'. 2010. Directed by Un-Magritt Nordseth. Performed by Liu Minzi, Dai Shaoting, Xie Xin, Jin Xing, Sun Zhuzhen, and Talisi as Nora. No. 22 Wangfujing Street, Dongcheng District, Beijing, China. October 22. *IbsenStage*, Event 77765. http://ibsenstage.hf.uio.no/pages/event/77765.
41. '*Casa de Boneca*'. 2001. Directed by Aderbal Freire-Filho. Performed by Ana Paula Arósio as Nora. Teatro Leblon, R. Conde Bernadotte, Rio De Janeiro, Brazil. October 16. *IbsenStage*, Event 77320. https://ibsenstage.hf.uio.no/pages/event/77320.
42. '*Casa de Muñecas*'. 2011. Directed by Alfredo Castro. Performed by Amparo Noguera as Nora. Teatro la Memoria, Santiago, Chile. November 3. *IbsenStage*, Event 85677. https://ibsenstage.hf.uio.no/pages/event/85677.
43. '*Persiguiendo a Nora Helmer*'. 2012. Directed by Alexandra von Hummel. Performed by Tamara Acosta as Nora. Teatro La María, Centro Cultural Gabriela Mistral, Sala N1, Santiago, Chile. June 15. *IbsenStage*, Event 85747. https://ibsenstage.hf.uio.no/pages/event/85747.
44. This online interview was translated by Gabriela Espinosa for this publication.

45. '*The Former Miss Barstow with Every Tom, Dick and Harry in a doll's house*'. 1987. Directed by Richard Newton. Performed by Nancye Ferguson. 315 South Hewitt Street, Los Angeles, California, USA. September 19. *IbsenStage*, Event 85351. https://ibsenstage.hf.uio.no/pages/event/85351. See also '*The Former Miss Barstow*' (2015).
46. This production has been the site of significant critical debate, see Helland (2015); Carlson (2011); Taucar (2011). '*Mabou Mines Dollhouse—From Henrik Ibsen's* A Doll's House *with snippets of* The Vikings of Helgeland'. 2003. Directed by Lee Breuer. Performed by Maude Mitchell. Mabou Mines, St Ann's Warehouse, 38 Water Street, Brooklyn, New York, USA. November 7. *IbsenStage*, Event 75826. https://ibsenstage.hf.uio.no/pages/event/75826.

Conclusion

Following our distant reading of the production history of Ibsen's play, are we any closer to understanding the global success of *Et dukkehjem*? Have new ways of looking produced fresh answers to this question?

The premise underlying this study has been that patterns in our distant visions are shaped by forces constraining the artistic diversity and complexity of *Et dukkehjem*, and our analyses have concentrated on the ways in which artists (and their audiences) comply with, contest, and oppose these forces. By following this premise and examining forces at work in the cultural transmission and adaptation of *Et dukkehjem*, we have arrived at new insights into the global success of Ibsen's play.

In Part I, we concentrated on forces that have encouraged artists to produce and adapt *Et dukkehjem*, thereby increasing the value of the play as a 'stake in the game', while simultaneously limiting the diversity of the repertoire of world theatre. The European women's movements of the late nineteenth and early twentieth centuries were social forces that created a sympathetic context for the first global dissemination of the play, as Chapter 2 outlined. These movements changed the personal and professional expectations of women and created the conditions necessary for the emergence of actress-managers as important figures in global commercial theatre markets. A significant number of these artists were attracted to *Et dukkehjem* and Nora became a major role in their personal repertoires, as well as a positive fictional character to justify their unconventional life

J. Holledge et al., *A Global Doll's House*, Palgrave Studies in Performance and Technology, DOI 10.1057/978-1-137-43899-7

choices. These early Noras marketed the play to audiences interested in contemporary debates about changes in the social organisation of gender. The first global transmission of *Et dukkehjem* managed by these actresses has been largely overlooked; Ibsen's early success has been attributed to his connections with the late nineteenth-century avant-garde of European theatre. Although there have been numerous accounts of early Ibsen productions outside of Europe, they have been framed as isolated studies. By mapping major touring productions across five continents, we have been able to connect these discrete histories of the play in different theatre cultures, to highlight the importance of the influence of the actress-managers in the world theatre markets, and to make the connection between the European women's rights movements and the first global cultural transmission of *Et dukkehjem*.

In Chapter 3, we considered the combined force of the Norwegian institutions that have 'peddled' the play. We uncovered the beginnings of an *Et dukkehjem* performance tradition in the Nordic region, and followed its consolidation in Norway and subsequent international dissemination. We traced artistic networks linking Nordic productions of *Et dukkehjem* from the Copenhagen premiere of 1879 to the present day, and explored their connections with Norwegian theatrical families. The existence of these networks highlights the importance of the rehearsal room as a site for transmission of the accumulated knowledge of generations regarding the performance of this canonical work. Finally, by following the funding trail associated with festivals, awards, and cultural aid, we concluded that Norway had become the engine driving the global distribution and production of the play in the twenty-first century.

In Part II, we traced the forces at work inside the creative process producing *Et dukkehjem*. The comparison of dramaturgical structures, character manipulations, and narrative substitutions alerted us to a range of social and aesthetic forces that have general applicability to theatrical adaptation, in particular constraints of time and place. We found that the materiality of performance spaces influenced the choice of genres in adaptations, and that cultural contestations were being played out in the parallel temporal structures of narrative time and performance time. We also charted the impact of cultural forces on the representation of social organisation and the depiction of symbolic power structures. We were surprised by the flexibility with which the dramaturgical structure of *Et dukkehjem* could be moulded to represent social dynamics in so many cultural contexts. It suggested that the skeletal structure of hierarchical relations of power together with horizontal relations between social groups could be used to reflect a wide variety of social models. This inherent malleability may be a contributing factor to the success of *Et dukkehjem*, but to establish whether this is the case will require comparative studies of other global dramas.

The analysis of dramaturgical structures highlighted a strong force that was specific to *Et dukkehjem*, concerning the representation of the female characters in multiple cultures. It was to be expected that the play would trigger taboos over representations of motherhood and the breaking of the mother–child dyad, particularly given Ibsen's own 'barbaric violence to the play' in which Nora looks at her children and says: 'Oh, this is a sin against myself; but I cannot forsake them. (*half sinks down by the door*)' (Ibsen 1880c, 27). Less expected were the widespread negative connotations associated with representations of a female agency dependent on sexual manipulation, which led to these aspects in Ibsen's characters being cut. We were intrigued by the fact that Ibsen's female characters had such a long history as contested sites in the adaptation process. Did this have any bearing on the success of the play? Did the challenge of combatting constraints over the depiction of female characters hold an attraction for adaptors? We looked in more detail at how these representational forces were being negotiated or deliberately confronted by artists.

The metatheatrical possibilities embedded in the tarantella rehearsal, the focus of Chapter 5, made this scene the obvious choice for an in-depth comparative study into constraints governing representations of Ibsen's character of Nora. We selected images of the scene from 150 adaptations and arranged them in a tree structure; the branches and sub-branches reflected different interpretative strategies shaped through cultural, aesthetic, and ideological forces. We found that taboos over the exhibition of the female performing body were present in a range of cultures, all stemming from an implied association between female display and prostitution. Where taboos over the display of the female body were not enforced, the obligation to provide visual pleasure for audiences was difficult to escape. This insistence that the female performing body please the eye was indulged, critiqued, and overdetermined in the adaptations. Yet when artists attempted to break through this constraint and create a transgressive female body, their interpretations relied on physical displays of madness, regression, or altered states of consciousness. When other dancing bodies began to rehearse the tarantella, the transgressive potential of the scene was more readily achieved. Viewed at a distance, the tree with all its branches highlights the limitations imposed on female performing bodies in the representational systems of many cultures. For artists to break through these limitations was problematic, but the challenge to do so may have had some bearing on the numbers of artists selecting *Et dukkehjem* for adaptation.

The analytical model we have developed to interrogate 3787 records of productions of a single play has yielded significant results. We have identified major forces at work in *Et dukkehjem* that have contributed to its success as a world drama: social movements and national interests have attached commercial and cultural value to Ibsen's play and contributed to its worldwide distribution; the signifying system has proved sufficiently flexible to adopt multiple forms through the dynamic interactions between ever-increasing artistic innovation and constraints imposed by culturally diverse representational systems. This summarises our research findings, but there are many more patterns in the distant visions of *Et dukkehjem* that need to be investigated. For this reason, readers are invited to conduct their own interpretations of the *Et dukkehjem* data set at IbsenStage: https://ibsenstage.hf.uio.no/pages/project/100.

Distant Visions as a Methodology

Applying the McShea and Brandon model of evolution to *Et dukkehjem* enabled us to comprehend the production history of the play. Rather than searching for elusive memes replicating themselves within the creative process, or explaining the diversity of adaptation through metaphors of natural selection, we argued that increasing diversity is the background condition of *Et dukkehjem* and therefore needs no explanation. Our efforts have been directed towards investigating the forces of constraint responsible for promoting the play within global theatre markets, and the forces of representational constraint at work in the adaptation process. Patterns in the distant visions defined the direction of this research. Previous studies of the play have selected sites for close analysis according to regional, temporal, or aesthetic criteria. We let the patterns determine the selection of sites and found that they were so varied that our close analyses relied on different traditions of theatre research: biography and artist interviews, close readings of performances, analyses of commercial touring and subsidised festival circuits, tracing theatrical families and artistic networks, studies of the performing body and gestural transmission, processes of adaptation, and the gathering and analysing of visual traces. Beyond our approaches to reading *Et dukkehjem* 'up close', an overarching visual logic of looking from a distance ordered the chapters. We began at the point furthest away in time and space, viewing the global trajectories of artists and productions of the play in the late nineteenth century; then focused on the Nordic region, still travelling through time to examine the changing relationship between *Et dukkehjem* and the nation state of Norway; a perspective shift took us inside the adaptation process where patterns in a sample of dramaturgical structures were compared with other performances from the production history of the play; and finally we isolated a single moment from Ibsen's play-script to look at a range of interpretative strategies used by artists in the staging of the tarantella rehearsal to negotiate representational constraints over depictions of sexuality and gender.

Perhaps one of the most startling realisations to emerge from this research methodology is its tendency to highlight contradictions. Not only has the evidence in each chapter contradicted assumptions about the play and its production history, the research findings also contain internal contradictions. The analysis of the Nordic network of artists uncovered a dominant performance tradition of interpreting *Et dukkehjem*, but when the last custodians of that tradition were interviewed, they were unaware of this theatrical heritage. The character of Nora is synonymous with *Et dukkehjem*, but adaptations have had a strong tendency to reduce the agency of this character within the dramatic action. The actress-managers who toured the world with *Et dukkehjem* were influential artists and business women, but their on-stage success as Nora was not matched by an equivalent off-stage success in combining a career with a marriage of equality and motherhood. We can only assume that this tendency towards internal contradiction is a product of letting the patterns in the distant visions determine the sites for close analysis rather than selecting them according to pre-existing criteria.

Maps and artistic networks were used to trace the cultural transmission of *Et dukkehjem*, and visual trees, character networks, and graphs were used to compare adaptations. The maps of *Et dukkehjem* provoked numerous questions; it was an unusual touring pattern of performances in Malawi that triggered our research into Norwegian soft diplomacy. Although we concentrated on touring productions, there are many more patterns to explore in the *Et dukkehjem* maps. We touched on the connections between post-colonial productions and the first global wave of touring from Europe, but more production records need to be gathered before this pattern will have the detail necessary for an in-depth analysis. Further work within Ibsen scholarship will involve comparative analyses on cultural transmission across the whole of the Ibsen repertoire. Doctoral research has begun on analysing both the early German and North American reception of all Ibsen's plays.

The greatest revelations regarding theatre historiography came from the network analyses that traced artistic links between productions. We were astounded to find such an extraordinary degree of interconnection between artists working on a single play, including unbroken lines of cultural transmission from the premiere in Copenhagen in 1879 to performances in 2014. We traced the major artistic network in the Nordic cluster, but the German cluster and many smaller clusters still await investigation. The next stage will be to interrogate IbsenStage to uncover the artistic networks that link productions of all Ibsen's plays. If the patterns we have found in *Et dukkehjem* are duplicated elsewhere, the importance of the transmission of production knowledge on interpretative traditions within the entire Ibsen repertoire will need to be addressed. We found that the dominant tradition of *Et dukkehjem* performance was being transmitted as embodied knowledge rather than rehearsal-room anecdotes; this suggests the need for further research into the body as the site of transmission for past performance knowledge in the staging of modern dramas. We can envisage a new strain of theatre historiography based on tracing artistic networks in twentieth-century theatres of modernity. These studies have the potential to destabilise assumptions about distinctions between theatres of modernity, which rely on professional structures of employment and training, and traditional theatre forms, with their systems of cultural inheritance based on biological or adopted theatrical families.

A study of so many productions of a single play is unprecedented in the historiography of modern drama, and the techniques of data analysis and visualisation that we used have far-reaching possibilities for the field. Plans to digitise the production records of the plays of Samuel Beckett and Federico García Lorca are already in motion to facilitate comparative analyses of the production histories of canonical playwrights. There are many directions that this research can take, from increasing our understanding of the dissemination of a European cultural heritage, to charting the importance of nation states in the creation and maintenance of the world theatre canon, to a deeper understanding of the transmission of aesthetic knowledge across cultures and between generations of artists, while comparative analyses of the production histories of significant global dramas will inevitably enrich our understanding of theatrical adaptation.

Afterword

In the Introduction we mentioned two strains of Ibsen scholarship regarding the interpretation of Ibsen's character of Nora: on the one hand she is seen as a representation of female subjectivity struggling for emancipation, on the other as a character that embodies a universal striving for subjective freedom. These interpretations are based on close readings of Ibsen's playscript, and scholars engaging in debates about the relative merits of these interpretations are apt to cite Ibsen's speech at the dinner held in his honour by the Norwegian Women's Rights League in Christiania, on 26 May 1898.

> I am not a member of the Women's Rights League. Whatever I have [created has not been based on a conscious tendency or wish to propagate]. I have been more poet and less social philosopher than people generally seem inclined to believe. I thank you for the toast, but must disclaim the honor of having consciously worked for the women's [cause]. I am not even quite clear as to what women's [cause] really is. [I have perceived it as a human cause]. And if you read my books carefully you will understand this. True enough, [it] is desirable to solve the women's [issue, beside] others; but that has not been the whole purpose. My task has been the description of human [beings]. (Ibsen [1898] 1910, 65–66)

Ibsen appeared in the Introduction, and so by rights he should appear in the conclusion, but his intentions have played no part in our analyses. Whatever was said at that dinner in 1898, *Et dukkehjem* has been *used* to represent sexual vectors of social change within the theatre. These vectors are not univocal: they encapsulate diverse sexual expressions and reorganisations of gendered paradigms. While the social changes associated with the women's emancipation movement are important in the early production history of the play, the social changes for men provoked by the second wave of the European women's rights movement are visible in the productions of the 1970s, and today it is normative heterosexuality that is being critiqued in cross-dressed, transgendered, and transsexual adaptations. Again a contradiction confronts us: the forces of cultural transmission link the play to changes in the social organisation of gender and sexuality, most significantly the influence of the actress-managers in the global theatre market and the Nora's Sisters programme of the Norwegian government, but within the adaptation process it has been the forces of theatrical conventions constraining representations of gender and sexuality that have confronted artists. As a consequence, the play has strong associations with struggles for change in both the social and representational worlds.

In the final words of any book there is a desire for closure, but we have avoided the ubiquitous sound of the *Et dukkehjem* slamming door throughout this study and will continue to do so. We prefer to leave the door wide open for future scholars to join our collaborative venture of rethinking Ibsen scholarship through interrogation of the many thousands of production records that are held in IbsenStage.

Bibliography

A Doll's House. 1973. Directed by Patrick Garland. Elkins Productions, Freeward Films, England. Film. Accessed July 31, 2015. ibsen.nb.no/id/6230.0.

A Doll's House. 1973. Directed by Joseph Losey. World Film Services, Les Films la Boétie, England, France. Film. Accessed July 31, 2015. ibsen.nb.no/id/6206.0.

Achurch, Janet. 1892. "Round the World with *A Doll's House*: An Interview with Miss Janet Achurch." *Pall Mall Gazette* (London), April 14: 1–2.

——. 1895. "Janet Achurch Chats." *Dramatic Mirror*, New York. May 18: 2. Accessed August 13, 2015. http://fultonhistory.com/Newspaper.

Achurch, Janet, and Charles Charrington. 1894. "A Confession of their Crimes by Janet Achurch and Charles Charrington from the Cell of Inaction to which They Were Condemned in the Latter Half of the Year of Grace, 1893." *New Review*, April 10: 488–98.

Ahmed, Leila. 1992. *Women and Gender in Islam*. New Haven, CT: Yale University Press.

Ahsanuzzaman, Ahmed. 2012. "Sambhu Mitra's *A Doll's House*: *Putul Khela* in Bengal." PhD Thesis, University of Oslo, Norway.

Akerholt, May-Brit. 2015. Email correspondence with Julie Holledge. December 12.

Angel, Christine Judith. 2014. "The Woman Who Did: Janet Achurch, Ibsen, and the New Woman in Australia 1889–1891." PhD Thesis, University of Tasmania, Australia.

Archer, William. 1883. "Two Dramas by Ibsen." *Academy*, xxiii, January 6: 5–6.

——, ed. and trans. 1906. *A Doll's House, Ghosts*. Vol. 7 of *Collected Works of Henrik Ibsen*. London: William Heinemann.

J. Holledge et al., *A Global Doll's House*, Palgrave Studies in Performance and Technology, DOI 10.1057/978-1-137-43899-7

——, ed. and trans. 1917. *The Works of Henrik Ibsen*. 12 vols. New York: Charles Scribner's Sons.

Armand, Gisken. 2011. Interview with Julie Holledge and Frode Helland. May 25. Archived at Centre for Ibsen Studies, University of Oslo.

Arthur, Paul Longley, and Katherine Bode. 2014. *Advancing Digital Humanities: Research, Methods, Theories*. Basingstoke and New York: Palgrave Macmillan.

Arthur, Thomas. 2000. "Female Interpreters of Ibsen on Broadway, 1896–1947: Minnie Maddern Fiske, Alla Nazimova, and Eva Le Gallienne." *Ibsen Studies* 1 (1): 54–67.

Asiedu, Awo Mana. 2011. "*Nneora: An African Doll's House*: A Study of the Virtues of Womanhood." In "Ibsen Intercultural: Nora's Door Slamming Around the Globe," edited by Antje Budde, special issue, *Canadian Review of Comparative Literature* 38 (2): 172–85.

AusStage. 2003–15. *AusStage*. www.ausstage.edu.au.

Azevedo, José Fernando Peixoto de, and Teth Maiello. 2012. Interview with Julie Holledge. August 1.

Baruch, Elaine Hoffman. 1980. "Ibsen's *Doll House:* A Myth for Our Time." *Yale Review* 69 (30): 374.

Bay-Cheng, Sarah. 2010. "Theatre History and Digital Historiography." In *Theatre Historiography: Critical Interventions*, edited by Henry Bial and Scott Magelssen, 125–36. Ann Arbor, MI: University of Michigan Press.

Beevor, Antony. 2004. *The Mystery of Olga Chekhova*. New York: Penguin.

Berry, David M., ed. 2012. *Understanding Digital Humanities*. Basingstoke and New York: Palgrave Macmillan.

Bery, Ashok. 2007. *Cultural Translation and Postcolonial Poetry*. Basingstoke: Palgrave MacMillan.

Birnbaum, Phyllis. 1999. *Modern Girls, Shining Stars, The Skies of Tokyo: 5 Japanese Women*. New York: Columbia University Press.

Blackmore, Susan. 1999. *The Meme Machine*. Oxford: Oxford University Press.

Blanc, Tharald. 1899. *Christiania Theaters Historie 1827–1877*. Christiania: Cappelen.

——. 1906. *Henrik Ibsen og Christiania Theater 1850–1899*. Kristiania: Dybwad.

Bøgh, Erik. (1879) 1980. "Udvalgte Feuilletoner ('Dit og Dat')" [Selected Serials ("This and That")]. In *Gyldendalske Boghandels Forlag*. Copenhagen: F. Hegel & Søn.

Bollen, Jonathan, and Julie Holledge. 2011. "Hidden Dramas: Cartographic Revelations in the World of Theatre Studies." In "Cartographies of Fictional Worlds," special issue, *The Cartography Journal* 48 (4): 226–36.

Bollen, Jonathan, Neal Harvey, Julie Holledge, and Glen McGillivray. 2009. "AusStage: e-Research in the Performing Arts." *Australasian Drama Studies* 54: 178–94.

Bourdieu, Pierre. 1993. *The Field of Cultural Production*. Cambridge: Polity Press.

——. 1996. *The Rules of Art: Genesis and Structure of the Literary Field*. Cambridge: Polity Press.

Bradbrook, Muriel C. 1982. "*A Doll's House* and the Unweaving of the Web." *Women and Literature 1779–1982*. Vol. 2 of *The Collected Papers of Muriel Bradbrook*. Brighton: Harvester Press.

Branigan, Tania. 2012. "Jin Xing: From Chinese Army Officer to Dancing TV Stardom." *Guardian*. September 11. Accessed December 4, 2015. www.theguardian.com/world/2012/sep/10/jin-xing-chinese-army-dancing-tv.

Braun, Edward, ed. 1991. *Meyerhold on Theatre*. By Vsevolod Meyerhold and translated with a critical commentary by Edward Braun. Revised Edition. London: Methuen Drama.

Brooks, Peter. 1984. *Reading for the Plot: Design and Intention in Narrative*. Cambridge, MA: Harvard University Press.

Bruni, Frank. 2002. "A Nation That Exports Oil, Herring and Peace." *New York Times*, December 21. Accessed December 21, 2015. http://www.nytimes.com/2002/12/21/world/a-nation-that-exports-oil-herring-and-peace.html.

Bucks, Dorothy. S., and Arthur. H. Nethercot. 1946. "Ibsen and Herne's *Margaret Fleming*: A Study of the Early Ibsen Movement in America." *American Literature* 17 (4): 311–33.

Budde, Antje, ed. 2011. "Ibsen Intercultural: Nora's Door Slamming Around the Globe," special issue of *Canadian Review of Comparative Literature* 38 (2).

Burdick, Anne, Johann Drucker, Peter Lupenfeld, Todd Presner, and Jeffrey Schnapps, 2012. *Digital Humanities*. Cambridge, MA and London: MIT Press.

Caretti, Laura. 2002. "Ibsen and Raphael." In *Ibsen and the Arts: Painting-Sculpture-Architecture, Acta Ibseniana I,* edited by Astrid Sæther, 81–89. Oslo: Centre for Ibsen Studies.

Carlson, Marvin. 2003. *The Haunted Stage: The Theatre as Memory Machine*. Ann Arbor, MI: University of Michigan Press.

——. 2011. "Ibsen's A Doll's House in America." In *Global Ibsen: Performing Multiple Modernities*, edited by Erika Fischer-Lichte, Barbara Gronau, and Christel Weiler, 39–52. New York and Abingdon: Routledge.

Carson, Christie. 2005. "Digitising Performance History: Where Do We Go From Here?" *Performance Research* 10 (3): 4–17.

Casanova, Pascale. 2004. *The World Republic of Letters*. Translated by M.B. Debovoise. Cambridge, MA: Harvard University Press.

——. 2007. "The Ibsen Battle: A Comparative Analysis of the Introduction of Henrik Ibsen in France, England and Ireland." In *Anglo-French Attitudes: Comparisons and Transfers between English and French Intellectuals since the Eighteenth Century*, edited by Christophe Charle, Julian Vincent, and Jay Winter, 214–32. Manchester and New York: Manchester University Press.

Catalogue du pavillion de la Norvège à l'exposition internationale de Paris 1937. 1937. Oslo: Blix.

Causey, Matthew. 2006. *Theatre and Performance in Digital Culture: From Simulation to Embeddedness*. London: Routledge.

Chakrabarty, Dipesh. 2000. *Provincializing Europe: Postcolonial Thought and Historical Difference*. Princeton: Princeton University Press.

Charrington, Charles. 1892. "The Statesman and Mr Charles Martin alias Charrington." *The Statesman*, Calcutta. February 20: 2.

——. to George Bernard Shaw. 1916. Charles Charrington's Account of his Wife, Janet (after her death). September 16. Rare Books, Music and Manuscripts Collection, British Library.

Christiania Intelligentssedler (Dagens Nyheter). 1885. May 24.

Cima, Gay Gibson. 1980. "Elizabeth Robins: The Genesis of an Independent Manageress." *Theatre Survey* 21 (2): 145–63.

——. 1983. "Discovering Signs: The Emergence of the Critical Actor in Ibsen." In "Aporia: Revision, Representation and Intertexual Theatre," special issue, *Theatre Journal* 35 (1): 5–22.

Colella, Sandra. 2007. "Tarantism and Tarantella in *A Doll's House*." Masters Thesis. Oslo University, Norway.

"Currency Converter." 2015. *OANDA*. Accessed December 25, 2015. http://www.oanda.com/currency/converter/.

D'Amico, Giuliano. 2014. "Six Points for a Comparative Ibsen Reception History." *Ibsen Studies* 14 (1): 4–37.

Dante Alighieri, and Gustave Doré. 1868. *Il Purgatorio; Paradiso*. Parigi: Hachette.

Darwin, Charles. 1871. *The Descent of Man*. London: D. Appleton and Company.

Davis, Tracy C. 1985. "Ibsen's Victorian Audiences." *Essays in Theatre* 4 (1): 21–38.

——. 2000. *The Economics of the British Stage, 1800–1914*. Cambridge: Cambridge University Press.

Dawkins, Richard. (1976) 1989. *The Selfish Gene*. 2nd ed. Oxford: Oxford University Press.

De Martino, Ernesto. (1961) 2002. *La terra del rimorso*, edited by Net Gruppo editoriale. Milano: Il Saggiatore.

Dean, Robert. 2011. "Diegetic Musical Motifs in Ibsen's *A Doll's House* and *John Gabriel Borkman*." *Ibsen Studies* 11 (1): 51–70.

Debray, Régis. 2004. *Transmitting Culture*. New York: Columbia University Press.

DECO. 2011. "Consultants." *DECO*. Accessed November 30, 2015. http://www.deco.no/.

"Director-General Condemns Killing of Norwegian Reporter Carsten Thomassen in Kabul Hotel." 2008. *UNESCO News Archive*. January 22. Accessed November 30, 2015. http://portal.unesco.org/ci/en/ev.php-URL_ID=25816&URL_DO=DO_TOPIC&URL_SECTION=201.html.

Dixon, Steve, with Barry Smith. 2007. *Digital Performance: A History of New Media in Theatre, Dance, Performance Art, and Installation*. Cambridge, MA and London: MIT Press.

Doloff, Steven. 1994. "Ibsen's *A Doll's House* and 'The Dead.'" *James Joyce Quarterly* 31 (2): 111–15.

Donohue, Joseph. 1989. "Evidence and Documentation." In *Interpreting the Theatrical Past: Essays in the Historiography of Performance*, edited by Thomas Postlewait and Bruce A. McConachie, 177–97. Iowa City: University of Iowa Press.

"Dramatic and Musical; Agnes Sorma Reappears in Ibsen's *A Doll's House* at the Irving Place Theatre." 1898. *New York Times,* March 15. Accessed August 13, 2015. http://query.nytimes.com/mem/archivefree/pdf?res=9B07E7D7163 8E433A25756C1A9659C94699ED7CF.

Dukore, Bernard F. 1990. "Karl Marx's Youngest Daughter and *A Doll's House*." *Theatre Journal* 42 (3): 308–21.

Ebadi, Shirin and Azadeh Moaveni. 2006. *Iran Awakening From Prison to Peace: One Woman's Struggle at the Crossroads of History*. London: Rider.

"Editorial: What We As Women Can Learn From *A Doll's House*." 1912. *Seito* (January): 62–114.

Eide, Elisabeth. 1987. *China's Ibsen: From Ibsen to Ibsenism*. Scandinavian Institute of Asian Studies Monograph Series 55. London: Curzon Press.

——. 1995. "*Peer Gynt* and *A Doll's House*: Or One Aspect of Modern Chinese Drama." In *I: Ibsen Research Papers,* 300–17. Beijing: Chinese Literature Press.

Ekman, Paul. 2003. *Emotions Revealed: Recognizing Faces and Feelings to Improve Communication and Emotional Life*. 2nd ed. London: Weidenfeld & Nicolson.

El-Robi, Mohammad. 2006. "*A Doll's House*, A True Model for Women's Theatre." *Al-Karama,* (39), July 4.

El-Ruweiny, Abla. 2006. "Nora: From Ibsen's Realism to Yakout's Romaticism." *Al-Akhbar Daily,* (16912), July 5.

Eveleigh, Melissa. 2009. Interview with Julie Holledge. April 8.

Fabre, M. Emile. 1907. "*La Maison d'Argile*" *(The House of Clay*). Comedie Française, Paris, France. February 25. Performance.

Finney, Gail. 1994. "Ibsen and Feminism." In *The Cambridge Companion to Ibsen*, edited by James McFarlane, 89–105. Cambridge: Cambridge University Press.

Fischer-Lichte, Erika, Barbara Gronau, and Christel Weiler, eds. 2011. *Global Ibsen: Performing Multiple Modernities.* New York and Abingdon: Routledge.

Fodstad, Lars August. 2006. "Refurbishing the Doll's House? The Theatre Programme as Paratextual Trace." *Ibsen Studies* 6 (2): 149–87.

Fonda. Jane. 2005. *My Life So Far*. New York: Random House.

"*The Former Miss Barstow with every Tom, Dick and Harry in a doll's house*." 1987. Directed by Richard Newton. *YouTube*. Accessed December 17, 2015. https://www.youtube.com/watch?v=NWRVIQt5ENg.

Friedman, Jonathan. 1994. *Cultural Identity and Global Process.* London: Sage.

Fulsås, Narve. 2005–10. "Innledning." In *Henrik Ibsens Skrifter,* edited by Vigdis Ystad et al. Vol. 12k (2005): 37–40 and 49–52; 13k (2008): 16–23; 14k (2009): 13–18; 15k (2010): 19–29. Oslo: University of Oslo and Aschehoug. Accessed December 16, 2015. http://www.ibsen.uio.no/BRINNL_brevInnledning_4.xhtml.

Gentz, Natascha. 2002. "Jiang Qing and the 'Year of Nora' 1935: Drama and Politics in the Republican Period." Draft Prepared for the International Conference "Women In Republican China," Berlin, 6–11 October 2002. *Ibseninchina.* Accessed November 5, 2006. http://www.ibseninchina.com.cn/Jiangqing.htm.

Gjervan, Ellen Karoline. 2010. "Creating Theatrical Space: A Study of Henrik Ibsen's Production Books, Bergen 1852–1857." PhD Thesis, University of Bergen, Norway.

Gold, Matthew. 2012. *Debates in the Digital Humanities.* Minneapolis, MN: University of Minnesota Press.

Gregersen, Halfdan. 1936. *Ibsen and Spain: A Study in Comparative Drama.* Cambridge, MA: Harvard University Press.

Grosz, Elizabeth. 2011. *Becoming Undone: Darwinian Reflections on Life, Politics and Art.* Durham and London: Duke University Press.

Gupta, Tapati. 2006. "*Putul Khela* on Page and Stage." In *Proceedings, International Ibsen Conference: Socio-Political Aspects of Ibsen's Plays: Dhaka, Bangladesh 11–13, May,* 81–90. Dhaka: Centre for Asian Theatre.

——, trans. 2015. Unpublished translation of "Jhulan." By Rabindranath Tagore.

"H." 1912. "A Letter to Nora." *Seito* (January): 133–41.

Habermas, Jürgen. 1985. *The Philosophical Discourse of Modernity.* Translated by F. Lawrence. Cambridge: Polity Press.

Halle, Jesper. 2005. *Nora's barn.* Unpublished play-script.

Hansen, Harald. 1888. "Kristiania Teater 1837–87." *Tilskueren,* (Kbh) 5: 71–96.

Hanssen, Eirik Frisvold. 2015. "*A Doll's House* and the Performance of Gender in American Silent Cinema." *Screening the Past.* Accessed October 4, 2015. http://www.screeningthepast.com/2015/08/a-doll's-house-and-the-performance-of-gender-in-american-silent-cinema/.

Harding, Sandra. 2008. *Science from Below: Feminisms, Postcolonialities, and Modernities.* Durham, NC and London: Duke University Press.

Haugen, Einar I. 1934. "Ibsen in America: A Forgotten Performance and an Unpublished Letter." *The Journal of English and Germanic Philology* 33 (3): 396–420.

Hayles, N. Katherine. 2012. *How We Think: Digital Media and Contemporary Technogenesis.* Chicago, IL and London: University of Chicago Press.

He, Chengzhou. 2003. "Ibsen and Chinese 'Problem Drama.'" *Ibsen Studies* 3 (1): 54–70.

——. 2004. *Henrik Ibsen and Modern Chinese Drama*. Oslo: Oslo University Press.
——. 2016. "Cross-dressing Ibsen on Contemporary Chinese Stage—On Yue Opera Adaptations of *Hedda Gabler* and *Lady from the Sea*." In *Ibsen Between Cultures*, edited by Frode Helland and Julie Holledge. Oslo: Novus forlag. In Press.
Helland, Frode. 2015. *Ibsen in Practice: Relational Readings of Performance, Cultural Encounters and Power*. London: Bloomsbury Methuen Drama.
Helland, Frode and Julie Holledge, eds. 2016. *Ibsen Between Cultures*. Oslo: Novus forlag. In Press.
Helland, Frode, and Julie Holledge. 2013. "*A Doll's House* as National Tradition: Understanding the Construction of Aesthetic Value." In *Assigning Cultural Values*, edited by Kjerstin Aukrust, 165–90. Frankfurt: Peter Lang Verlag.
Henrikson, Alan K. 2005. "Niche Diplomacy in the Public Arena: Canada and Norway." In *The New Public Diplomacy: Soft Power in International Relations*, edited by Jan Melissen, 67–87. Houndmills: Palgrave Macmillan.
Herbert, Ian. 1986. "Computer Databases for Theatre Studies." *New Theatre Quarterly* 2 (6): 175–80.
Herrnstein Smith, Barbara. 1984. "Contingencies of Value." In *Canons*, edited by Robert von Hallberg, 5–39. Chicago, IL: University of Chicago Press.
"High Salaries Are Doomed: English Actresses Out of Work Because They Demand Too Much." 1896. *New York Times*. November 28. Accessed February 2, 2015. http://query.nytimes.com/mem/archive-free/pdf?res=9800E4DA1 03BEE33A2575AC2A9679D94679ED7CF.
HIS (Henrik Ibsens skrifter), BREV 1844–1905. [*Henrik Ibsen's Writings. Letters 1844–1905*.] 2005–10. Volumes 12–14, edited by Narve Fulsås. Oslo: University of Oslo and Aschehoug.
——. 2015. Accessed November 17. http://www.ibsen.uio.no/.
Hoare, Eileen. 2003. "*A Doll's House* in Australia." In *Proceedings of the 10th International Ibsen Conference, Ibsen Society of America and Long Island University, New York, 1–7 June 2003*. New York: Long Island University. Accessed November 13, 2015. http://www.ibsensociety.liu.edu/conference-papers/adollhouse.pdf.
——. 2004. "The New Woman in the New World: Reception of *A Doll's House* in Australia and New Zealand 1889–1891." Masters Thesis, Macquarie University, Sydney, Australia.
Hockey, Susan. 2000. *Electronic Texts in the Humanities: Principles and Practices*. Oxford: Oxford University Press.
Holledge, Julie. 1981. *Innocent Flowers: Women in Edwardian Theatre*. London: Virago.
——. 2006. "O Gu: A Cross Cultural Case Study of Emotional Expression in Contemporary Korean and Australian Theatre." *Australasian Drama Studies* 49: 76–88.

——. 2008. "Addressing the Global Phenomenon of *A Doll's House*: An Intercultural Intervention." *Ibsen Studies* 8 (1): 13–28.

——. 2010a. "Pastor Hansen's Confirmation Class: Religion, Freedom, and the Female Body in *Et Dukkehjem.*" *Ibsen Studies* 10 (1): 3–16.

——. 2010b. "Seeing Nora in Your Mirror: The Role of Theatrical Characters in the Playing of Self." *Ibsen and Identity* Conference Papers, Hong Kong Open University and Centre for Ibsen Studies. In *Ibsen and the Modern Self*, edited by Kwok-kan Tam, Terry Siu-han Yip, and Frode Helland, 204–23. Hong Kong: Open University of Hong Kong Press.

——. 2011. "Sharing a Doll's House with Islamic Neighbours." In "Ibsen Intercultural: Nora's Door Slamming Around the Globe," edited by Antje Budde, special issue, *Canadian Review of Comparative Literature* 38 (2): 154–71.

——. 2015. "Gurrya ka Ghar: Part of a Global Tradition." In *Tees Aur Aik Saal: Gender Politics and Performance in South Asia,* edited by Sheema Kermani, Asif Farrukhi, and Kamran Asdar Ali, 130–45. Karachi: Oxford University Press.

Holledge, Julie, and Joanne Tompkins. 2000. *Women's Intercultural Performance.* London and New York: Routledge.

Hov, Live. 2007. *Med fuld natursandhed. Henrik Ibsen som teatermann.* København: Multivers Academic.

——. 2010. "Enter Nora: The First Three Productions of *A Doll's House*, in Denmark, Sweden and Norway." *Nordic Theatre Studies* 22: 30–45.

Hoyt, Eric, Kevin Ponto, and Carrie Roy 2014. "Visualizing and Analyzing the Hollywood Screenplay with ScripThreads." *Digital Humanities Quarterly* 8 (4). Accessed December 17, 2015. http://www.digitalhumanities.org/dhq/vol/8/4/000190/000190.html.

Hutcheon, Linda. 2006. *A Theory of Adaptation.* London and New York: Routledge.

Hutcheon, Linda, and Siobhan O'Flynn. 2013. *A Theory of Adaptation.* 2nd ed. London: Routledge.

Ibsen Awards. 2014. "*Nora/Nurê.*" *Ibsen Awards.* Accessed November 20. http://www.ibsenawards.com/scholarship/winners/nora-nure/#blog.

Ibsen Awards. 2015. "Winners of International Ibsen Scholarships." *Ibsen Award.* Accessed August 26. http://www.ibsenawards.com/scholarship/winners.

"Ibsen in English Again, this Time at the Hoyt's Theatre." 1895. *New York Times,* June 7. Accessed February 4, 2015. http://query.nytimes.com/mem/archive-free/pdf?res=9807EEDF103DE433A25754C0A9609C94649ED7CF.

Ibsen International. 2010. "About." *Ibsen International.* Accessed November 30, 2015. www.ibseninternational.com/about.

Ibsen, Henrik. (1851) 2010. Review of "'Huldrens Hjem,' Originalt Skuespil i tre Akter med Sange og Chor" ("'The Wood-Nymph's Home,' Original Play in Three Acts with Songs and Choir"). In *Manden/Andhrimner.* June 22. In vol. 16 of *Henrik Ibsens skrifter,* 78–83. Oslo: University of Oslo and Aschehoug.

——. (1867) 1963. *Peer Gynt*. Translated by Michael Meyer. London: Rupert Hart-Davis.

——. 1878a. Letter to Harald Holst, November 21. In vol. 13s of *Henrik Ibsens skrifter*, edited by Narve Fulsås, 463–65. Oslo: University of Oslo and Aschehoug.

——. (1878b) 1917. "Notes for a Modern Tragedy." October 19. Translated by William Archer. In vol. 12 of *The Works of Henrik Ibsen*, 91. New York: Charles Scribner's Sons.

——.1879a. Letter to Edmund Gosse, July 4. In vol. 13s of *Henrik Ibsens skrifter*, edited by Narve Fulsås, 498–99. Oslo: University of Oslo and Aschehoug.

——. 1879b. Letter to Frederik Hegel, September 15. In vol. 13s of *Henrik Ibsens skrifter*, edited by Narve Fulsås, 505–06. Oslo: University of Oslo and Aschehoug.

——. 1880a. Letter to Editor of Nationaltidende, February 17. In vol. 14 of *Henrik Ibsens skrifter*, edited by Narve Fulsås, 24–25. Oslo: University of Oslo and Aschehoug.

——. 1880b. Letter to Erik af Edholm, January 3. In vol. 14s of *Henrik Ibsens skrifter*, edited by Narve Fulsås, 11–12. Oslo: University of Oslo and Aschehoug.

——. 1880c. Letter to Heinrich Laube, February 18. In vol. 14 of *Henrik Ibsens skrifter*, edited by Narve Fulsås, 25–27. Oslo: University of Oslo and Aschehoug.

——. 1883. Letter to August Lindberg, August 2. In vol. 14s of *Henrik Ibsens skrifter*, edited by Narve Fulsås, 192–94. Oslo: University of Oslo and Aschehoug.

——. 1887. Letter to Hans Schrøder, January 2. In vol. 14s of *Henrik Ibsens skrifter*, edited by Narve Fulsås, 379–80. Oslo: University of Oslo and Aschehoug.

——. 1891. Letter to Moritz Prozor, January 23. In vol. 15 of *Henrik Ibsens skrifter*, edited by Narve Fulsås, 92–94. Oslo: University of Oslo and Aschehoug.

——. (1898) 1910. "Speech to Norwegian League for Women's Rights in Christiania." May 26. In *Speeches and New Letters*, translated by Arne Kildal with an introduction by Lee M. Hollander, 65–66. Boston: Gorham.

"Ibsen's Nora is haute couture in London." 2006. *Royal Norwegian Embassy in London*. October 26. Accessed July 29, 2015. http://www.norway.org.uk/norwayandcountry/culture/fashion/nora/#.Vl0PeMr8FsN.

IbsenStage. 2015. https://ibsenstage.hf.uio.no.

International Ibsen Award. 2015. "About the International Ibsen Award." *International Ibsen Award*. Accessed November 30. www.internationalibsenaward.com/about.

Jafri, Anwer. 2009. Interview with Julie Holledge. November 21. Dhaka, Bangladesh.

Jakovljevic, Branislav. 2002. "Shattered Back Wall: Performative Utterance of *A Doll's House*" *Theatre Journal* 54 (3): 431–48.

"Joan Crawford and Basil Rathbone Perform *A Doll's House* for Lux Radio Theatre." 1938. *YouTube*. June 6. Accessed December 17, 2015. https://www.youtube.com/watch?v=4V2OsexLDg0.

Kalb, Jonathan. 2004. "Nora the Killer Doll." *New York Times*. November 7. Accessed December 2, 2015. www.nytimes.com/2004/11/07/theater/newsandfeatures/nora-the-killer-doll.html?_r=0.

Kano, Ayako. 2001. *Acting Like a Woman in Modern Japan: Theater, Gender and Nationalism*. New York: Palgrave Macmillan.

Kapp, Yvonne. 1972–76. *Eleanor Marx*. London: Lawrence and Wishart.

Kermani, Sheema. 2009. Interview with Julie Holledge. November 21. Dhaka, Bangladesh.

Khedr, Mona. 2010. "Negotiating an Islamic Identity on Egyptian, Australian and Malaysian Stages, a Comparative Study." PhD Thesis, Flinders University, Adelaide, Australia.

——. 2012. Email Communication with Julie Holledge. July 1.

Koht, Halvdan. 1971. *Life of Ibsen*. Translated and edited by E. Haugen and A.E. Santaniello. New York: B. Blom.

Komisarjevsky, Theodore. 1929. *Myself and the Theatre*. Kingswood, Surrey: The Windmill Press.

Koski, Pirrko. 2006. "Nora Dances on the Finnish Stage." Presented at the International Ibsen Conference 11. *The Living Ibsen*, 525–31. Oslo: Centre for Ibsen Studies, University of Oslo.

Krook, Dorothea. c1969. *Border Cases: Ibsen's* A Doll's House, Hedda Gabler, The Wild Duck, The Master Builder. New Haven, CT: Yale University Press.

La Gallienne, Eva. 1965. *The Mystic in the Theatre: Eleonora Duse*. Carbondale, IL: Southern Illinois University Press.

Lambert, Gavin. 1997. *Nazimova: A Biography*. New York: Alfred A. Knoff.

Langås, Unni. 2005. "What Did Nora Do? Thinking Gender with *A Doll's House*." *Ibsen Studies* 5 (2): 148–71.

Leitch, Thomas. 2009. *Film Adaptation and Its Discontents: From* Gone with the Wind *to* The Passion of the Christ. Baltimore, MD: Johns Hopkins University Press.

"Looking Forward to a Week of Serious Drama: Nazimova's Achievements and Future Possibilities A Creative Artiste Who Promises to Become a Stage Figure of International Prominence." 1907. *New York Times*, January 20. Accessed August 13, 2015. http://query.nytimes.com/mem/archive-free/pdf?res=9A03E0D9153EE033A25753C2A9679C946697D6CF.

Loranger, Françoise. (1967) 2011. "*Encore Cinq Minutes (Five Minutes More)*." Translated by Louise H. Forsyth. In "Ibsen Intercultural: Nora's Door Slamming Around the Globe," edited by Antje Budde, special issue, *Canadian Review of Comparative Literature* 38 (2): 283–328.

Luce, Clare Boothe. 1970. "*A Doll's House* 1970: A Classic Play About a Woman Who Wanted to be Equal to a Man, Rewritten in the Light of Recent Events (With Apologies to Henrik Ibsen)." *Life Magazine,* New York 69 (16): 54–67.

Ly, Singko. 1979. *The Fall of Madame Mao.* New York: Vantage.

Magaldi, Sábato. 2005. "Presença da França no teatro brasileiro." In *Revista Brasileira*, Fase VII, Ano XI (43): 285. http://www.academia.org.br/sites/default/files/publicacoes/arquivos/revista-brasileira-43.pdf.

Mahmood, Saba. 2005. *Politics of Piety: The Islamic Revival and the Feminist Subject.* Princeton: Princeton University Press.

Mankell, Henning. 2006. *Nora's Daughters.* Directed by Manuela Soeiro. Teatro Avenida, Maputo, Mozambique. Performance.

Manovich, Lev. 2011. "What is Visualization?" *Visual Studies* 26 (1): 36–49.

Mansfield, Richard. (1895) 1965. "Letter to George Bernard Shaw dated April 14, 1895." In *Collected Letters 1874–1897.* By George Bernard Shaw. Edited by Dan H. Laurence, 523–24. New York: Dodd, Mead and Company.

Marcus, J.C. 1973. "Elizabeth Robins: A Biography." PhD Thesis, Northwestern University, United States of America.

Marker, Frederick J., and Lise-Lone Marker. 1989. *Ibsen's Lively Art: A Performance Study of the Major Plays.* Cambridge: Cambridge University Press.

——. 1996. *A History of Scandinavian Theatre.* Cambridge: Cambridge University Press.

——. 1999. *Ingmar Bergman: A Project for the Theatre.* New York: Continuum.

Massey, Doreen. 2005. *For Space.* London: Sage.

Matsui, Sumako. 1912. "Problems on Stage." Translated by J. McGory, *Seito* (January): 162–63.

McAuley, Gay. 2000. *Space in Performance: Making Meaning in the Theatre.* Ann Arbor, MI: University of Michigan Press.

McCarty, Willard. 2005. *Humanities Computing.* Basingstoke: Palgrave Macmillan.

McClary, Susan. 1992. *Georges Bizet Carmen.* Cambridge Opera Books. Cambridge: Cambridge University Press.

McFarlane, James. 1993. "Norwegian Literature 1860–1910." In *A History of Norwegian Literature*, edited by Harald S. Naess, 107–99. Lincoln, NE: University of Nebraska Press.

McGann, Jerome J. 2001. *Radiant Textuality: Literature after the World Wide Web.* New York and Basingstoke: Palgrave Macmillan.

McShea, Daniel W., and Robert N. Brandon. 2010. *Biology's First Law: The Tendency for Diversity and Complexity to Increase in Evolutionary Systems.* Chicago, IL and London: University of Chicago Press.

Meyer, Michael. 1971. *Ibsen.* New York: Doubleday.

"Midori." 1912. "*A Doll's House.*" *Seito* (January): 118–25.

Min, Anchee. 2001. *Becoming Madame Mao.* New York: Mariner Books.

Min, X. 1962. "The Stage Performance of *Nora* and Others." *Wen Hui Bao*. February 16: n.p.

Mir-Hosseini, Ziba. 1993. "Women, Marriage, and the Law in Post-Revolutionary Iran." In *Women in the Middle East: Perceptions, Realities, and Struggles for Liberation*, edited by H. Afshar, 59–84. Hampshire: Macmillan.

"Miss Achurch at the Avenue Theatre." 1892. *Western Mail* (1885–1954), Perth, WA, June 25: 45.

Mitchell, Maude. 2009. Email correspondence with Julie Holledge. October 19.

Moi, Toril. 2006. *Henrik Ibsen and the Birth of Modernism: Art, Theater, Philosophy*. Oxford: Oxford University Press.

Moretti, Franco. 2000. "Conjectures on World Literature." *New Left Review* 1 (1): 54–68.

——. 2005. *Graphs, Maps, and Trees: Abstract Models for Literary History*. London and New York: Verso.

——. 2013. *Distant Reading*. London and New York: Verso.

Mori, Mitsuya. 2011. "Women's Issues and a New Art of Acting." In *Global Ibsen: Performing Multiple Modernities*, edited by Erika Fischer-Lichte, Barbara Gronau, and Christel Weiler, 74–88. New York and Abingdon: Routledge.

Mukhopadhyay, Saranya, trans. 2014. *Putul Khela* by Sambhu Mitra. Unpublished translation of play-script.

Mulvey, Laura. 1975. "Visual Pleasure and Narrative Cinema." *Screen* 16 (3): 6–18.

Murjas, Teresa. 2007. "Introduction." *The Morality of Mrs Dulska*. By Gabriela Zapolska. Translated by Teresa Murjas, xii–lxxxvii. Bristol and Chicago, IL: Intellect Books.

Nakamura, Toshiko. 1985. "Three *A Doll's House* in Japan." *Edda: Scandinavian Journal of Literary Research* 73 (3): 163–71.

Nasjonalbiblioteket. 2012. *The International Ibsen Bibliography*. Accessed November 17, 2015. http://www.nb.no/baser/ibsen/english.html.

Natanson, W. 1958. "*A Doll's House* Revisited Polish Perspectives." *Warszawa* 1: 64–67.

National Library of Norway. 2015. "Ibsen Repertoire Database." *National Library of Norway*. Accessed November 17. http://ibsen.nb.no/id/110728.0.

Nationaltheatret. 2010. *International Ibsen Festival Programme 2010*. Oslo: Nationaltheatret.

Newton, Richard. 2009. Email Correspondence with Julie Holledge, May 25.

——. 2012. "The Former Miss Barstow with every Tom, Dick and Harry." Inaugural Artists' Panel, *XIII International Ibsen Conference: Ibsen and World Drama(s), Tromsø, June 18–23*.

Nilu, Kamaluddin, ed. 2003. *The Relevance of* A Doll's House—*Translation and Adaptation. Proceedings of the International Ibsen Conference*. Bangladesh: Centre for Asian Theatre.

Nora. 1922. Directed by Berthold Viertel. Performed by Olga Chekhova as Nora. Projektions-AG Union, Berlin. Silent Film.

Nora. 2003. Directed for the stage by Thomas Ostermeier and for television by Hannes Rossacher. Performed by Anne Tismer as Nora. ZDF Theaterkanal, Berlin and ARTE, France. Television Movie.

Nora's Sisters. 2006. Norwegian Ministry of Foreign Affairs. Accessed December 21, 2015. https://www.regjeringen.no/globalassets/upload/kilde/ud/bro/2006/0042/ddd/pdfv/295903-norasisters1.pdf.

"Nora's Sisters Seminar—Women in Politics, 8–9 March 2008." 2008. *The Representative Office of Norway to the Palestinian Authority*. March 19. Accessed August 25, 2015. http://www.norway.org.ps/ARKIV/Nora_Sisters/#.Vlvfi8r8HRl.

Nordau, Max. 1895. *Degeneration*. New York: D. Appleton and Co.

Northam, John. 1953. *Ibsen's Dramatic Method: A Study of the Prose Dramas*. London: Faber and Faber.

"Notes of the Stage." 1895. *New York Times*, June 9. Accessed February 4, 2015. http://query.nytimes.com/mem/archivefree/pdf?res=9806EFDC1039E033A2575AC0A9609C94649ED7CF.

Nye, Jr., Joseph S. 2004. *Soft Power: The Means to Success in World Politics*. New York: Public Affairs.

Ohnstad, Liv Kirsten. 1984. "The Treatment of 'Nora' in Selected Sequels to Ibsen's *A Doll's House*." Masters Thesis, University of Wisconsin, United States of America.

Oliver, Roger W. 1992. "Bergman's Trilogy: Tradition and Innovation." *Performing Arts Journal* 14 (1): 74–86.

Østbye, Marit. 2011. Interview with Julie Holledge and Frode Helland. May 27. Archived at Centre for Ibsen Studies, University of Oslo.

Ostermeier, Thomas. 2005. "Presenter Interview: In pursuit of the Theater for the Playwright. Talking with Artistic Director Ostermeier of the Shaubuehne." *Performing Arts Network*, Japan. August 18. Accessed December 15, 2015. http://www.performingarts.jp/E/pre_interview/0508/pre_interview0508e.pdf.

——. 2010. "Reading and Staging Ibsen." *Ibsen Studies* 10 (2): 68–75.

Østerud, Erik. 1997. "*A Doll's House*: Ibsen's Italian masquerade." *Proceedings of the International Seminar and Workshop on Gender Issues in Ibsen's Plays*. Dhaka: Centre for Asian Theater. *Nordic Theatre Studies* 10: 23–35.

——. 2004. "Nora's Watch: Time, Space and Image in Ibsen's *A Doll's House*." *Ibsen Studies* 4 (2): 147–75.

——. 2005. "Sex, Sensuality and Death: Nora's Tarantella." In *Ibsen: The Dark Side*, edited by Gianna De Martino, Stefano Bajma Griga, Ruth Anne Henderson, 157–68. Rome: Carocci Editore.

Oxfeldt, Elisabeth. 2005. *Nordic Orientalism: Paris and the Cosmopolitan Imagination 1800–1900*. Copenhagen: Museum Tusculanum Press.

Paletschek, Sylvia, and Bianka Pietrow-Ennker. 2004. *Women's Emancipation Movements in the Nineteenth Century: A European Perspective*. Stanford, CA: Stanford University Press.

Penley, Constance, ed. 1998. *Feminism and Film Theory*. New York and London: Routledge.

Perrelli, Franco. 2001. "Some More Notes about Nora's Tarantella." In *Ibsen and the Arts: Painting-Sculpture-Architecture, Acta Ibseniana I*, edited by Astrid Sæther, 119–27. Oslo: Centre for Ibsen Studies.

Peters, Margot. 1980. *Bernard Shaw and the Actresses: A Biography*. New York: Doubleday.

Polenov, Vasily. 1874. "Le Droit Du Seigneur." Moscow, Tretyakov Gallery. Oil painting on canvas.

Pontiero, Giovanni. 1982. *Duse on Tour: Guido Noccioli's Diaries, 1906–07*. Translated and edited with an introduction and notes by Giovanni Pontiero. Amherst: University of Massachusetts Press.

Porter, Cathy. 1980. *Alexandra Kollontai: A Biography*. London: Virago.

Postlewait, Thomas. 1986. *Prophet of the New Drama: William Archer and the Ibsen Campaign*. Westpoint, CT: Greenwood Press.

Puccini, Giacomo. 1918. *Gianni Schicchi*. Libretto by Giovacchino Forzano. Metropolitan Opera, New York. December 14. Performance.

Quigley, Austin E. 1984. "Ibsen: *A Doll's House*, The Modern Stage and Other Worlds." *Modern Drama* 27 (4): 584–603.

Quinn, Bernadette. 2010. "Arts Festivals, Urban Tourism and Cultural Policy." *Journal of Policy Research in Tourism, Leisure and Events* 2 (3): 264–79.

Reich, Pauline C., and Atsuko Fukuda. 1976. "Japan's Literary Feminists: The 'Seito' Group." *Signs* 2 (1): 280–91.

Review of *Et dukkehjem* at Christiania Theater. 1880. *Dagbladet*, Kristiania, 12 (17), January 21.

Review of *Et dukkehjem*. 1885. *Aftenposten*, Kristiania. May 23. Press clipping held in Centre for Ibsen Studies, University of Oslo.

Review of *Et dukkehjem*. 1885. *Dagbladet*, Kristiania. May 24. Press clipping held in Centre for Ibsen Studies, University of Oslo.

Review of Janet Achurch in *A Doll's House*. 1891. *Auckland Evening Star*, New Zealand, 22 (12), January 15: 5.

Review of Janet Achurch in *A Doll's House*. 1891. *New Zealand Herald*, 28 (8464), January 18: 5.

Rhys, Jean. 1966. *Wide Sargasso Sea*. London: Andre Deutsch.

Ringdal, Nils Johan. 2000. *Nationaltheatrets historie 1899–1999*. Oslo: Gyldendal.

Riordan, Shaun. 2005. "Dialogue-based Public Diplomacy: A New Foreign Policy Paradigm?" In *The New Public Diplomacy: Soft Power in International Relations*, edited by Jan Melissen, 180–95. Houndmills: Palgrave Macmillan.

Riviere, Joan. 1929. "Womanliness as a Masquerade." *International Journal of Psychoanalysis* 10: 303–13.

Roberts-Smith, Jennifer, Shawn DeSouza-Coelho, Teresa M. Dobson, Sandra Gabriele, Marcelo Hong, Diane Jakacki, Alexandra Kovacs, David Lam, Lesley Northam, Helle Porsdam, Manuel Portela, Omar Rodriguez-Arenas, Stan Ruecker, Robert Schoenbeck, Stéfan Sinclair, and Daniel So. 2013. "Visualizing Theatrical Text: From Watching the Script to the Simulated Environment for Theatre (SET)." *Digital Humanities Quarterly* 7 (3). Accessed May 5, 2014. http://www.digitalhumanities.org/dhq/vol/7/3/000166/000166.html.

Robertson, Raylene. 2011. Review of *A Doll's House*—Theatre Delicatessen: Picton Place, London. *The Reviews Hub.* January 10. Accessed December 4, 2015. www.thereviewshub.com/a-dolls-house-theatre-delicatessen-picton-place-london/.

Robins, Elizabeth. 1932a. *Ibsen and the Actress.* Hogarth Essays, Second Series, No. XV. London: Hogarth Press.

—. 1932b. *Theatre and Friendship.* Life and Letters Series. London: Jonathan Cape.

Rodd, L.R. 1991. "Yosana Akiko and the Taisho Debate over the 'New Woman.'" In *Recreating Japanese Women, 1600–1945,* edited by Gail Lee Bernstein. 175–98. Los Angeles, CA: University of California Press.

Roger, Edith, Joachim Calmeyer, and Espen Skjønberg. 2011. Interview with Julie Holledge and Frode Helland. May 26. Archived at Centre for Ibsen Studies, University of Oslo.

Romeo, Jacqueline. 2004. "Vera Kommissarzhevskaia: The American Tour." *Toronto Slavic Quarterly* 20: n.p. http://www.utoronto.ca/tsq/archive.shtml.

Rosenberg, Marvin. 1969. "Ibsen vs. Ibsen, or: Two versions of *A Doll's House.*" *Modern Drama* 12 (2): 187–96.

Roy, Kumar. 2003. "Ibsen's *A Doll's House* in Indian Perspectives and Bohurupee's Production of *Putul Khela* (1958) through 10.01.1958 to 11.06.1978." *Proceedings of the International Ibsen Seminar 2002*, 141–48. Dhaka: Centre for Asian Theater.

"Russian Actress Appears as Nora." 1908. *New York Times.* March 3. Accessed December 28, 2015. http://query.nytimes.com/gst/abstract.html?res=9B07E1DC1639E333A25750C0A9659C946997D6CF.

Saltz, David Z. 2004. "Performing Arts." In *A Companion to Digital Humanities*, edited by Susan Schreibman, Ray Siemens, and John Unsworth, Chapter 11. Oxford: Blackwell. http://www.digitalhumanities.org/companion/view?docId=blackwell/9781405103213/9781405103213.xml&chunk.id=ss1–2-11&toc.depth=1&toc.id=ss1–2-11&brand=default.

Sandberg, Mark B. 2015. *Ibsen's Houses: Architectural Metaphor and the Modern Uncanny.* Cambridge: Cambridge University Press.

Sanders, Julie. 2006. *Adaptation and Appropriation.* Abingdon and New York: Routledge.

Sato, Toshihiko. 1981. "Ibsen's Drama and the Japanese Bluestockings." *EDDA: Scandinavian Journal of Literary Research* 5: 265–93.

Schanke, Robert, A. 1988. *Ibsen in America: A Century of Change*. Metuchen, NJ and London: Scarecrow Press.

——. 1998. "Alla Nazimova: 'The Witch of Makeup.'" In *Passing Performances: Queer Readings of Leading Players in American Theatre History*, edited by Robert A. Schanke and Kimberley Marra, 129–50. Ann Arbor, MI: University of Michigan.

Schmiesing, Ann. 2006. *Norway's Christiania Theatre, 1827–1867*. Madison, NJ: Farleigh Dickinson University Press.

Schreibman, Susan, Ray Siemens, and John Unsworth, eds. 2004. *A Companion to Digital Humanities*. Oxford: Blackwell. http://www.digitalhumanities.org/companion/.

Scott, John. 2000. *Social Network Analysis: A Handbook*. London: Sage.

Selaiha, Nehad. 2006. "Ibsen at the National: The National's *A Doll's House* Leaves Nehad Selaiha Puzzled as to the Where and When of the Action." *Al-Ahram Weekly Online*. Accessed December 17, 2015. http://weekly.ahram.org.eg/2006/810/cu1.htm.

——. 2006. "Ibsen in Egypt." *Al-Ahram Weekly Online*, July 13–19. Accessed February 25, 2009. http://weekly.ahram.org.eg/2006/810/cu1.htm.

Sen, Amartya. 2005. *The Argumentative Indian: Writings on Indian Culture, History and Identity*. London: Penguin Books.

Senelick, Laurence. 1980. "Vera Kommissarzhevskaya: The Actress as Symbolist Eidolon." *Theatre Journal* 32 (4): 475–87.

Shahidian, Hammed. 1997. "Women and Clandestine Politics in Iran, 1970–1985." *Feminist Studies* 23 (1): 7–42.

Shaikevich, B.A. 1974. *Ibsen and Russian Culture*. Kiev: Izd Vysshaia shkola.

Shaw, George Bernard. 1891. *The Quintessence of Ibsenism*. London: Walter Scott.

——. 1892. Letter Written on a Train. April 21. In *Collection of Letters by George Bernard Shaw*. Rare Books, Music and Manuscripts. British Library, London.

——. 1929. Letter to Ashley Dukes, December 14. *Collection of Letters by George Bernard Shaw*. Rare Books, Music and Manuscripts. British Library, London.

——. 1965. *Collected Letters 1874–1897*. Edited by Dan H. Laurence. New York: Dodd, Mead and Company.

Sheehy, Helen. 2003. *Eleonora Duse: A Biography*. New York: Alfred A. Knoff.

Shepherd-Barr, Kirsten. 1997. *Ibsen and Early Modernist Theatre 1890–1900*. Westport, CT: Greenwood Press.

——. 2012. "Ibsen in France from Breakthrough to Renewal." *Ibsen Studies* 12 (1): 56–81.

——. 2015. *Theatre and Evolution from Ibsen to Beckett*. New York: Columbia University Press.

Shih, Frank Y. 2010. *Image Processing and Pattern Recognition: Fundamentals and Techniques*. Hoboken, NJ: John Wiley.

Shim, Jung Soon. 2004. "Recasting the National Motherhood: Transactions of Western Feminisms in Korean Theatre." *Theatre Research International* 29 (2): 143–54.

Shulman, Alix Kates, ed. 1998. *Red Emma Speaks: An Emma Goldman Reader*. Amherst, NY: Humanity Books.

"*Si prega di non discutere di casa di bambola*." 2015. *Vimeo*. Accessed July 29. http://vimeo.com/10061728.

Silva, Jane Pessoa da. 2007. "Ibsen no Brasil: historiografia, seleção de textos críticos e catálogo bibliográfico." Dissertação de Mestrado, Faculdade de Filosofia, Letras e Ciências Humanas, São Paulo. http://www.teses.usp.br/teses/disponiveis/8/8151/tde-01112007-141703/pt-br.php.

"Sorma at M'Vicker's." 1898. *Chicago Tribune*, April 4. Accessed August 13, 2015. http://archives.chicagotribune.com/1898/04/04/page/8/article/sorma-at-mvickers.

Stanford Friedman, Susan. 1998. *Mappings: Feminism and the Cultural Geographies of Encounter*. Princeton, NJ: Princeton University Press.

Stark, Mirian T., Brenda J. Bowser, Lee Horne, and William A. Longacre. 2008. *Cultural Transmission and Material Culture: Breaking Down Boundaries*. Tucson, AZ: University of Arizona Press.

Stetz, Margaret D. 2007. "Mrs Linde, Feminism, and Women's Work, Then and Now." *Ibsen Studies* 7 (2): 150–68.

Stevens, Ashton. 1898. "Blanche Bates as the Ibsen Missionary of the Woolly West." *San Francisco Call*, November 6, 84 (159): 29.

Støre, Jonas Gahr. 2006. "Ibsen's Calling Is to Ask Questions, Not to Give Answers." *Dagbladet*. January 28. Accessed December 21, 2015. https://www.regjeringen.no/en/aktuelt/ibsens-calling-is-to-ask-questions-not-t/id420835/.

——. 2012. "Åpning av Ibsen-festivalen 2012." *Regjeringen*. August 23. Accessed October 23, 2015. https://www.regjeringen.no/no/aktuelt/apning-av-ibsen-festivalen-2012/id697962/.

Sunde, Vivi. 2011. Interview with Julie Holledge and Frode Helland. May 24. Archived at Centre for Ibsen Studies, University of Oslo.

Synnøve Berg, Marit. 2011. Interview with Julie Holledge and Frode Helland. March 26. Archived at Centre for Ibsen Studies, University of Oslo.

Tagore, Rabindranath. 2001. *Selected Writings on Literature and Language*, edited by Sisir Kumar Das and Sukanta Chaudhuri. New Delhi: Oxford University Press.

Talal, Asad. 2003. *Formations of the Secular: Christianity, Islam, Modernity*. Stanford, CA: Stanford University Press.

Tam, Kwok-kan. 1985. *Ibsen in China: Reception and Influence*. Urbana, IL: University of Illinois.

Tanahasi, Y., and Ma, Kwan-Liu. 2012. "Design Considerations for Optimizing Storyline Visualizations." *IEEE Transactions On Visualization and Computer Graphics* 18 (12): 2679–88.

Tandberg, Monna. 2011. Interview with Julie Holledge and Frode Helland. May 27. Archived at Centre for Ibsen Studies, University of Oslo.

Taucar, Jacqueline. 2011. "Playing (with) Gestic Dolls in Mabou Mines Doll House." In "Ibsen Intercultural: Nora's Door Slamming Around the Globe," edited by Antje Budde, special issue, *Canadian Review of Comparative Literature* 38 (2): 268–82.

Taussig, Michael. 1993. *Mimesis and Alterity.* London and New York: Routledge.

Taylor, Paul. 2011. Review of *A Doll's House*, Picton Place, London. *The Independent.* January 11. Accessed December 4, 2015. www.independent.co.uk/arts-entertainment/theatre-dance/reviews/a-dollrsquos-house-picton-place-london-2181078.html.

Templeton, Joan. 1997. *Ibsen's Women.* Cambridge: Cambridge University Press.

Terrill, Ross. 1984. *The White Boned Demon: A Biography of Madame Mao Zedong.* London: Heinemann.

Thanhouser, Edwin. 1911. Advert in *The Moving Picture World.* July 11. Accessed October 5, 2015. http://www.thanhouser.org/tcocd/.

"The Theatrical Week: Dullness from London and Vivacity from Paris." 1895. *New York Times.* March 24. Accessed August 13, 2015. http://query.nytimes.com/mem/archivefree/pdf?res=9C03EFDE133DE433A25757C2A9659C94649ED7CF.

"The Theatrical Week: Mme Rejane's Facile Art Exhibited in Various Plays: Her Technique is Wonderful." 1895. *New York Times.* March 31. Accessed August 13, 2015. http://query.nytimes.com/mem/archivefree/pdf?res=9402EED6163CE433A25752C3A9659C94649ED7CF.

Thompson, E.P. (1976) 1994. Review of *Eleanor Marx* by Yvonne Kapp. *Persons and Polemics, Historical Essays.* By E.P. Thompson, 66–76. London: Merlin Press. Accessed November 22, 2015. https://www.marxists.org/archive/thompson-ep/1976/eleanor-marx.htm.

Thorkildsen, Inga Marte. 2008. Nora's Sisters Seminar, Ramallah, March 8–9. Accessed August 25, 2015. http://www.norway.org.ps/ARKIV/Nora_Sisters/#.VdvuZ3gVfzI.

Thorson, Gerald. 1978. "When Nora Helmer Came to Chicago." *MELUS* 5 (1): 31–37.

Timmers, Gerrit. 2009. Telephone Interview with Julie Holledge. February 3.

Tompkins, Joanne. 2006. *Unsettling Space: Contestations in Contemporary Australian Theatre.* Basingstoke: Palgrave Macmillan.

Tømta, Hanne. 2015. Interview with Julie Holledge. October 16.

Törnqvist, Egil. 1995. "Ibsen: *A Doll's House.*" Plays in Production. Cambridge: Cambridge University Press.

Toulmin, Stephen. 1990. *Cosmopolis: The Hidden Agenda of Modernity*. Chicago, IL: University of Chicago Press.

Tung, Constantine. 1995. "Why Doesn't the Chinese Nora Leave Her Husband?: Women's Emancipation in Post-1949 Chinese Drama." *Modern Drama* 38 (3): 298–307.

Ueda, Makoto. 1961. "Zeami on Art: A Chapter for the History of Japanese Aesthetics." *Journal of Aesthetics and Art Criticism* 20 (1): 73–79.

UNESCO (United Nations Educational, Scientific, and Cultural Organisation). 2005. "Vimbuza Healing Dance." *Intangible Cultural Heritage*. Accessed December 15, 2015. http://www.unesco.org/culture/ich/en/RL/vimbuza-healing-dance-00158.

—. 2015. "Henrik Ibsen: *A Doll's House*." *Memory of the World*. Accessed August 4, 2015. http://www.unesco.org/new/en/communication-and-information/flagship-project-activities/memory-of-the-world/register/full-list-of-registered-heritage/registered-heritage-page-4/henrik-ibsen-a-dolls-house/.

Uthaug, Gro Ann. 2011. Interview with Julie Holledge and Frode Helland. May 23. Archived at Centre for Ibsen Studies, University of Oslo.

Utoh-Ezeajugh, Tracie C. 2005. *Nneora: An African Doll's House*. Anambra State: Valid Publishing Company.

Venuti, Lawrence, ed. 1992. *Rethinking Translation: Discourse, Subjectivity, Ideology*. London: Routledge.

von Bergen, Louise. 2006. *Nordisk Teater i Montevideo: Kontextrelaterad reception av Henrik Ibsen och August Strindberg*. Acta Universitatis Stockholmiensis. Stockholm Studies in History of Literature, No. 51. Stockholm: Almqvist and Wiksell International.

Von Hummel, Alexandra. 2013. Interview. Accessed February 11. http://www.3tv.cl/index.php?m=video&v=25123.

Waal, Carla Rae. 1967. *Johanne Dybwad: Norwegian Actress*. Oslo: Universitetsforlaget.

Warnken, William P. 1974. "Kate Chopin and Henrik Ibsen: A Study of *The Awakening* and *A Doll's House*." *Massachusetts Studies in English* 4 (4–5): 43–49.

Wicklund, Beret. 2003. "Death and Pain: Liberation and Infection in *A Doll's House*." *The Relevance of* A Doll's House—*Translation and Adaptation Proceedings of International Ibsen Conference, Dhaka, Bangladesh, 8-14 November 2002*. Centre for Asian Theatre in collaboration with Centre for Ibsen Studies, 35–41. Dhaka: Centre for Asian Theatre.

Wiles, David. 2003. *A Short History of Western Performance Space*. Cambridge: Cambridge University Press.

Williams, Raymond. 1969. *Drama From Ibsen to Brecht*. New York: Oxford University Press.

Winter, William. 1910. *Life and Art of Richard Mansfield with Selections from his Letters to William Winter*. New York: Moffart, Yard and Co.

Witke, Roxane. 1977. *Comrade Chiang Ching*. Toronto: Little, Brown.

Witoszek, Nina. 2011. *Origins of the "Regime of Goodness": Remapping the Cultural History of Norway.* Oslo: Universitetsforlaget.

Women's Learning Partnership for Rights, Development, and Peace. 2009. Accessed March 2. http//www.learningpartnership.org/en/advocacy/alerts/morocco 0204.

Wu, X. 1956. "Before the Performance of *Nora*." *People's Daily,* July 28: n.p.

Yakout, Gamal. N.d. "*A Doll's House*, Between the Text and the Performance." Translated by Mona Khedr. Unpublished.

Yeazell, Ruth Bernard. 2000. *Harems of the Mind: Passages of Western Art and Literature*. New Haven, CT: Yale University Press.

Ystad, Vigdis, and Asbjørn Aarseth. 2008. "Innledninger og kommentarer." In Vol. 7k of *Henrik Ibsens skrifter*, edited by Vigdis Ystad and Asbjørn Aarseth, 191–304. Oslo: University of Oslo and Aschehoug.

Zaman, Niaz, and Sadrul Amin, eds. 2006. *Centennial Essays on Ibsen*. Dhaka: Department of English, University of Dhaka, Mother Printers.

Zangwill, Israel, and Eleanor Marx Aveling. 1891. "*A Doll's House* Repaired." *Time*, 24: 239–53.

Zapolska, Gabriela. 2007. *The Morality of Mrs Dulska*. Translated and introduced by Teresa Murjas. Bristol and Chicago, IL: Intellect Books.

Index[1]

[1] Note: Page numbers with "n" denote notes.

J. Holledge et al., *A Global Doll's House*, Palgrave Studies in Performance and Technology, DOI 10.1057/978-1-137-43899-7

www.ingramcontent.com/pod-product-compliance
Ingram Content Group UK Ltd.
Pitfield, Milton Keynes, MK11 3LW, UK
UKHW021833200226
R4131900001B/R41319PG468211UKX00002B/3
* 9 7 8 1 3 4 9 6 8 3 7 8 9 *